Justice, Community and Dialogue in International Relations

Shapcott investigates the question of justice in a culturally diverse world, asking if it is possible to conceive of a universal or cosmopolitan community in which justice to difference is achieved. Justice to difference is possible, according to Shapcott, by recognising the particular manner in which different humans identify themselves. Such recognition is most successfully accomplished through acts of communication and, in particular, conversation. The account of understanding developed by H. G. Gadamer provides a valuable way forward in this field. The philosophical hermeneutic account of conversation allows for the development of a level of cosmopolitan solidarity that is both 'thin' and universal, and which helps to provide a more just resolution of the tension between the values of community and difference.

RICHARD SHAPCOTT is Lecturer in International Relations, Deakin University. His research interests lie in international relations theory, international ethics and the hermeneutic philosophy of Hans-Georg Gadamer.

CAMBRIDGE STUDIES IN INTERNATIONAL RELATIONS

Justice, Community and Dialogue in International Relations

CAMBRIDGE STUDIES IN INTERNATIONAL RELATIONS

Justice, Community and Dialogue in International Relations

Richard Shapcott

CAMBRIDGE
UNIVERSITY PRESS

PUBLISHED BY THE PRESS SYNDICATE OF THE UNIVERSITY OF CAMBRIDGE
The Pitt Building, Trumpington Street, Cambridge, United Kingdom

CAMBRIDGE UNIVERSITY PRESS
The Edinburgh Building, Cambridge CB2 2RU, UK
40 West 20th Street, New York, NY 10011-4211, USA
10 Stamford Road, Oakleigh, VIC 3166, Australia
Ruiz de Alarcón 13, 28014 Madrid, Spain
Dock House, The Waterfront, Cape Town 8001, South Africa

http://www.cambridge.org

First published 2001

Printed in the United Kingdom at the University Press, Cambridge

Typeface Palatino 10/12.5 pt   *System* LATEX 2$_\varepsilon$ [TB]

A catalogue record for this book is available from the British Library.

ISBN 0 521 78028 4 hardback
ISBN 0 521 78447 6 paperback

Contents

Acknowledgements

This book would never have been completed, or even undertaken, without the support, advice, encouragement and inspiration of the following people and institutions (in no particular order).

The School of Australian and International Studies and the Faculty of Arts at Deakin University granted me six months leave to complete this project in 2000. The Faculty of Social Sciences and the Department of Politics of the University of Bristol awarded me a university scholarship, as did the Overseas Research Scholarship scheme, to undertake the PhD thesis out of which this book evolved. I would be remiss were I not to acknowledge the benefits I gained from teaching on Bristol's Master's degree in World Politics. At Bristol I received the support and friendship from the staff in general and the administrative staff – Veronica Scheibler, Anne Jewell and Elisabeth Grundy in particular. In addition, the Department of International Relations at the University of Keele provided me with a fertile, stimulating and welcoming environment for the seven months in which I was a visiting scholar there in 1994 when crucial early research was conducted. Alex Danchev, John Macmillan, Hidemi Suganami and Chris Brewin all expressed interest and enthusiasm as well as provided constructive input. Rosarie McCarthy, Peter Newell, Matt Paterson and Jo Van Every all helped to make my transition to English life easier and my time at Keele enjoyable. The Department of Politics at Monash University also supported the early stages of my investigation and awarded me an Australian Postgraduate Research Award in 1993. The book also benefited from the time I spent at La Trobe University, Australia, as a Post-doctoral Fellow in 1998. Steven Slaughter of Monash University stepped in at the last minute to take over my teaching responsibilities at Deakin; without this assistance the book would have been a much longer time coming.

In England I was fortunate enough to receive real encouragement and enthusiastic support from a number of colleagues and friends which went way beyond my expectations and made for a thoroughly hospitable and welcoming intellectual environment. Chris Brown, Mervyn Frost, Steve Smith, Nick Rengger, Mark Hoffman, Tim Dunne, Molly Cochran, Eddie Keane, Charlotte Hooper and Ewan Harrison, are just a few of the people who contributed to this work. Professor Steve Smith has shown an interest and support for my work since an early stage and has continued to do so. As an examiner and as managing editor of this series his input has been crucial to the development of this project.

At Bristol, Professor Richard Little as both Head of Department, and as examiner, always gave me useful, intelligent advice and support. Most importantly, he understood the value of supporting a vibrant graduate student body. He, along with Dr Judith Squires, encouraged our participation in every aspect of departmental life. Furthermore without the time, effort and contributions of Judith Squires I am certain this would be a much poorer piece of work. During her time as supervisor of the PhD from which this book grew she was more than generous with her time, and provided crucial directions, constructive criticism and detailed advice. She provided the best possible supervision a PhD candidate could ask for.

This book would certainly never have been completed without the friendship of Charlotte Hooper, Ian Douglas, Debbie Lisle, Will Gallois, Matt Patterson, Marinês Garcia, Mark Ogge and Michele Wilson. I would also like to thank Christie and colleagues at The Beach Café, and the staff at The Turtle Café, in Elwood.

I would especially like to acknowledge my friend and colleague Richard Devetak. He has been an excellent conversational partner (though our conversations sometimes get rather heated and resemble arguments!) since we shared an office at Keele, and ever since. His critical mind and close readings have served to engage and correct me many times since. He has also provided a constant reminder of the importance of really reading a text.

My major intellectual debt is to Professor Andrew Linklater who, since my earliest days as an undergraduate, has been able to inspire me, and others, with the scope of his vision and the fairmindedness of his criticism. He has set intellectual and professional standards to which I can only aspire, but which I hope have informed and guided my work.

Several people read and commented on drafts of the various chapters, in particular Dr Michael Janover of Monash University, who graciously

Acknowledgements

agreed to read, meet and talk with me on several occasions. Michael's is one of the finest minds I have ever encountered and I am grateful to have been the recipient of its insights. Richard Devetak and Andrew Linklater gave close readings and provided invaluable comments and insights at crucial stages. My father, Thomas Shapcott, invaluably, proof-read the penultimate draft, somehow fitting it into his truly enormous reading load. Needless to say all the inadequacies present are mine. Thanks also to Janey who read and commented on the early chapters.

Thanks are also due to John Haslam and Susan Beer for their help in editing and copy-editing. Finally, as always, my largest debts go to my mother and father, Margaret Grace and Thomas Shapcott, who have provided support in too many ways to mention here.

Sections of this book were presented as papers in a number of places, including the Department of Politics, Latrobe University, 1998; the International Studies Association Annual Conference, Toronto, March 1997; the Department of Politics, Monash University, March 1997 and June 2000; the British International Studies Conference, Durham, December 1996; the Millennium 25th Anniversary Conference, London, October 1996; Keele University, Department of International Relations, May 1994; the Contemporary Research in International Political Theory (CRIPT) session at the London School of Economics, June 1994.

Various sections of this book have also appeared, in slightly different formats, in the following publications: 'Solidarism and After: Global Governance, International Society and the Normative "Turn" in International Relations', *Pacifica Review*, vol. 12, no. 2, June 2000; 'Beyond the Cosmopolitan/Communitarian Divide: Justice, Ethics and Community in International Relations', in J. S. Fritz and M. Lensu (eds.), *Value Pluralism, Normative Theory and International Relations*, London: Macmillan, 2000; 'Conversation and Coexistence: Gadamer and the Interpretation of International Society', *Millennium: Journal of International Studies*, Spring 1994, vol. 23, no. 1.

Introduction

Insofar as hermeneutics is more than a theory of the human sciences, it also has the human situation in the world in its entirety in view. Thus it must be possible to include different cultures, religions, and so on, and their relations. What is at issue here is that when something other or different is understood, then we must also concede something, yield – in certain limits – to the truth of the other. That is the essence, the soul of my hermeneutics: to understand someone else is to see the justice, the truth, of their position. And this is what transforms us. And if we then have to become part of a new world civilisation, if this is our task then we shall need a philosophy which is similar to my hermeneutics: a philosophy which teaches us to see the justification for the other's point of view and which thus makes us doubt our own.[1]

No one can say what will become of our civilization when it has really met different civilisations by means other than the shock of conquest and domination. But we have to admit that this encounter has not yet taken place at the level of an authentic dialogue. That is why we are in a kind of lull or interregnum in which we can no longer practice the dogmatism of a single truth and in which we are not yet capable of conquering the scepticism into which we have stepped.[2]

This book faces an impossible task and suggests an impossible solution. It investigates the question of justice in a culturally diverse world and asks: is it possible to conceive of a universal or cosmopolitan community in which justice to difference is achieved? In order to answer this question it is necessary to investigate what may count as a just relationship

---

[1] H. G. Gadamer, 'Interview: The 1920s, 1930s and the Present: National Socialism, German History and German Culture', pp. 135–53, in D. Misgeld and G. Nicholson, *Hans-Georg Gadamer on Education, Poetry and History* (Albany: SUNY, 1992), p. 152.

[2] P. Ricoeur, *History and Truth* (Evanston: Northwestern University Press, 1966), p. 283.

to 'otherness' or 'difference'. These questions are part of an impossible task for several reasons: the term community itself implies a collectivity exhibiting a high degree of homogeneity of identity and consensus among its members and, therefore, a lack of 'difference' between them. A universal community, one that in principle includes all members of the species, must by virtue of being a community, exclude or deny important differences amongst its members. The idea of a universal community suggests that underlying apparent differences of identity there exists an essential unity. Such a statement itself denies the possibility of truly radical 'difference'. For this reason this book and its subject are guided by a tension between the desire for community and the recognition of difference.

The impossible solution to the task presented here originates in the work of H. G. Gadamer and the tradition of hermeneutics. Gadamer's philosophical hermeneutics arises from a tradition of thought which emphasises the possibility for understanding across both temporal and linguistic distances. The hermeneutic interest in understanding arises from the encounter between the familiar and the strange, usually in the form of historical texts. The primary argument presented here is that the account of understanding developed by Gadamer in *Truth and Method*[3] provides the basis for a conceptualisation of a cosmopolitanism more able to accommodate the tension between community and difference in a productive manner.

While the tension between community and difference is expressed differently according to the context both this problematic, and testimony to the impossibility of resolving it, can be witnessed throughout all of the positions discussed in this investigation. Be it as a tension between equality and identity, cosmopolitanism and communitarianism, abstract and concrete otherness, limitation and legislation, universalism and particularism or citizenship and humanity, this problem characterises all discussions of moral life in international relations (IR). Of course this dilemma goes well beyond the terms employed in this investigation and can rightly be understood to have characterised almost all western thought about politics and society. It is this same tension which informs the discourses of citizenship and statehood, rights and obligations, duties and freedoms. This book restricts itself, with some minor exceptions, to an examination and assessment of the resolutions offered by different theories of IR. It argues that while certain approaches

---

[3] H. G. Gadamer, *Truth and Method*, 2nd edn (trans. J. Weinsheimer and D. Marshall), (London: Sheed and Ward, 1989).

'Community' defined by moral world relativism.
NOT common beliefs etc.

Introduction

provide better resolutions than others none escapes the tension entirely, including the 'solution' suggested by philosophical hermeneutics. For this reason the development of an approach informed by philosophical hermeneutics should be understood as a contribution to the effort to better accommodate this tension rather than a claim to have finally resolved it.

The meaning of community

The identification of a tension between the values of community and difference raises the possibility of doubt as to the accuracy of the term 'community' to describe the goal being pursued here. However, because what is being attempted here is a reconceptualisation of community which captures this tension, the term community is employed in the loosest possible sense. Community here refers to the act of inclusion in the 'moral world'. It refers to the range of subjects who are included within moral calculations or within the range of moral considerateness. This definition is loose in the sense that it is not restricted to those united by common beliefs, religion, culture or political institutions. The advantage of formulating community in this way is that emphasis is placed on the moral realm *per se* rather than any particular understanding of morality. It is adopted here because it is the nature of community, morality and justice in the absence of commonly held norms or normative discourse that is the focus of this investigation. This definition both allows for and problematises the assumption that morality and justice can only be practised within a shared discourse. It allows for the fact that individuals and societies can and do understand themselves as having moral obligations and duties to those who do not necessarily belong to their 'group' and for the possibility of moral action where norms and values are either openly in dispute or not shared, this conception therefore does not restrict the scope of moral action to the like-minded community. Most importantly it suggests that the act of engaging in conversation is an act of community and solidarity that extends the range of moral inclusion. Understanding community in this fashion is central to the task of developing a cosmopolitan community that achieves justice to difference, because this community itself is instantiated in a conversation between diverse positions, agents and discourses. It is important to note that underlying the account presented here is the loosely Kantian understanding that morality consists fundamentally, but not exclusively, of treating other humans as equals, or ends in themselves. It is for this reason that the task of pursuing both moral community and

3

justice are intertwined in this book: inclusion can only be moral if it is just.

What this book does and does not do

Before proceeding with the argument it is necessary to clarify some key terms and concepts and to set out exactly what it is this argument seeks to do and not do. The argument in this book should be understood as an attempt to think philosophically about certain moral dimensions of international politics. It does not provide a defence of the normative project itself. Such a defence has been made, rather conclusively I think, by more capable authors. Andrew Linklater, Mervyn Frost, Charles Beitz, Stanley Hoffman are just a few of those who have demonstrated the centrality of moral and ethical concerns to international relations. Those who seek more elaborate discussion of this project need go no further than the works of these authors (cited in chapters 1 and 2).

This book engages in a largely philosophical discussion regarding the conception of a cosmopolitan community and the nature of good dialogue. It does not attempt a substantive defence of the principles of inclusion, universality and the value of 'difference'. The discussion which follows should be understood as one largely occurring within the cosmopolitan tradition. It does not seek to defend the ideals of universal equality nor cosmopolitan community as such. Rather it assumes, for the purposes of argument that these are 'goods' which have been successfully defended elsewhere. The argument does problematise these concepts and offer some alternative interpretations of them.

The language of the discussion is at times necessarily abstract. While the final chapter engages with some less abstract questions and begins to investigate the implications of the philosophical positions developed in the earlier chapters there is relatively little in the way of concrete policy advice, prescription or analysis of specific moral problems such as humanitarian intervention. This is not a result of an in-principle refusal to engage with this level, nor still less a belief that philosophical reflection should be unsullied by the 'real world'. Rather, it stems from a belief that before 'real' moral and ethical problems can be adequately addressed it is essential to be clear about the issues at stake as well as their possible solutions. This being the case, this book is an attempt to think through the meanings of justice, morality, community and dialogue and their relationship to each other. Incorporating the results of this reflection into any attempt to address the myriad concrete ethical and moral issues characterising the international realm can only take place once the philosophical ground work has been undertaken. That said, as Gadamer and others emphasise, the meaning of the concepts explored here are incomplete as long as they remain exclusively in the abstract realm. Therefore this book should be seen as merely the first step along the way of developing a thin cosmopolitanism informed by philosophical hermeneutics.

The moral problematique of international relations and the problem of community

Before this argument can proceed it is first necessary to outline the developments in normative theorising in international relations which have led to the posing of the questions with which this study is concerned. Recent years have seen a small but significant expansion of interest in what can broadly be called normative IR theory.[4] The literature involved in this expansion covers a wide variety of normative, theoretical and methodological approaches. Critical theory, constitutive theory, constructivism, international political economy and others have all contributed to a transformation of how international relations as a whole approaches normative issues. Not all of this literature has been exclusively concerned with debating moral issues and the meaning of justice but most of it has sought to include normative reflection of some sort or another in its ambit, whether it be on the normative orientation of theory itself, the role of norms in constituting and changing the international realm, or possibilities for international justice. Nonetheless there is still a relative dearth of genuine normative reflection within the discipline as a whole. With some notable exceptions IR as a discipline steers clear of directly posing the difficult questions normally associated with political theory and moral philosophy; such as 'What is the good life?', 'How shall we live?', 'What is a just society?' The current work is an attempt, amongst other things, to help redress this imbalance and to erode the divide between IR and other branches of the humanities.

Despite the relatively recent expansion of moral reflection evidenced in the publications of Linklater, Hutchings, Frost, Cochran, Beitz, Brown and Campbell, the presence of the questions which concern this volume can be identified in most of the central works of the discipline.

---

[4] As Molly Cochran has recently reminded us, all theory is normative theory. See M. Cochran, *Normative Theory in International Relations* (Cambridge: Cambridge University Press, 1999).

Indeed it is possible to follow Linklater's lead and argue that almost all theorising about international relations has at its heart the question of community.[5] According to Linklater, following Martin Wight, the three dominant traditions of Realism, Rationalism and Revolutionism (or Idealism) identify the determination of the boundaries of moral obligations in the absence of a universal state or universal moral community as one of the central problems of IR. The question of community is at the heart of international relations to the degree that most IR theory addresses or refers to either or both of the following questions: 'What are the possibilities for moral community beyond the state?', and 'What are the qualities and characteristics of any such community?' Indeed the dominant question addressed by most studies of international relations relates to the obstacles and possibilities for a transformation of international politics arising from a war-prone system of independent political communities, usually nation-states, into something less war-prone. For instance, the central question identified by Waltz in *Theory of International Politics*[6] is 'How is it possible to explain the reproduction of the anarchic system of states?' In other words what are the conditions that restrict the transformation of political community? Viewed in this light, the realist account of the international system stresses those forces which encourage particularity and the restriction of moral duties and obligations to the state-based community.

In contrast to realists, rationalists such as Hedley Bull suggest that not all moral ties stop at the state border. They argue that states have been able to commit themselves to international principles of order and co-existence which constitute a minimal international moral order. In this way, states admit to a limited and partial recognition of human community mediated through a society in which states, not individuals, are the members. Such a reading of the Rationalist school and of the meaning of international society is of course contested. But certain comments made by Hedley Bull suggesting that the society of states can only be judged according to how well it serves the human species, who are its ultimate moral referents, indicate the way in which the society of states mediates relations between the nascent community of humankind.[7] Linklater argues that the existence of such a community of states might provide the grounds upon which moral community may be developed even

[5] A. Linklater, 'The Problem of Community in International Relations', *Alternatives*, 15 (1990), 135–53.
[6] K. Waltz, *Theory of International Politics* (Reading: Addison Wesley, 1979).
[7] H. Bull, *The Anarchical Society* (London: Macmillan, 1977).

further. In this reading the principles of coexistence evident in theories of international society are testament to the possibility of overcoming those processes identified by Realism as inhibiting the expansion of community.[8]

The achievement of a universal community is the primary defining aim for Revolutionists. The revolutionist and idealist traditions assert the primacy of the 'latent' universal community of humankind and argue that this community requires the transformation of the states-system into a cosmopolitan order. Cosmopolitanism refers to a form of moral and political community characterised by laws which are universal. The central proposition of cosmopolitanism as a moral and political doctrine is that humans can and should form a universal (that is global) moral community. Cosmopolitans argue that in addition to being members of our national and local communities we also belong to the human community. The task facing cosmopolitans, idealists and revolutionists is to transform the international realm and to bring it into line with moral law.

It is also true that culture, cultural difference and the obstacles to developing more inclusive communities presented by them have also been a concern for thinkers in each of these traditions. Most discourses of IR have cited the presence of radical cultural difference as one of the principal obstacles to the development of cosmopolitan tendencies in the states-system. For example, one of the standard arguments attributed to Realism is that the diversity of moral standards in different states contributes to the conflict accompanying the international anarchy and to the impossibility of moving beyond an international state of nature.[9] Realism suggests that genuinely morally motivated action remains impossible because the plurality of different standards rules out any possible agreement on what constitutes either the 'right' or the 'good' in the international realm. Furthermore, the Realists argue that any aspiration to cosmopolitanism, or any claim to be acting for the good of the species, is merely a mask, conscious or not, for the self-interest of particular states. In this account cosmopolitanism is seen both as a lie and one that is hostile to particular cultural differences. Traditionally, this account has led to the endorsement of a moral bifurcation, whereby

---

[8] See A. Linklater, *Beyond Realism and Marxism: Critical Theory and International Relations*, 2nd edn (London: Macmillan, 1990).

[9] See the discussions in E. H. Carr, *The Twenty Years Crisis* (London: Macmillan, 1939) and H. Morgenthau, *Politics Among Nations: The Struggle for Power and Peace* (New York: Alfred A. Knopf, 1954).

7

substantive moral life is possible only within the state, and the interstate realm is portrayed as the realm of necessity possessing a different and restricted morality, the morality of states (the chief virtue of which is prudence).

The account of community presented by the rationalists holds a somewhat different place for culture. In the works of Wight, Bull and Watson the existence of a certain degree of shared cultural inheritance provides the conditions of possibility for an ordered society of states.[10] However, for Bull and others the presence of major cultural difference within the modern universal society of states raises the possibility for a decrease in world order and an increase in conflict. Amongst the tasks of international society then, is the mediation of cultural differences and the identification of shared interests or goals across cultural boundaries.[11]

As the discussion in chapter 2 demonstrates, cosmopolitans have also identified cultural heterogeneity as an obstacle to progress in the international realm. Where they tend to differ from Realists is in the aspiration to transcend these differences and either to replace or incorporate them in a universal community. For this reason cosmopolitanism has often been identified as hostile to the existence of diverse societies and value systems. While a full discussion of the place of culture in IR theory is beyond the scope of this investigation it is possible to suggest from this brief overview that the question of cultural difference is central to the question of community in IR.

The task of this book is to contribute to the development of alternative understandings of the relationship between community and cultural difference in the international realm. It addresses both parts of the question: is moral community possible beyond the state or the particular community and, if so, what are the characteristics of that larger community? In answer to the first part, it argues that a morally inclusive but 'thin' cosmopolitanism capable of doing justice through recognition is possible. In answer to the second, it argues that such a community should embody the values of communication and the characteristics of dialogue in which recognition of differences can occur.

---

[10] H. Bull, *Justice in International Relations* (The Hagey Lectures), (University of Waterloo, 1983). M. Wight, (Wight, G. and Porter, B. eds.) *International Theory: The Three Traditions* (Leicester University Press, 1991). M. Wight, 'De Systematibus Civitatum', in *Systems of States* (Leicester University Press, 1977).

[11] H. Bull and A. Watson (eds.), *The Expansion of International Society* (Oxford University Press, 1984).

Rawls' "veil" of "ignorance" for neutral theory of justice

Introduction

Justice as recognition of difference

For many years moral theory in international politics focused largely on the moral critique of the states-system. Moral theory in the sense of thinking about the meaning of justice is a relatively recent arrival in international relations. Perhaps the most important publication in this regard is Charles Beitz's 1979 *Political Theory and International Relations* which represents the best known attempt to apply moral theory to the international realm via the work of John Rawls. Rawls's landmark *Theory of Justice* has, above all else, served to reinvigorate thinking on the meaning of justice, community and the good life across the board. The gradual emergence of a small literature of this type, including the works of Henry Shue, Onora O'Neill, Michael Walzer and, more recently, Janna Thompson and Andrew Linklater, reflects what might be called, paraphrasing Quentin Skinner, 'the return of grand moral theory' to the realm of international politics.

It was the reaction to Rawls's work that largely spurred the development of what has come to be called the communitarianism approach and the associated liberal/communitarian debate. Communitarian critics of Rawls drew attention to the way in which liberal conceptions of justice either ignored or were blind to the manner in which individuals were situated in real communities. The major criticism of Rawls's position was that a recognition of this dimension undermines the possibility of judging from behind a 'veil of ignorance', the central intellectual device of his theory. Attention to this dimension of human agency could reveal the limitations of the attempt to establish an impartial or neutral theory of justice. The result of this insight was the development of a variety of approaches which attempted to take the specifics of cultural context into account. These differed in scope and approach, from the broad alternative provided by Michael Walzer, in *Spheres of Justice*[12] (which in many ways represents the communitarian attempt to offer a comprehensive theory of justice similar in scope and ambition to Rawls's) to those interested in the way in which liberal theories (and some communitarian ones) articulated a masculinist view of justice which ignored or excluded the concerns of women. Writers such as Iris Marion Young, Seyla Benhabib, Carol Gilligan and Jean Bethke Elshtain, have all sought to correct the masculinist blindness of conventional, especially liberal, moral theory. Their efforts have sought to direct moral theory away from the exclusive emphasis on abstract,

[12] M. Walzer, *Spheres of Justice* (Oxford: Blackwell, 1983).

9

Justice as recognition of Identity

impartial justice in which the aim is to establish the nature of moral obligations, either within communities or across them, towards an attempt to develop theories which are equally, if not more, attentive to the arguably more 'feminine' perspectives of care, benevolence and compassion.

For the purposes of this book the most important development to come out of these debates has been a concern with the development of a moral theory in which 'difference', either 'cultural' or gender based, is accorded an appropriate place. The identification of 'difference' as an element in calculations of justice is indicative of a change of emphasis away from distributive issues. It is possible to sum up this change in emphasis as one which focuses on justice as *recognition*. As Iris Marion Young has argued, justice for most theorists has referred to questions of the distribution of material goods and services or the distribution of rights and duties of equal individual citizens.[13] For many theorists, including Young, the distributive definition of justice fails to capture the full nature of inequality in most societies and across the globe. As a result of the perceived limitations of the distributive paradigm there has been an attempt to broaden and redefine the concept of justice. Justice understood as recognition embodies the assumption that discrimination and inequality occur not only in the realm of material well-being but are equally experienced in the realm of identity. In this formulation, justice involves recognising the particular identities and claims of distinct ethnic, cultural or gender groupings. The idea of justice as recognition asks how is it possible to do justice to those who are marginalised or excluded because of their different identities or because they are seen as 'other'.

The idea of justice as recognition suggests that justice should refer to a more complete and inclusive account of well-being than those provided by purely economic or legalistic accounts. Justice as recognition extends well-being to include external recognition of the identity, or identities, constituting any individual or group. As Charles Taylor argues, recognition rests on the argument that:

> a person or group of people can suffer real damage, real distortion, if the people or society around them mirror back to them a confining or demeaning or contemptible picture of themselves. Non-recognition or misrecognition can inflict harm, can be a form of oppression, imprisoning someone in a false, distorted, and reduced mode of being.[14]

[13] See I. M. Young, *Justice and the Politics of Difference* (Princeton University Press, 1990).
[14] C. Taylor, 'The Politics of Recognition', in C. Taylor and A. Gutman, *Multiculturalism: Examining the Politics of Recognition* (Princeton University Press, 1994), p. 25.

ID distorted by group treatment

[handwritten annotations: equality as sameness dictated by white = injustice at level of identity]

The politics of recognition refers not only to people's relationships to the things of the world but to their fundamental modes of being-in-the-world. The issue of recognition therefore adds an ontological dimension to the problem of justice whereby justice is related to recognition of who 'we' *are*.

For example, in many societies today the concern with class discrimination has been replaced or overshadowed by debates on how to recognise the place of various cultures or groups which go to make up society as whole. In multicultural and immigrant societies such as Canada, the United States and Australia the issue of cultural recognition is at the forefront of current political debate. In these societies justice as recognition extends to the relations between white Anglo-Saxon majorities and various migrant communities as well as to the relationship between both these communities and the indigenous populations of their countries. (In Australia today one of the most pressing issues facing the government and society is how to recognise the cultural and identity costs born by the indigenous populations since white settlement. The demand for an apology from the Federal Government for its role in the forced separation of Aboriginal children from their parents and the creation of what have been called the 'stolen generations' is, contrary to current government thinking which sees such an apology as an acknowledgement of financial responsibility, a demand for recognition of the experiences of indigenous Australians and the impact this has had on their lives and identities.)

According to their critics, liberal theories of politics and justice, such as the work of John Rawls, do not recognise substantive differences, in fact are predicated on their denial, and therefore fail in the goal of achieving justice. Advocates of the politics of recognition argue that the attempt to provide an impartial and universal theory of justice constitutes a violence to different identities because they assume one particular identity as the standard universal model for human agency.

These arguments will be examined in more depth in chapter 1. What can be noted here is that injustice at the level of identity is a consequence of the formulation of the meaning of equality. The principal objection to these models is that in them, equality comes to mean sameness or a shared identity, usually derived from a white, European male. To be equal means to share not only the same rights and duties but also to be constituted as similar agents sharing the same identity. The aspiration for an account of justice as recognition on the other hand involves the attempt to redefine equality so that it incorporates difference.

The principle of justice to difference, in so far as it is an account of justice, pursues equality but defines it differently. The issue of recognition suggests, adopting the vocabulary of Michael Walzer, a 'thin' notion of equality. It suggests that insofar as equality requires some quality to be shared, then different agents are equal in the manner of sharing the 'thin' quality of 'identity' rather than any particular substantive identity. Thus justice is achieved by recognising the particular manner in which different humans identify themselves.

Justice as recognition has, like many other ideas, crossed over from political theory and moral philosophy into the domain of IR. Attention to cultural questions in the moral theory of international politics, while often present, has only recently come to take a more central place. The emergence of the idea of justice as recognition has in recent times served to transform much of how normative IR is conducted and in particular which questions now form the focus of moral debate and ethical reasoning. It is only fitting that these developments should be echoed in attempts to theorise international justice. The work of feminists and critical theorists in particular has focused on the goal of reframing how the issue of difference can be approached in IR. The single most important text in this regard has been Andrew Linklater's *The Transformation of Political Community*.[15] Detailed discussion of this text occurs in chapters 2, 3 and 4. What can be acknowledged here is that while Linklater sits firmly within the cosmopolitan tradition, he has sought to engage in a rethinking of cosmopolitanism so that a concern with the inclusion of difference becomes a central goal. As a result he has seriously engaged with the work of 'difference' theorists and attempted to incorporate their insights into the cosmopolitan project. A central component of Linklater's approach is the utilisation of Jürgen Habermas's critical theory and in particular the idea of discourse ethics. The introduction of discourse ethics allows the cosmopolitan project to be reformulated along communicative lines. In particular it introduces the idea that justice to difference can be achieved through communicative, dialogic, inclusion.

The argument presented in this book begins with that insight. It is argued that recognition is most successfully (though not exclusively) accomplished through acts of communication and understanding, and in particular, through conversation. The recognition of the shared quality

[15] A. Linklater, *The Transformation of Political Community: Ethical Foundations of the Post-Westphalian Era* (Cambridge: Polity Press, 1997).

12

of identity in turn rests on, and is mediated through, the shared quality of language. Because human identity is shaped and constituted linguistically (though not exclusively so) it is capable of articulation through language; in other words, it can be communicated. This being the case, recognition becomes a dialogical task to be achieved through understanding the 'other' in conversation. For this reason the work of Gadamer is used to demonstrate how the dialogical character of understanding constitutes an act of communication between differently constituted agents. The major task proceeding from these insights is to theorise the nature of a good dialogue in which justice to difference is achieved. Linklater's work contains one theorisation of the nature of good inclusive dialogue and, to date, represents the most consistent attempt offered in international relations to think through the meaning of inclusion in a universal dialogue. The work of David Campbell and other poststructuralists has also contributed to a serious effort to think through the relationship of 'self' to 'other' in the international context. However, as is noted in chapter 2, this has not, for a variety of reasons, involved sustained reflection on the meaning of dialogue and conversation. The aim of this work is to contribute to the project of thinking about the nature of communication and dialogue in an international context and, in particular, about what a universal community in which justice to difference is achieved might look like.

However, before proceeding further down this track one important task needs to be undertaken. The best means for understanding the importance of communication as an ethical/moral relationship is to compare it to its alternatives. It is only when having examined the ways in which communication differs from certain other modes of interaction that it is possible to understand both how communication provides a superior form of self/other relation and what exactly is involved in communicating. For this reason the discussion below turns to the work of Tzvetan Todorov and his now classic discussion of self/other relations in *The Conquest of America*.[16] The principal task performed by this discussion is to elaborate on the ways in which communication is related to both knowledge and belief. While it says little about what 'good' dialogue itself might consist of, Todorov's reading of the encounter between Europeans and the occupants of the Americas provides an essential service by making the argument for communication over and against its alternatives of assimilation and coexistence.

[16] T. Todorov, *The Conquest of America* (New York: Harper), 1982.

2 Cultures meeting for 1st time…

Self/other relations in the conquest of America: annihilation, assimilation, coexistence and communication

In the *Conquest of America*, Todorov attempts to understand how the 'enigma' of otherness was apprehended by the Spanish in the Americas. His enquiry examines the relationship between self and other that developed when two different cultures encountered each other for the first time.[17] In particular, he examines the relationship between knowledge of the other and evaluation of them in the century after the Spanish conquest. Todorov asks the question: if one's knowledge of understanding of the other is inaccurate or deficient then can one truly have a just relationship? Following this is a further question: what is the relationship between one's knowledge (or ignorance) of the other and one's actions towards them? In this way Todorov's study addresses the question of the content of recognition: what does recognition consist of? The aim of *Conquest of America* is to examine the relationship between knowledge and evaluation of the other from the Spanish perspective. The ensuing discussion will attempt to reveal and explain the most important problems that stand in the way of knowing and conversing with the other.

The answers to these questions generate four different possibilities for self–other relations which can be used to assess different accounts of community and justice in IR.[18] For the purposes of this work, the

---

[17] The meeting of the Spanish and the Indians in the years after 1492 is of interest to this investigation for several reasons. The inhabitants of the Americas, indeed the Americas themselves, had no place in the Christian cosmology prior to 1492, and were truly 'other'. Thus, upon encountering them, the Europeans had to interpret this new phenomenon and decide how it might fit their old cosmology. It can be argued that this encounter began the process of decentring the European identity. The difficulties and problems involved in such a decentring are a necessary step towards communication. For another reading of this encounter see B. Jahn, 'The Power of Culture in International Relations: The Spanish Conquest in the Americas and its Theoretical Repercussions' (San Diego: paper presented at ISA Annual Conference, April 1996). See also D. Blaney and N. Inayatullah, 'Prelude to a Conversation of Cultures in International Society? Todorov and Nandy on the Possibility of Dialogue', *Alternatives*, 19 (1994), 23–51; C. Brown, 'The Modern Requirement?: Reflections on Normative International Theory in a Post-Western World', *Millennium: Journal of International Studies*, 17.2 (1988), 339–48; C. Brown, 'Cultural Diversity and International Political Theory: From the Requirement to "Mutual Respect"', *Review of International Studies* (2000), 26, 199–13 and, W. E. Connolly, 'Identity and Difference in Global Politics', in J. Der Derian and M. J. Shapiro, *International/Intertextual Relations: Postmodern Readings of World Politics* (Lexington, 1989).

[18] Todorov's account is not without its critics. While the following argument draws heavily on Todorov it is an interpretation and application of ideas found in *Conquest of America* and not a wholesale endorsement of his position. The purpose of this discussion is merely to use his categories to pursue a certain line of thinking.

14

significance of Todorov's book lies in the introduction of a set of categories derived from these possibilities. These four categories are: annihilation, assimilation, coexistence and communication. Annihilation involves the complete physical or ideational destruction of the other. Assimilation involves the other's incorporation into one's own world, but not as an equal, for it also involves the destruction or denial of important differences in the name of a greater similarity. Coexistence involves toleration and neutrality but suggests no genuine engagement with the other. Communication suggests that it is possible to understand the other and to move towards an exchange of knowledge. It also suggests the possibility of agreement and a reciprocity of subjectivity, two possibilities denied by the alternative categories. Thus, it is only the last category that permits a just relation to the other. The goal of justice to difference involves communication and conversation. This section examines these categories and demonstrates the relationship of thought and practice in them.[19]

In addition to developing these descriptive and evaluative categories Todorov's study permits a defence of the category of communication. If the vocabulary of international justice, at least in philosophical circles, has now become one of recognition then Todorov provides an argument that recognition, or justice, is best achieved through communication and conversation.

The four modes of engagement: annihilation, assimilation, coexistence and communication, not only represent practices but also correspond to normative and philosophical positions. The ensuing discussion attempts to reveal and explain the most important problems that stand in the way of knowing and conversing with the other.

Todorov argues that the relation of self to other and knowledge to action exists on three axes of alterity:

> First of all, there is a value judgement (an axiological level); the other is good or bad, I love or do not love him, or as was more likely to be said at the time, he is my equal or my inferior (for there is usually no question that I am good and that I esteem myself). Secondly, there is the action of *rapprochement* of distancing in relation to the other (praxeological level): I embrace the other's values. I identify myself with him, or else I identify the other with myself, I impose my own image upon him;

---

[19] Todorov himself does not use these terms, I have adapted them for my own purposes. Todorov uses the terms enslavement, colonialism and communication, conquest, love and knowledge to describe various manifestations of similar phenomena. See Todorov, *Conquest of America*, pp. 169, 185.

between submission to the other and the other's submission there is also a third term, which is neutrality, or indifference. Thirdly, I know or am ignorant of the other's identity (this would be the epistemic level); of course there is no absolute here, but an endless gradation between the lower or higher states of knowledge.[20]

Annihilation, assimilation, coexistence and communication exist primarily on only one of the planes of alterity, namely that of practice. Practice here should be taken very broadly to include the *act* of identification. While Todorov is at pains to assert that there is no direct causal relation between these three levels, we can nonetheless see how one may lead to the next and how they are mutually implicated. The key question of Todorov's enquiry, therefore, is what relationships exist between one's knowledge (or ignorance) of the other and one's actions towards the other.

Discovery and conquest

Todorov establishes his categories by analysing the encounters between a series of Spaniards: Columbus, Cortés, Sepúlveda, Las Casas, Dúran, Sahagún, and the Indians. To varying degrees these encounters correspond to the progression: Discovery (Columbus), Conquest and Annihilation (Cortés and Sepúlveda) and Assimilation (Las Casas, Dúran and Sahagún), with the last two authors also beginning the act of Communication.

Cortés and Columbus are instances of discovery and conquest. They both comprehend the other as inferior and themselves as superior; in the case of Columbus it is because of their difference, in the case of Cortés, in spite of it. It is because they begin with the assumption of superiority that their knowledge or lack of knowledge of the Indians does not affect their judgement. As far as understanding the Indians, Columbus at first insists that he can understand their language (because he believes that all words have a common origin and if they sound alike they must mean roughly the same thing) but later, as his attempts at interpretation fail him, he goes so far as to suggest that the Indians not only cannot speak Spanish but that they do not possess language at all, nor do they have religion. Indeed they are completely without culture, the evidence of this being their proclivity for nakedness.[21] Columbus, it seems, never really encounters the other, in the sense that he leaves with almost no

---

[20] *Ibid.*, p. 185. [21] *Ibid.*, pp. 31 and 35.

Understanding an "other":
knowledge, valuation & action towards the other
Introduction

more knowledge of the Indians than when he arrived. Instead, he sees only what he expected to see: the Indies and China.

In the case of Cortés, we see a more complicated relationship between knowledge, valuation and action towards the other. Cortés, despite being an agent of the Indians' destruction, knows them relatively well. He understands the Indian language, and even manipulates their cosmology and beliefs in order to further his conquest. Furthermore, of all the conquistadors Cortés, surprisingly enough, is liked by many Indians.[22] He demonstrates his knowledge and communicative skill most famously by using the Indian belief that the Spanish are gods and that he is the god Quetzalcoatl to assist his victory over them. Cortés is also an admirer of the products of Indian civilisation and rates them highly in comparison to those of Spain: 'I shall not attempt to describe it all, save to say that in Spain there is nothing to compare with it.'[23] It is, however, not the Indians he admires but their works: 'Cortés goes into ecstasies about the Aztec productions but does not acknowledge their makers as human individualities to be seen on the same level as himself.'[24] Thus, knowledge does not necessarily lead to a positive valuation or relation of equality. Cortés understands and knows the other but values them (the Indians, not their handiwork) as inferior. There is no self-reflection involved in the encounter, nor any reflection upon the justice of the Spanish occupation or his own part in it. He takes it as self-evident that the European Christians are superior. No amount of knowledge of the Indians' culture will change the fact that they are pagans and idolaters and it is Spain's duty to conquer and convert them.[25]

According to Todorov, the moral of the story of Cortés is '... unless grasping is accompanied by a full acknowledgement of the other as subject, it risks being used for purposes of exploitation, of "taking", knowledge will be subordinated to power.'[26] It is this inability or refusal to recognise the other's equality, as a subject like oneself, that allows and condones the Spanish conquest and their massacres: '... this conduct is ... conditioned by their notion of the Indians as inferior beings, halfway between men and beasts. Without this essential premise, the destruction could not have taken place.'[27] For all his knowledge,

---

[22] *Ibid.*, pp. 176–7.   [23] *Ibid.*, p. 128.   [24] *Ibid.*, p. 129.
[25] 'There is no doubt that the natives must obey the royal orders of your majesty, whatever their nature.' *Ibid.*, p. 130.
[26] *Ibid.*, p. 132.   [27] *Ibid.*, p. 147.

17

Cortés does not communicate, in the sense intended here, with the Indians because his evaluation of them as inferior remains and is unaffected by his knowledge, thereby ruling out communication from the beginning.[28]

Assimilation

In the case of the Spanish priest and Bishop Bartolomeo de Las Casas, probably the principal advocate of the Indians' equality in the sixteenth century, the relationship between knowledge and evaluation becomes more complex. Las Casas' relation to the Indians is that of assimilation. This is a more complex relationship to the other than the ones discussed earlier because although it allows for the possibility of equality, such equality comes at the expense of identity.

Las Casas has his *alter ego* in the figure of the scholar, lawyer and philosopher Ginês de Sepúlveda. Where Las Casas argues against the policies of conquest and enslavement, Sepúlveda defends the wars against the Indians as just on the grounds that the Indians are naturally inferior. The two figures engaged in a debate at Valladolid in Spain in 1550, the content of which illustrates the category of assimilation. The basic arguments were simple: Las Casas argued that the Indians were the Europeans' equals and should be treated as such, while Sepúlveda argued that the Indians' inferiority legitimated their destruction. Las Casas' position, however, is not as straightforward, nor as desirable,

---

[28] Despite the ease with which Cortés undertakes the conquest and despite the general Spanish assumption of superiority, the Spanish felt the need to provide some moral and legal means by which they could justify the conquest and dispossession of the Indians. The example of the *requirimiento* is the most famous illustration of this. The *requirimiento* was a Spanish proclamation required to be read upon encountering Indians in the new world. It presented the Indians with a history and explanation of how the Spanish came to be laying claims to the new world. It suggested that the Spanish claim was Just and God-given, and gave the Indians two alternatives: voluntary surrender and recognition of Spanish legitimacy, or enslavement and war. The *requirimiento* illustrates the lack of choice presented to the Indians. It paid lip service to moral discourse but was, in fact, an ultimatum, and one that was beyond the comprehension of those to whom it was addressed (literally so because it was in Spanish!). The requirement is a parody of conversation, as it implies that the Indians can partake in the discussion, while at the same time completely ruling out the possibility of such a discussion and assuming the inequality of the other. 'The Indians can choose only between two positions of inferiority: either they submit of their own accord and become serfs; or else they will be subjugated by force and reduced to slavery . . . (they) are posited as inferiors from the start, for it is the Spaniards who determine the rules of the game. The superiority of those who promulgate the *requirimiento* . . . is already contained in the fact that it is they who are speaking while the Indians listen.' *Ibid.*, p. 148. For further discussion of the requirement see R. Shapcott, 'Conversation and Coexistence, Gadamer and the Interpretation of International Society', *Millennium: Journal of International Studies*, 23.1 (1994).

as it seems and reveals the difficulties and problems of the category of equality. The remainder of this section examines the core arguments of this debate in order to articulate more clearly the category of assimilation.

Sepúlveda's argument for the Indians' inequality is drawn from Aristotle. For Sepúlveda '. . . hierarchy, not equality, is the natural state of human society'.[29] Sepúlveda's world is made up of dichotomies of superiority/inferiority; the body must be subject to the soul, matter to form, children to parents, women to men, and slaves to masters.[30] Thus, when it comes to judging the Indians, the calculation is quite simple: the Indians are different and therefore inferior. For Sepúlveda, it is self-evident that 'our' (Spanish) identity is good, as we are Christians, and therefore we are superior to those who are not. It therefore follows that the Indians, being different, are inferior and evil. This 'natural' inferiority makes it not only possible, but just, to wage war against the barbarians: 'The greatest philosophers declare that such wars may be undertaken by a very civilised nation against uncivilised people who are more barbarous than can be imagined.'[31] The name of Sepúlveda's relation to the other is Annihilation.

Equality

Whereas Sepúlveda's starting point is a premise of human inequality and the 'natural fact' of hierarchy, Las Casas starts from the Christian principle of equality. All humans are equal before God, because they are equally capable of accepting God. Indians are human beings and potential Christians and to wage war against them is wrong and a denial of their fundamental humanity. Thus, Las Casas demonstrates their equality by asserting not only how like the Spaniards they are, but how like Christians. His argument for the Indians' equality is premised upon a Christian identity, the Indians' 'human nature' is their 'Christian nature'. As Todorov points out, the universalism of Christianity implies a fundamental lack of difference between all persons.[32] In the case of the Indians this is not only a matter of recognising them as human beings capable of understanding and converting to Christianity, but also of their particular predisposition toward it: 'At no other time and in no other people has there been seen such capacity, such predisposition,

---

[29] *Ibid.*, in note 3, p. 152. [30] See *ibid.*, p. 153.
[31] *Ibid.*, p. 156. [32] *Ibid.*, p. 162.

and such facility for conversion...'[33] They are so predisposed because they already resemble and embody basic Christian qualities. According to Las Casas, '[t]hese peoples considered in general, are by their nature all gentleness, humility and poverty, without weapons or defences not the least ingenuity, patient, enduring as none other in the world'.[34] Las Casas only sees those things he wants to see in the Indians, in particular those attributes he can interpret as essentially Christian, such as humility and poverty. There are two important points to note from this account: first, that *all* the Indians of the Americas bear these same traits and, second, that all these traits are psychological states of mind. The first denies any difference between the various Indian groups, and the second is blind to social practices and behaviour that will enable *knowledge* of who the Indians are, that is, what they believe, the reasons and meanings of their practices, and how they understand themselves; again a form of denial of differences. Las Casas proceeds to account for all differences as, in fact, similarities. For example, the Indians' disinterest in material wealth is in harmony with '... the divine law and the evangelical perfection which praise and approve that man be content with no more than what is necessary'.[35] It is therefore seen as evidence of their essential Christianity. There is, then, a major catch in Las Casas' defence, the price of the Indians' equality is their identity; according to natural law, humans exist 'without any difference'.[36]

Las Casas attempts to demonstrate the Indians' equality by minimising the differences that Sepúlveda, for instance, draws attention to. Ironically, this means that Las Casas is, in many ways, even further away from knowledge and communication with the other than Sepúlveda. The Indians themselves never speak in Las Casas' account; they are certainly not present at Vallodolid, and we learn little or nothing of them in the course of the debate. For all Las Casas' love of the Indians it is at the cost of knowing them. For all Sepúlveda's hatred of them he knows them better. Todorov asks 'Can we really love someone if we know little or nothing of his identity, if we see, in place of that identity, a projection of ourselves or of our ideals?... Does one culture risk trying to transform the other in its own name, and therefore risk subjugating it as well?'[37] The name for Las Casas' relation to the other is Assimilation.

---

[33] *Ibid.*, p. 163.   [34] *Ibid.*   [35] *Ibid.*, p. 165.   [36] *Ibid.*, p. 162.   [37] *Ibid.*, p. 168.

annihilate : assimilate
as
enslave :Colonize

So far in this account we have seen the development of the nexus difference/inferiority, identity/equality. Sepúlveda believes the Indians are different and, therefore, inferior. Las Casas believes they are equal and, therefore, the same. While we may applaud Las Casas and sympathise with his attempts to bring justice to the Indians by ending the wars against them, the realm of practice reveals another layer to this story. We know Sepúlveda wishes the Indians' destruction and justifies the wars against them, but what of Las Casas? What is the relation of thought to practice in his case?

Las Casas supports the colonisation and occupation of the Americas; what he rejects is the Conquest or, more correctly, its means and practitioners: 'Las Casas does not want to put an end to the annexations of the Indians, he merely wants this to be effected by priests rather than soldiers.'[38] The Indians are potential Christians, they are equals but they must be converted in order to achieve their full equality. Las Casas, believing the Indians to be ripe for conversion, seeks the end of the bloodshed but not the occupation.

According to Todorov, the difference between Las Casas and Sepúlveda is the difference between two ideologies: Enslavement and Colonialism.[39] The move to Colonialism may be an improvement on Enslavement, but it is not a recognition of the other's being a subject 'like oneself', as the Indians still remain subjugated to the colonial power. Las Casas' defence of the Indians is only in the name of Colonialism, and their continued subjugation. As in the *requirimiento*,[40] the Indians only have a choice between two forms of subjugation (though of course in reality they rarely even have a choice about this).

Colonialism denies justice in the particular form that Todorov desires, that of communication: '... if colonialism opposes enslavement, it simultaneously opposes that contact with the other which I shall simply call communication. To the triad understand/seize/destroy corresponds this other triad in inverted order: enslavement/ colonialism/ communication.'[41]

---

[38] *Ibid.*, p. 171.
[39] An *'enslavement'* ideology reduces the other to the status of an object, to be bought or sold. A *'colonialist'* ideology recognises the other's subjectivity but only to the extent that 'the other is seen as a subject capable of producing objects that one can then possess'. *Ibid.*, p. 176.
[40] See note 28 above regarding the *requirimiento*.   [41] *Ibid.*, p. 177.

Christianizing is: unjust b/c ignores difference, imposes new identity

Equality and inequality exist on the axiological level, concerning values and judgement. However, they are almost inevitably accompanied by counterparts on the praxeological level of practice and identification. The issues revealed at Valladolid no longer just oppose equality to inequality, but also identity to difference. Specifically, '. . . difference is corrupted into inequality, equality into identity. These are the two great figures of the relation to the other that delimit the other's inevitable space.'[42] It is in this space that the category of assimilation provides a relationship more familiar to modern, liberal approaches to difference and otherness. Where the categories of annihilation and conquest value difference as inequality, the category of assimilation asserts equality, intended as a defence of the weak and the different, but ironically at the *expense* of difference: 'If it is incontestable that the prejudice of superiority is an obstacle in the road to knowledge, we must also admit that the prejudice of equality is a still greater one, for it consists in identifying the other purely and simply with one's own "ego ideal" (or with oneself).'[43] In the category of assimilation the defence of the other is purchased at the cost of identity.

Las Casas' justice for the Indians is an attempt at Christian justice, but it is a justice to be imposed on the Indians at a considerable continued cost to them. It is unjust because it is premised on the denial of their difference and, therefore, it denies them the articulation of their own concerns. Starting from the assumption of identity, Las Casas' justice lies in awakening the Indians to this identity and denying or eradicating their cultural difference and own self-understanding. It is an imposition of an identity upon them and, thus, an unwitting denial of what Las Casas values so highly: their equality. The relation of assimilation is, therefore, an unjust or less just relation to the other in that it insufficiently embodies the recognition of the other's equality.

Coexistence

Before exploring Todorov's notion of communication, there is one other option, adopted by Las Casas in his later life and certainly prevalent in discussions of cultural difference today, especially in IR. This is the stance of tolerance, neutrality or coexistence.

Todorov argues that after the Valladolid encounter, Las Casas underwent a change that gradually led him to a 'perspectivist' position. At Valladolid, Las Casas had to find a way to make the seemingly

---

[42] *Ibid.*, p. 146.   [43] *Ibid.*, p. 165.

barbaric practice of human sacrifice appear a Christian act. He did this by demonstrating examples of sacrifice in the Bible, not least of which is the sacrifice of Christ. However, he also had another, and perhaps more interesting, argument which leads him to a more directly relativist position. Las Casas argued that the Indians' practice of sacrifice should be understood as a gesture of religiosity: '[M]en worship God according to their capacities and in their fashion, always trying to do the best they can... the greatest proof one can give of one's love for God consists of offering Him what is most precious to oneself, human life itself.'[44] The Indians therefore demonstrate their love of God through the (misguided) practice of human sacrifice. While the practice itself may be condemned, the gesture is worthy. Las Casas even argued that, in the intensity of their worship, the Aztecs exceeded the Christians.

For Las Casas the Indians' ignorance of Christian belief is not in itself an argument against their *religiosity*. The value they place on their gods is equal to that of the Christians. Their error is to believe their gods to be the true gods. In these arguments, Las Casas comes very close to an acknowledgement of the relativity of all belief. If their gods are true for them, ours is true for us: 'what then remains common and universal is no longer the God of the Christian religion... but the very idea of divinity, of what is above us; the religious rather than religion'.[45] Las Casas argued that the Indians believed their gods to be true and demonstrated this height of religiosity by sacrificing human life to them. This is a definite shift from the perception of the Indians as exclusively barbarian and inferior because it perceives them as equal yet different.

At this point in Las Casas' argument, the relationship between equality and identity changes: 'equality is no longer bought at the price of identity; it is not an absolute value that we are concerned with: each man has the right to approach god by the path that suits him. There is no longer a true god (ours) but a coexistence of possible universes...'[46] Las Casas has moved to the stage of equality as coexistence.

Though he does not surrender the idea of evangelism and the conversion of the Indians, there is really only one practice Las Casas can condone: the withdrawal of the Spanish from the Americas in order to 're-establish in their sovereignties all their kings and natural lords'.[47] Where previously Las Casas' sequence ran equal, same, assimilate, it

---

[44] *Ibid.*, p. 188–9.   [45] *Ibid.*, p. 189.   [46] *Ibid.*, p. 190.   [47] *Ibid.*, p. 193.

now runs something like same, equal, tolerate.[48] Equality becomes tolerance, neutrality and coexistence. The question that needs to be put here is whether coexistence is enough, is this truly where justice to otherness lies? The answer of this book is that it is not enough, and it is to what lies beyond tolerance, coexistence and neutrality that it now turns.

Communication

What remains is the option of communication. In none of the scenarios previously explored have we come across an instance of equality leading to communication. Even Las Casas' final position, coexistence, forestalls and withholds from understanding and communicating with the Indians. Coexistence denies any possibility of communicating or judging across cultures. Equality here means autonomy but extends no further. The other is both like me (equal) and unlike me (different) and being unlike me I cannot engage with them. Put in terms of the identity/difference nexus Todorov offers us this formulation: '... we want equality without its compelling us to accept identity; but also difference without its degenerating into superiority/inferiority. We aspire to reap the benefits of the egalitarian model and of the hierarchic model; we aspire to rediscover the meaning of the social without losing the quality of the individual.'[49] To recognise truly the humanity of the other, to have a relationship with them that meets this aspiration, one must communicate, or at least attempt communication. Of course, communication and conversation is itself problematic and requires more space than is available here to articulate fully and explore it. However, Todorov begins to sketch the requirements of communication and it is with this that we will leave this section.

Assuming, Todorov argues, that we want to have interaction between cultures and go beyond coexistence, then such interaction must proceed in the form of proposition, not imposition. Communication, therefore, is opposed to assimilation as proposition is opposed to imposition:

> The essential thing ... is to know whether they [changes] are *imposed* or *proposed*. Christianization, like the export of any ideology or technology, can be condemned as soon as it is imposed, by arms or otherwise. A civilisation may have features we can say are superior or inferior; but this does not justify their being imposed on others. Even more, to

[48] Both of these, of course, contrast with the view of Sepúlveda: different, inferior, destroy/enslave.
[49] *Ibid.*, p. 249.

Imposition of Christ.. denies communion + reciprocity inequality inherent in orientation ("not listening")

impose one's will on others implies that one does not concede to that other the same humanity one grants to oneself . . .[50]

Proposition allows communication and reciprocity, imposition denies it. Communication involves not only mutual recognition of the other's status as both different and like oneself, but also an orientation towards mutual understanding and enlightenment.

After the false conversation of the *requirimiento*, the Spanish discourse is never addressed to the Indians, but instead to the Crown, and their praxis is concerned with what the Spanish should *do to* the Indians, and never with what the *Indians* desire. It is never conducted as proposition but as imposition, and that is what makes the relationship unjust.[51]

Thus, to encounter the other as different we need to suppose as little as possible regarding their identity beforehand. We need only suppose, unlike Columbus, that we are capable of communicating with them and they with us. Understanding and agreement are possible because the other is seen neither as absolutely other nor essentially identical. The idea of communication suggests an encounter with the other that is premised on the possibility of mutual understanding.

What such a morality suggests is a continual ongoing conversation, that itself contributes to the building of community, of shared understandings and practices. It is possible that through engagement with others and through a commitment to communication and understanding that new understandings of self and of the other can come about. A real conversation Todorov suggests '. . . contributes to the reciprocal illumination of one culture by another, to "making us look into the other's face" . . . we know the other by the self, but also the self by the other.'[52] The second great tragedy of the Spanish in the Americas (after the genocide of the Indians, that is) was that the Spanish never attempted genuine conversation with the Indians nor sought 'illumination' in their encounter. This book is committed to the task of preventing the repetition of such tragedies through the formulation of an adequate account of conversation.

In light of this discussion it is concluded that communication represents the practice most capable of delivering a more just relationship

---

[50] *Ibid.*, p. 179.
[51] 'No one asked the Indians if they wanted the wheel, or looms or forges; they were obliged to accept them. Here is where the violence resides, and it does not depend on the possible utility of these objects. But in whose name would we condemn the unarmed preacher, even if his avowed goal is to convert us to his own religion?' *Ibid.*, p. 181.
[52] *Ibid.*, p. 241.

to otherness. Communication involves a formulation of equality that does not require the assimilation of the identity of the other, nor restrict equality to coexistence. Communication suggests that equality is achieved through discursive engagement. However, the implications of communication go beyond this. Communication also suggests the possibility of developing more inclusive moral arrangements that do not require the annihilation or assimilation of the other.

The category of communication suggests the possibilities of conversation across moral boundaries and between radically different agents. In so doing, it suggests the further possibility that dialogue may result in the expansion and/or reconfiguration of moral boundaries. This is so because the principle of communication is universally inclusive: no agent capable of communication can be ruled out in principle. Communication, therefore, suggests that moral boundaries remain open. It suggests that no communicative agent can be excluded on the grounds of their linguistic or cultural difference.

The idea of communication being pursued here should be understood as a relationship involving a reciprocity between actors and not just the transmission of information or knowledge from one actor to another. It is communication as equality. While communication might seem a straightforward concept there are in fact varieties to it, some of which are more reciprocal and 'communicative' than others. Discussion of these issues is the task of the remainder of the book.

Chapter structure

This discussion has provided a preliminary case for communication as a model of self–other relations capable of providing a more just relationship to difference, of fulfilling the requirement of justice as recognition. The remainder of this book consists of an examination and evaluation of approaches to justice and community in IR in terms of this typology: annihilation, assimilation, coexistence and communication. In so doing, it explores the relations between the axiological, epistemic and praxeological positions of a variety of thinkers and perspectives. The next two chapters will attempt to assess the contributions of Normative IR theories according to the degree to which they approximate, account for, contribute to or embody the idea of communication.

Chapter 1 proceeds from this discussion to an assessment of the so-called cosmopolitan/communitarian divide. An application of the category of communication to this divide suggests the possibility of effecting a reconciliation between cosmopolitan and communitarian positions. The discussion here shifts the critique to the level of agency. At this level cosmopolitanism contains a significant assimilatory logic. Communitarianism on the other hand comes closest to the category of coexistence. The case is presented that the positions represented by Charles Beitz, Onora O'Neill, Michael Walzer and Chris Brown do not take sufficient account of the possibilities for communication between radically diverse agents. The category of communication allows a critique of both sides of this divide by revealing their limitations, while also offering the possibility of incorporating their key insights into a new position. By correcting these tendencies with an account of communication between particular, situated agents it can be argued that a communitarian path to cosmopolitanism becomes available.

Chapter 2 discusses three attempts to move beyond the cosmopolitanl communitarian divide. Constitutive, poststructuralist and critical theories are examined as accounts which attempt to incorporate a discursive, communicative dimension into the question of community. Starting from broadly communitarian premises these approaches aspire to more genuinely universal and inclusive positions. Constitutive, poststructuralist and critical theories all proceed from the hermeneutic premise that the social world is constituted by the meanings it has for its inhabitants and that this applies as equally to norms and values as it does to boundaries and institutions. Despite sharing this common ground with communitarians, they all attempt to extend the possibilities for recognition and communication beyond the state-based community. Chapter 2 outlines these positions and demonstrates how they go beyond cosmopolitan and communitarian positions by incorporating a discursive element. The chapter concludes with the acknowledgement that Linklater's application of Habermasian discourse ethics to the cosmopolitan project represents the most sophisticated and thorough incorporation of a communicative dimension to these issues. One of Linklater's principal contributions is the use of discourse ethics to develop a model of conversation between concrete situated agents. In so doing he moves the debate to another plane.

Having established the category of communication as the basis for recognition of difference, the debate then moves to the question of what communication consists of and, in particular, what might constitute an appropriate model of conversation. It is this question which forms the substance of chapter 3 which engages in more detailed discussion of the limits and potentialities of both poststructuralist and critical theoretical accounts of communication. It argues that despite their differences both approaches exhibit a tension between the concern with freedom and a concern with communication. Discourse ethics in particular is revealed to contain a tension between its principle of universal freedom in dialogue and the requirements of a dialogue characterised as providing 'the moral point of view'.

Chapter 4 presents the case for the philosophical hermeneutic account of communication. Philosophical hermeneutics provides a theory of what understanding consists of and, as such, develops an account of communication. In philosophical hermeneutics, understanding is an act of communication that is essentially dialogical or conversational in nature. In Gadamer's model of conversation self and other are seen as partners in discussion concerning an object or subject (*die sache Selbst*) which is placed before them. It is this model of conversation that is most consistent with a practice of communication in which the other is seen as different and yet equal. In this model the other is seen as holding the same potential for truthful interpretation as the self and as being capable of conveying that interpretation in conversation. It is argued that the claim to universality of philosophical hermeneutics suggests a model of conversation which is radically inclusive because it is open to any linguistically constituted agent. This radical inclusiveness relieves philosophical hermeneutics of the task of creating a homogenous realm of similarly constituted agents. At this juncture the Aristotelian concept of *phronesis* or practical reasoning is introduced in order to strengthen the case for the philosophical hermeneutic model of the self/other relationship and its application to the goal of 'thin' cosmopolitanism. Chapter 4 also involves a comparison of the philosophical hermeneutic and discourse ethics models and suggests that philosophical hermeneutics provides a less assimilatory model.

Chapter 5 examines the principal limitations and criticisms of philosophical hermeneutics. It begins with an examination of the so-called Habermas/Gadamer debate which focused on the role of tradition and the capacity of reason to provide emancipation. Discussion then turns to the relationship between philosophical hermeneutics and deconstruction as witnessed in the interaction between Gadamer and Jacques Derrida. The chapter concludes by arguing that philosophical hermeneutics, rather than constituting a polar opposite, can be distinguished from both critical theory and deconstruction by its distinctive

Stimmung, or mood, which emphasises continuity over discontinuity or rupture.

Chapter 6 incorporates the insights of philosophical hermeneutics into a reformulated and 'thin' cosmopolitanism. It suggests that among the characteristics of a cosmopolitanism informed by philosophical hermeneutics is the never-completed pursuit of understanding and agreement. Furthermore, the flexibility of the philosophical hermeneutic approach leaves open the possibility that different parts of the international system may develop or engage in different types of conversations and correspondingly develop different levels of 'thick or thin' agreement. The primary characteristic of such a thin cosmopolitanism is that it does not prescribe the moral content of the community, instead, it allows that content to be filled in by the participants themselves. The chapter concludes with some reflections on how the perspective adopted in this book might inform thinking about universal human rights.

1   Beyond the cosmopolitan/ communitarian divide

> we want equality without its compelling us to accept identity; but also difference without its degenerating into superiority/inferiority. We aspire to reap the benefits of the egalitarian model and of the hierarchic model; we aspire to rediscover the meaning of the social without losing the quality of the individual.[1]

In recent years the question of community in IR has been discussed increasingly in terms of a cosmopolitan/communitarian divide. According to Chris Brown the cosmopolitan/communitarian divide concerns argument over whether the state or the species represent the limit of human community.[2] Cosmopolitans, Brown argues, place

[1] T. Todorov, *The Conquest of America* (New York: Harper, 1982), p. 249.
[2] While these terms are relatively new to the discourse of IR Chris Brown argues that the positions themselves have a pedigree that goes back a long way. The formulation cosmopolitan/communitarian echoes the formulation, of 'man and citizen'. Though the pedigrees of these two discourses are different, the central question is the same: which comes first, membership of the community or the species? What the cosmopolitan/communitarian formulation captures at this particular juncture, however, is the question of cultural difference, as it theoretically opens up the possibility of substate communities, whereas the men and citizens formulation focuses on the state/citizenship relationship. It is interesting to note that Andrew Linklater argues that citizenship can go higher and lower to include the species and the substate community, whereas Brown – a sympathiser with communitarianism – resists the claims of non-state communities. See C. Brown, *International Relations Theory: New Normative Approaches* (London: Harvester Wheatsheaf, 1992); C. Brown, 'International Political Theory and the Idea of World Community' in Smith, S. and Booth, K. *International Relations Theory Today* (Cambridge: Polity, 1995) and C. Brown, 'Ethics of Coexistence: The International Theory of Terry Nardin', *Review of International Studies*, 14 (1988), 213–22; also J. Thompson, *Justice and World Order: a Philosophical Enquiry* (London: Routledge, 1992); M. Cochran, *Normative Theory in International Relations* (Cambridge: Cambridge University Press, 1999); M. Cochran, 'Cosmopolitanism and Communitarianism in a Post-Cold War World', in J. Macmillan and A. Linklater (eds.), *Boundaries in Question: New Directions in International Relations* (London: Pinter, 1995); A. Linklater, *Men and Citizens in the Theory of International Relations*, 2nd edn (London: Macmillan, 1990).

Cosmopolitanism : champion universal justice; human comm.
Communitarianism: champion particular communities

ultimate moral significance on the individual and the species, while communitarians situate it in the local or national community, or the individual's relationship to the community. Central to this debate have been the questions of universal justice and cultural diversity. As it presently stands, the formulation of the problem of community in IR suggests that these two goals are necessarily oppositional. Cosmopolitanism, on one hand, is seen as championing universal justice and membership of the human community at the expense of cultural diversity and membership of particular communities. On the other, communitarianism is seen to be hostile to universal projects and sees any attempt to develop universal moral vocabularies as necessarily destructive of the particular communities in which people exist. The constitution of this issue in terms of a divide has meant that universal cosmopolitan justice has continued to be seen as in conflict with the goal of maintaining cultural diversity and justice to difference. The cosmopolitan/communitarian divide, therefore, restates the opposition between community and difference.

The aim of this chapter is to assist in overcoming this divide, as a step towards achieving a more just relationship to difference. In order to begin this task it is necessary to examine both cosmopolitan and communitarian positions. This chapter argues that neither cosmopolitanism nor communitarianism, in their most widely understood formulations, are adequate in themselves to the task of providing a satisfactory relationship to 'difference'. The inadequacy of both cosmopolitan and communitarian positions can be demonstrated by analysing them according to the criteria of 'communication' as categorised in the Introduction. In particular it is argued that both cosmopolitan and communitarian positions exclude or marginalise the possibility of moral communication and conversation between diverse groups.

The aim of this exercise, however, is not the total rejection of either cosmopolitan or communitarian positions; rather it is to effect a reconciliation. The problem lies in neither communitarianism nor cosmopolitanism, as such, but rather in aspects of the dominant formulations and, most importantly, the divide between them. The absence of an adequate account of communication on either side of the divide leads to a too-quick foreclosure of the possibilities for what may be called a communitarian path to cosmopolitanism.[3] There are two goals in this chapter: the assessment of both cosmopolitan and communitarian positions according to the category of

[3] It is these possibilities that form the focus of chapters 3 to 6.

communication; and beginning the task of overcoming the divide between them.

For the sake of clarity the discussion here is restricted to the liberal-cosmopolitanism of Charles Beitz, the obligations-based cosmopolitanism of Onora O'Neill, and the communitarianism of Michael Walzer and Chris Brown. Liberal-cosmopolitanism designates rights-based cosmopolitanism, as distinct from other forms such as Marxism or those endorsed by critical theorists like Andrew Linklater and David Held. While Beitz, O'Neill, Walzer and Brown are by no means the only important advocates of these positions, they are nonetheless useful representatives of these categories. In particular Beitz's use of early Rawls ties him directly to the principal focus of the liberal/communitarian debate and brings the concerns of that debate to the discussion of cosmopolitanism. Second, not only has Michael Walzer been one of the most important critics of Rawls, he has also been one of the few communitarians to attempt to think systematically about the international realm. Chris Brown can also be understood as attempting an application of aspects of communitarian thought to the international realm. Onora O'Neill presents an alternative reading of cosmopolitanism that expressly attempts to address some of the concerns of communitarianism. In focusing on these authors, the purpose is to depict them as representatives of correlate positions in political theory, on which the cosmopolitan/communitarian debate in IR draws.

The key to moving beyond the cosmopolitan/communitarian divide lies in a better understanding of the origins and nature of both positions. One of the problems with the cosmopolitan/communitarian framework is that it misrepresents the nature of the issues at stake, constructing debate as one over moral/political *boundaries*. However, much of the literature on which this debate draws is not concerned with boundaries as such but with disputes over the nature, source or grounding of morality *per se*. Characterised as a debate between liberals and communitarians, the central question is about how we acquire *knowledge* of the good, and the relationship between the right and the good, rather than over the *boundaries* of the moral community.[4] The Liberalism of the early Rawls, for example, appears to attempt definition of the nature of the moral point of view and pursues the possibility of defining a universal

---

[4] See S. Mulhall and A. Swift, *Liberals and Communitarians* (Oxford: Blackwell, 1992); also D. Morrice, 'The Liberal–Communitarian Debate in Contemporary Political Philosophy and its Significance for International Relations', *Review of International Studies*, 26 (2000), 233–51.

procedural account, in which the qualities of the right are defined once and for all time. Communitarianism, on the other hand, suggests that the contextual and historical nature of human social life prevents such an exercise from succeeding. Both liberalism and communitarianism begin with premises relating to the nature of morality itself and only then move on to positions regarding the scope of moral boundaries; in particular whether morality is transcendental, or universal, or whether it is contextualised and particular.[5]

There is an important qualifier that needs to be made here. Because they are not concerned with boundaries *per se* very few, if any, communitarians argue that we have *no* obligations to others, or more correctly, that community borders work as strict walls preventing expressions of moral solidarity and action between peoples. Most accept that humans on the whole are moral beings capable of treating each other morally regardless of their particular origins or situations. What the definition or expression of morality might consist of is disputed, in the sense that we may have different obligations to those who do not belong to the immediate community, but this is secondary to the charge that communitarians restrict moral actions to the domestic sphere entirely. Likewise, many liberals, such as Rawls, accept that their theories presuppose consensus and existent levels of community, and, therefore, cannot be applied unproblematically to the international realm.[6]

However, what does distinguish these positions are their conceptions of selfhood and moral agency. Liberal and communitarian positions begin with different conceptions of the moral self, and derive from them different conceptions of community. What is at issue here is the nature of

---

[5] This is what the framework suggests. What the participants themselves argue is often different. Some communitarians, such as Charles Taylor, give more specific endorsement to the possibility of heterogeneous community. See C. Taylor and A. Gutman, *Multiculturalism: Examining the Politics of Recognition* (Princeton University Press, 1994). See also his discussion of communitarianism in C. Taylor, 'Cross-Purposes: The Liberal–Communitarian Debate', in N. L. Rosenblum (ed.), *Liberalism and the Moral Life* (Harvard University Press, 1989). Taylor argues that the liberal/communitarian debate runs together two issues which should be kept separate, namely ontology and advocacy. It blurs the distinction between 'the factors you will invoke to account for the good life' and 'the moral stand or policy one adopts'. Taylor, 'Cross-Purposes', p. 159. The two are not necessarily related he argues and to conflate them is to conflate description with prescription.

[6] For instance see M. Walzer, 'The Distribution of Membership' in P. G. Brown and H. Shue (eds.), *Boundaries: National Autonomy and its Limits* (New Jersey: Rowman and Littlefield, 1981); J. Rawls, 'The Law of Peoples', in S. Shute and S. Hurley, *On Human Rights: The Oxford Amnesty Lectures* (New York: Basic Books, 1993); J. Rawls, *Political Liberalism* (Columbia University Press, 1993).

the 'selves', or moral agents, that populate the moral community and the relationship to otherness suggested by the different conceptions of the self. Understanding these various levels will allow assessment of both cosmopolitan and communitarian positions and a movement beyond the divide at the level of boundaries.

The cosmopolitan/communitarian divide in international relations theory

This section demonstrates how the cosmopolitan approaches to international justice articulated by Charles Beitz and Onora O'Neill display many characteristics of the assimilationist attitude. The following section demonstrates how communitarian positions, such as that articulated by Michael Walzer and Chris Brown, too quickly settle for coexistence at the expense of communication. In order to argue this case the work of Seyla Benhabib is employed.[7] The discussion concludes by suggesting how both cosmopolitan and communitarian positions can contribute to the development of a communicatively based universalism that does justice to difference.

The positions occupied at the level of practice in cosmopolitan and communitarian thought stem from the conception of the moral self and of human agency that underpin liberal and communitarian thought, respectively. In particular, liberal thought relies on a highly abstracted, idealised conception of human agency and selfhood. Communitarian thought alternatively focuses on the embedded and contextual nature of human morality and agency and on how selfhood is relative to particular social circumstances. These different understandings of selfhood result in divergent understandings of the relationship between self and other in the moral community and involve two different standpoints towards otherness.

Benhabib argues that moral debates of the kind represented by cosmopolitanism and communitarianism privilege either the 'generalised' other or the 'concrete' other. The standpoint of the generalised other has been the dominant standpoint in Western thought from Hobbes to Rawls. It corresponds to the liberal–cosmopolitan position. This standpoint

> requires us to view each and every individual as a rational being entitled to the same rights and duties we would want to ascribe to

[7] S. Benhabib, *Situating the Self* (Oxford: Blackwell, 1992).

ourselves. In assuming the standpoint, we abstract from the individuality and the concrete identity of the other. We assume the other, like ourselves, is a being who has concrete needs, desires and affects, but that what constitutes his or her moral dignity is not what differentiates us from each other, but rather what we, as speaking and acting rational agents, have in common. Our relation to the other is governed by the norms of formal equality and reciprocity: each is entitled to expect and to assume from us what we can expect and assume from him or her.[8]

Liberal–cosmopolitanism privileges the generalised other. It employs abstract and impartial conceptions of human capacities, removed from their particular social, cultural contexts. By privileging the generalised other, liberal–cosmopolitanism performs an assimilative task. In particular, it reduces plurality to unity.

The standpoint of the concrete other, in contrast, corresponds roughly to the priorities of the communitarian position. It

> requires us to view each and every rational being as an individual with a concrete history, identity, and affective-emotional constitution . . . (it) abstract[s] from what constitutes our commonality and focuses on individuality. We seek to comprehend the needs of the other, his or her motivation, what she searches for and s/he desires. Our relation to the other is governed by the norms of equity and complementary reciprocity: each is entitled to expect and to assume from the other forms of behaviour through which the other feels recognised and confirmed as a concrete, individual being with specific needs, talents and capacities. Our differences in this case complement rather than exclude each other . . . I confirm not only your *humanity* but your *individuality*.[9]

Benhabib uses these categories to help negotiate a position transcending, yet incorporating, both the concrete 'ethic of care' offered by writers like Carol Gilligan, and the justice of rights and responsibility offered in most liberal theories of justice.[10] Benhabib argues that an adequate account of moral reasoning and justice cannot afford to privilege either standpoint.[11] Instead, she argues that what is required is an account that mediates between them.[12] What is of importance at this juncture is not

---

[8] *Ibid.*, p. 159.   [9] *Ibid.*

[10] see V. Held, (ed.) *Justice and Care: Essential Readings in Feminist Ethics* (Boulder: WestView, 1995) for the debates surrounding this approach.

[11] In this sense the categories are intended to be descriptive and not prescriptive.

[12] Such an account, she suggests, is provided by Habermasian discourse ethics. For reasons of space Benhabib's argument concerning discourse ethics cannot be addressed in this chapter. However, as later chapters will argue it is not entirely clear whether discourse ethics meets the criteria of communication as articulated here. See the discussion in ch. 3.

the issue of Benhabib's solution but her categories of analysis. In the first instance, it is the assimilative function of the generalised other that preoccupies this enquiry.

Liberal–cosmopolitanism: Beitz

Liberal rights-based approaches, in one form or another, form the basis of the most widely held interpretations of cosmopolitanism. Rights-based approaches, for example, underlie the advocacy of international human rights laws and of arguments for global redistributive justice.[13] One of the most systematic and widely known formulations of the cosmopolitan position in recent times is offered by Charles Beitz who has outlined a cosmopolitan philosophy derived from the work of John Rawls.[14]

According to Beitz, a cosmopolitan morality must be universal: it must consider the good of the individual and, therefore, of the species. It is concerned '... with the moral relations of members of a universal community in which state boundaries have merely derivative significance. There are no reasons of basic principle for exempting the internal affairs of states from external moral scrutiny...'[15] What defines Beitz's cosmopolitanism as liberal, in addition to its individualism, is the commitment to universal and *impartial* principles. According to Beitz, a cosmopolitan position is impartial because it 'seeks to see each part of the whole in its true relative size... the proportions of things are accurately presented so that they can be faithfully compared'.[16] Cosmopolitan morality must also, therefore, remain neutral in relation to different conceptions of the good. A cosmopolitan perspective cannot privilege any one group in relation to any other or any group over any individual. It must be non-perspectival, claims Beitz.[17] In other words, cosmopolitanism aspires to treat all individuals alike, regardless of their situation.

For Beitz, this aspiration comes closest to fulfilment in a Rawlsian social contract. The cosmopolitan quest for impartiality requires that 'we must... regard the world from the perspective of an original position

---

[13] See for example H. Shue, *Basic Rights* (Princeton University Press, 1980).

[14] C. R. Beitz, *Political Theory and International Relations* (Princeton University Press, 1979) and J. Rawls, *A Theory of Justice* (Oxford University Press, 1972).

[15] Beitz, *Political Theory and International Relations*, p. 182.

[16] C. R. Beitz, 'Cosmopolitan Liberalism and the States System', in C. Brown (ed.), *Political Restructuring in Europe: Ethical Perspectives* (London: Routledge, 1994), p. 124.

[17] 'By, "non perspectival", I mean that a cosmopolitan view seeks to see each part of the whole in its true relative size... the proportions of things are accurately presented so that they can be faithfully compared. If local viewpoints can be said to be partial, then a cosmopolitan viewpoint is impartial.' *Ibid.*, p. 124.

from which matters of national citizenship are excluded by an extended veil of ignorance'.[18] The Rawlsian 'contract' is arrived at through a hypothetical conversation in which rational choosers are placed behind a 'veil of ignorance', where 'individuals are ignorant of their society's history, level of development and culture, level of natural resources, and role [for Beitz] in the international economy'.[19] The 'veil of ignorance' is a levelling device meant to articulate a neutral and impartial principle that mediates between different conceptions of the good in establishing a universal conception of the right. According to Rawls, rational actors choosing from behind a veil of ignorance would agree upon principles whereby society would be organised for 'the greatest benefit of the least advantaged'.[20] The aim of the Rawlsian original position is to determine principles of justice that could be agreed upon by all. It is meant to encapsulate the liberal principles of equality, freedom and impartiality.

Liberal–cosmopolitanism, as articulated by Beitz, privileges the generalised other in several ways. The commitment to impartiality, as specifically formulated by Beitz, privileges the generalised other by attempting to found a position outside of context and above all particularities. The cosmopolitan focus on individuality in Beitz's interpretation of early Rawls, means that ties of context, sectional affiliations and particularistic loyalties, such as family, clan or nation, are to be disregarded for the purposes of moral reasoning; '... when sectional values come into conflict with the requirements of an impartial view, why should the sectional values not simply lose out?'[21] To be impartial towards all particular affiliations, associations and contexts, to take account of the good of the whole means, in Beitz's formulation, to judge from a detached, dispassionate and abstracted position.

According to Iris Marion Young the ideal of impartiality, and thereby the standpoint of the 'generalised' other, denies or represses differences, or assimilates, in three ways.[22] First, it denies the particularity of situations. In it '[t]he reasoning subject ... treats all situations according to the same moral rules, and the more the rules can be reduced to a

---

[18] Beitz. *Political Theory and International Relations*, p. 176.
[19] D. R. Mapel, 'The Contractarian Tradition in International Ethics', in T. Nardin and D. R. Mapel, *Traditions of International Ethics* (Cambridge: Cambridge University Press, 1992), p. 193.
[20] Rawls, *Theory of Justice*, p. 83. 'Rawls argues that in such situations it is rational to choose principles of justice that maximise one's minimum share should one turn out to be the least advantaged member of society.' Maple, 'The Contractarian Tradition', p. 193.
[21] C. Beitz, 'Sovereignty and Morality in International Affairs', in D. Held. (ed.), *Political Theory Today* (Cambridge: Polity, 1991), p. 24.
[22] I. M. Young, *Justice and the Politics of Difference* (Princeton University Press, 1990).

Veil of ignorance denies differences!

single rule or principle, the more this impartiality and universality will be guaranteed'.[23] Second, the variety and particularity of feelings of individual subjects are excluded from the moral realm: '... reason stands opposed to desire and affectivity as what differentiates and particularise persons'.[24] Third, impartiality 'reduces the (actual) plurality of moral subjects to one (abstract) subjectivity'.[25] It is this third description that is the most important in terms of the moment of assimilation. To be universally impartial, the cosmopolitan position must abstract from the particularity of agents and replace them with a generalised, and, therefore, universal, conception of agency. By reducing actual agents/subjects to abstract subjectivity, to the reasoning dispassionate (male) ego, liberal-cosmopolitanism performs an act of assimilation regarding the other's identity. The other's moral identity is taken to be the same in matters of moral reasoning: 'Because it already takes all perspectives into account, the impartial subject need acknowledge no subjects other than itself to whose interests, opinions and desires it should attend.'[26] Young correctly describes this as a monological account of human agency and morality.

The ideal of impartiality, according to Young, constitutes a further threat or denial of difference, in that the claim to theoretical impartiality obscures real particularity. No vantage point is completely impartial and all positions are situated in some sort of context. In other words, there is no 'non-perspectival' perspective. As Young argues: '[i]t is impossible to adopt an unsituated moral point of view, and if a point is situated, then it cannot be universal, it cannot stand apart from and understand all points of view'.[27] Thus, liberal–cosmopolitanism involves insufficient recognition that the abstract, idealised, supposedly impartial, principle of justice is, in fact, the product of a particular history and context of social meanings, of a particular culture, and represents a particular conception of human agency.[28]

---

[23] *Ibid.*   [24] *Ibid.*
[25] *Ibid.*   [26] *Ibid.*, p. 101.   [27] *Ibid.*, p. 104.
[28] According to Benhabib this observation does not undermine the universalist project altogether, instead it merely provides a corrective to it. Under the conditions of the 'veil of ignorance' it becomes impossible to know what 'like' might mean: 'Without assuming the standpoint of the concrete other, no coherent universalizability test can be carried out, for we lack the necessary epistemic information to judge my moral situation to be, like, or unlike, yours.' Accordingly Benhabib argues a coherent universalism must take into account the plurality of concrete others. Benhabib, *Situating the Self*, p. 164.

In defence of Rawls and Beitz, it could be argued that the 'original position' attempts to take into account the plurality of subjects, and indeed that this is a central motivation behind the 'veil of ignorance'. However, while the Rawlsian contract may recognise plurality, it does not incorporate it into moral reasoning itself. Instead, the 'veil of ignorance' actually works to exclude any meaningful differences from the deliberation regarding justice. The 'veil of ignorance' is premised on the assumption that if all are situated equally behind it, then all will be able to take the position of others into account. However, behind the 'veil of ignorance' both the 'other' and the 'self' are robbed of any identity. The 'other' disappears because the 'veil of ignorance' requires that participants be ignorant of their own identity as well as that of others. The agents here are rational, autonomous, Kantian selves freely capable of choosing their own ends. However, in Rawls's theory '. . . this moral and political concept of autonomy slips into a metaphysics according to which it is meaningful to define a self independently of all the ends it may choose and all and any conceptions of the good it may hold'.[29] Thus, individuals are defined purely in terms of the capacity, but not the substance, of their agency. They are defined 'prior to their individuating characteristics'.[30] Defining individuals this way means that behind the 'veil of ignorance' there is in fact no plurality at all; instead there is what Benhabib calls 'definitional identity'. Where there is definitional identity and no plurality, it is impossible to know what the other might want or desire, because nothing is known about the other that is different from what is known about the self. Under conditions of the 'veil of ignorance', 'the *other as different from the self* disappears'.[31] In other words, a significant moment of assimilation occurs.

This leads to the second criteria by which we can judge the cosmopolitan/communitarian debate, namely the issue of conversation. The 'veil of ignorance' is premised on a form of conversation, and it is this conversation that is intended to incorporate the plurality of human agents. However, the conversation is a hypothetical conversation/contract, not an actual one. Justice in this formulation amounts to anticipating what abstracted reasoning individuals would choose in an ideal situation, instead of what embedded, contextualised individuals might agree upon in a real conversation. Furthermore, the outcome of this conversation is anticipated in advance: 'appropriate principles of justice', we are to

[29] *Ibid.*, p. 161.   [30] *Ibid.*, p. 162.   [31] *Ibid.*, p. 161.

suppose, would be those arrived at by all participants from behind a 'veil of ignorance'. But, as Walzer argues: '[R]ational men and women, constrained this way or that will choose one, and only one, distributive system.'[32] Mapel, likewise, notes that in Rawls's theory '. . . the agreement of the contractors is all but dictated by the normative constraints built into Rawls's initial situation of the "original position"'.[33] This account of justice is too prescriptive, and, therefore, unjust in relation to particularism, because it calculates the outcome on behalf of all others and, unsurprisingly, it arrives at the same outcome for all. The other is like us and, therefore, we can know in advance what they would choose under certain circumstances. Therefore, while the idea of conversation is included, it is not communication in the sense intended by Todorov. The other's voice is not heard here at all, instead it is imputed to it, the other's identity is already assumed in advance.

At the level of agency, we can see that Beitzian liberal–cosmopolitanism involves a high degree of assimilation and disregards the plurality of concrete others. It is assimilative in that it reduces all 'concrete' others to the same identity, that of the 'generalised' other.[34] The claim to impartiality both reduces the other's identity to insignificance and masks the situated identity of liberal–cosmopolitanism. In this sense it equates equality with identity and privileges identity over difference.

Not all accounts of cosmopolitanism are necessarily liberal in the above sense. According to Onora O'Neill it is possible to argue for a reading of Kant that suggests a cosmopolitanism that emphasises obligations over rights and that also is sensitive to the needs of real embedded agents. O'Neill distinguishes between accounts that provide idealised and abstract conceptions of agency: 'A theory or principle is abstract if it gives a general account of some matter – one that literally abstracts from details so is indeterminate.'[35] Abstraction necessarily leaves out details and involves selective omission. Idealisation, on the other hand, involves selective addition. Abstraction is necessary

[32] What Walzer means here is that for those behind the veil there really is no choice, to act rationally in this situation can have only one meaning. M. Walzer, *Spheres of Justice* (Oxford: Blackwell, 1983), p. 5.
[33] Mapel, 'The Contractarian Tradition', p. 183.
[34] According to Benhabib this is usually a western, male, public identity. She argues 'Universalistic moral theories in the Western tradition from Hobbes to Rawls are substitutionalist, in the sense, that the universalism they defend is defined surreptitiously by identifying the experiences of a specific group of subjects as the paradigmatic case of the human as such. These subjects are invariably white, male, adults who are propertied or at least professional.' Benhabib, *Situating the Self*, p. 153.
[35] O. O'Neill, *Faces of Hunger* (London: Allen and Unwin, 1986), p. 28.

in order to think about justice but idealisation is not: 'Abstraction enables us to reach audiences who disagree with us (in part); idealisation disables us from reaching audiences who do not fit or share the ideal.'[36] Rights-based and contractarian approaches are based on an over-idealised conception of agency and so will not be heard by those to whom they are addressed. Additionally these agents, O'Neill suggests, are often in most need of a rigorous account of justice, such as those in the poorest countries of the world. The degree of idealisation precludes their applicability and accessibility to real embedded agents. Idealisation, in presupposing and proposing forms of agency and identity on participants, speaks in a language that is deliberately removed from local contexts and in so doing makes itself unintelligible or inapplicable to the actual agents:

> For ethical reasoning to be accessible to the individuals, institutions and collectivities to whom it is addressed they must have some capacities for guiding their action by deliberation, to which the proposed reasoning can be appropriately adjusted. They do not need ideal capacities ... accessible ethical reasoning has to address the actual and varied capacities for agency of different individual institutions and collectivities.[37]

What is required for this is only a degree of abstraction. Abstraction, O'Neill argues, allows us to think globally, about people who we do not know, without imputing an identity to them. Idealisation requires some imposition of identity upon the agent; the ethical process comes to involve assumptions or argument about individuals that are too prescriptive and assimilative. According to O'Neill, an obligation-based Kantian morality attempts to take into account and accommodate the plurality of contexts and meanings in arriving at a universal morality, and it does so by refusing the level of idealisation of agents adopted by contractarian approaches. Abstract accounts of agency are preferable to O'Neill because they allow for a variety of agents and contexts. This is necessary if any moral universalism is to be achieved. To be universal, moral laws must be accessible to a variety of agents and circumstances. In this way O'Neill attempts to counter the problems of agency that affect other cosmopolitan perspectives. In particular, her argument suggests that a Kantian perspective of this type achieves a balance between the

---

[36] O. O'Neill, 'Ethical Reasoning and Ideological Pluralism', *Ethics*, 98, July (1988), 714.
[37] O' Neill, *Faces of Hunger*, p. 37.

generalised and the concrete other. Nonetheless, this position remains problematic and contains some threads that may undermine its claim.

The Kantian approach offered by O'Neill still claims both impartiality and a specific account of agency. In particular, the categorical imperative seems necessarily to convey a specific image of individual agents as capable of making free, rational choices as to their own ends. This implies that individuals choose their ends, goals and interests free from the influence of their cultural contexts and those other factors which go to make up their identities (and, therefore, their definition of their ends). Furthermore, the mediation between the universal and the particular in the categorical imperative is deliberated monologically, and abstractly, in advance of any real conversation. O'Neill's perspective attempts to balance the 'generalised' and the 'concrete' other by making principles of moral action reconcilable with local beliefs. For O'Neill, however, this should only be understood in the context of the categorical imperative. For Kantian ethics, the task is to discover and formulate universal principles and to make them accessible to particular local contexts and all this requires is really an act of translation from the abstract to the concrete. The categorical imperative, therefore, is a universal principle worked out monologically in advance and for this reason O'Neill remains committed to a monological account of moral deliberation.

This section has demonstrated the moment of assimilation and the place of conversation in liberal–cosmopolitan thought through an application of Benhabib's categories of the 'generalised' and the 'concrete' other. It argued that a commitment to impartiality as conceived by Beitz, following Rawls, reduces the real plurality of human agents, of concrete others, to a single abstract and idealised human subject. The reduction of many voices to one repeats the moment of assimilation present in Las Casas's approach to the other by replacing knowledge of the other with a form of one's own 'ego ideal'; by seeing not the other, but oneself.

Communitarianism

If the cosmopolitan position appears biased too heavily in favour of the generalised other, then the communitarian position appears to favour the concrete other. At the level of agency, communitarians take the position of the concrete other as the starting point of their deliberations on justice. As Walzer argues

> ... the question most likely to arise in the minds of members of a political community is not, What would rational individuals choose under

universalising conditions of such and such a sort? But rather, What would individuals like us choose, who are situated as we are, who share a culture and are determined to go on sharing it?[38]

Communitarians, therefore, share the critique of the standpoint of the generalised other outlined above and instead focus on the concerns of the embedded and particular individual in coming to an understanding about justice.

In contrast to the liberal–cosmopolitan advocacy of universally impartial principles based on idealised conceptions of agency, communitarians argue that justice and morality are relative and particular. In these accounts, justice stems from, and is defined by, the members of the community, and morality is local and contextual:

> ... if individuals are constituted wholly or in part by the social relations of their communities, if their goals, their ethical judgements and their sense of justice are inextricably bound up with community life, then why should they accept the criteria or evaluations of cosmopolitans?[39]

Communitarian approaches argue that if morality is context-dependent and can only be decided within a culture/community, attempts to propound universal conceptions of justice come up against the barrier of cultural difference. They ask '[w]here do these "external" criteria get their authority?'[40]

According to communitarians, cosmopolitans are particularly prone to attempts to define justice once and for all, universally across time and space. Thus, the cosmopolitan commitment to impartiality between different conceptions of the good life is itself an articulation of a particular conception of the good life.[41] The communitarian critique implies that, given that knowledge is particular and contextual, there will be no way of knowing or judging between the many contextual definitions of the good and establishing which is the correct or best one. In addition, this is sometimes accompanied by a supporting claim that contextual

---

[38] Walzer, *Spheres of Justice*, p. 5.
[39] Thompson, *Justice and World Order*, p. 22.   [40] *Ibid.*, p. 22.
[41] As Walzer notes regarding Rawls: '... the rules of engagement are designed to ensure that the speakers are free and equal, to liberate them from domination, subordination, servility, fear and deference ... but once rules of this sort have been laid out, the speakers are left with few substantive issues to argue and decide about ... The thin morality is already very thick – with an entirely decent liberal or social democratic thickness. The rules of engagements constitute a way of life ...' M. Walzer, *Thick and Thin: Moral Argument at Home and Abroad* (University of Notre Dame Press, 1994), p. 13.

Justice rooted in distinct understanding of differences

knowledge is necessarily incommensurable. The existence of differing conceptions of the good life, of morality and community, place effective limits on cosmopolitan and universalist arguments for the existence and desirability of transcultural norms. From the communitarian position cosmopolitan morality is seen as the universalisation, and imposition, of one particular morality or agency at the expense of other local or particular moralities. Cosmopolitanism requires a degree of cultural and moral homogeneity. Communitarians see the development of substantive moral universalism in itself as an injustice. Particular norms and cultures are to be valued and protected, and any imposition of universal standards upon them is an unjustifiable denial of integrity or group autonomy. According to Walzer, 'Justice is rooted in the distinct understanding of places, honours, jobs, things of all sorts, that constitute a shared way of life. To override those understandings is (always) to act unjustly.'[42] Given the existence of cultural particularism, we might abandon the quest for more universally inclusive forms of social life, morality and community altogether.

By adopting the standpoint of the concrete other, communitarian positions imply a position of coexistence. If universal norms and principles, appropriate to the position of the generalised other, are seen as doing an injustice to difference, the bias towards the concrete other would seem to suggest that an 'ethics of coexistence' between different communities is the best that can be hoped for.

One expression of communitarianism as an ethics of coexistence can be seen in the work of Chris Brown.[43] Starting from essentially communitarian premises, Brown has argued that the idea of an international society of states represents the best means of coping with value pluralism in the international arena. According to Brown, the society of states is the means by which particular conceptions of the good life, represented by sovereign states, are mediated by mutual recognition of interest in the maintenance of (state) autonomy. In international society states acknowledge that domestic conceptions of the good are not necessarily shared and, more importantly, can only be secured by a pact of coexistence between these competing conceptions which guarantees freedom from undue outside influence. International society is seen as providing the framework of rules that enables separate realms to pursue their own

[42] Walzer, *Spheres of Justice*, p. 314.
[43] I have elaborated on this aspect of Brown's thought elsewhere and what follows is drawn directly from that discussion. See R. Shapcott, 'Conversation and Coexistence, Gadamer and the Interpretation of International Society', *Millennium*, 23. 1, Spring (1994).

goals, aims or versions of the good life. 'The general function of international society is to separate and cushion, not to act.'[44] R. J. Vincent has described this as the 'egg box' conception of international society.

For Brown, Terry Nardin has provided the best articulation of this aspect of international society.[45] In establishing the nature of international society Nardin makes a distinction between 'purposive' and 'practical' associations. Purposive association is concerned with pursuing common and shared goals, such as a Trade Union might do. Practical association concerns the relationship between those '. . . who are associated with one another, if at all, only in respecting certain restrictions on how each may pursue his own purposes'.[46] This type of association covers those areas concerned with the rule of law and standards of conduct, it is '. . . a set of considerations to be taken into account in deciding and acting . . .'[47] or, in other words, the rules of engagement. Nardin himself draws on the work of Michael Oakeshott for this distinction.[48] The point is that Brown wants us to see that in Nardin's version '. . . the nature of international society is such that all-inclusive association can only be practical'.[49] Because the rules of international conduct are premised on the lack of agreed common purposes, the type of conversation in this community is limited to the terms of its continued existence. Nardin's version of international society is that of the 'egg-box'. In such an association the objective is merely to keep the various purposive associations apart; it has no role in facilitating understanding or agreement on matters of substance. This notion of ethics extends the possibility of shared values only so far as the maintenance of minimal order. Moral relativism is tempered only by need to manage diversity, to define rules of engagement and procedure; to establish a secure cushioning environment, an egg box. Thus for

[44] R. J. Vincent, *Human Rights and International Relations* (Cambridge: Cambridge University Press, 1986).
[45] See T. Nardin, *Law, Morality and the Relations of States* (Princeton University Press, 1983). For Brown's discussion of Nardin see Brown, 'Ethics of Coexistence' and also *International Relations Theory: New Normative Approaches*.
[46] Nardin, *Law, Morality and the Relations of States*, p. 9. Brown refers to these as the '. . . general arrangements of society'. Brown, 'Ethics of Coexistence', p. 215.
[47] Nardin, *Law, Morality and the Relations of States*, p. 6.
[48] See *ibid.* and M. Oakeshott, *On Human Conduct* (Oxford University Press, 1975). This argument closely parallels 'realist' views which emphasise difference as intractable (though it doesn't echo the realist distinction between domestic and international realms and the ensuing rejection of normative concerns in relations between states). In Brown's reading of Nardin 'Individual states are independent actors, mirroring Oakeshott's free human beings . . . and for all the play that is made with the notion of interdependence reducing barriers between states, is likely to remain so'. Brown, 'Ethics of Coexistence', p. 218.
[49] *Ibid.*, p. 215.

Brown, international society has been conceptualised as the means by which different particular thick cultures maintain their separateness.[50]

Difference and exclusion in Walzer

Communitarian thinking in International Relations attempts a formulation of community that does justice to the other by including and recognising a wide range of moral and cultural diversity. However, by settling on coexistence, this type of communitarian thought is also exclusive of difference. It is exclusive in the sense that it defines a more strict boundary between those inside the community of 'concrete others' and those outside. In so doing it defines a boundary between those we are capable of communicating with and those who are essentially outside of the conversation.

While an ethics of coexistence resists an articulation of difference as inferiority, it nonetheless consigns some concrete 'others' to a place outside the realm of moral conversation. According to communitarian thought, moral conversation can only take place within a community of shared values. Walzer argues that communities of this type are necessarily particularistic '. . . because they have members and memories, members with memories not only of their own but also of their common life. Humanity by contrast, has members but no memory, so it has no history and no culture, no customary practices, no familiar lifeways, no festival no shared understanding of social goods.'[51] In other words, the absence of shared social goods, of a common discourse of meaning, places limits on the capacity to communicate. Communitarian thought, therefore, implies a morally exclusive community.

While Walzer defends the communitarian emphasis on the concrete other, he also attempts to include, to a limited degree, those outside the immediate moral community. Walzer wishes to acknowledge that there are concrete others outside our community of shared discourse, towards whom we can act ethically and morally. Therefore, while the existence or non-existence of a shared language or culture places limits on the possibility for universal community, these limits are not absolute.

---

[50] This approach corresponds with what is known as the pluralist interpretation of international society. However, a solidarist interpretation is also available. The advantages of the solidarist interpretation will be discussed in later chapters; all that needs to be noted at this point is that the interpretation of the role of international society provided by Brown and Nardin can be contested by a more cosmopolitan or solidarist reading, see N. Wheeler and T. Dunne, 'Hedley Bull's Pluralism of the Intellect and Solidarism of the Will', *International Affairs*, 72 (1996), 1–17.

[51] Walzer, *Thick and Thin*, p. 8.

Walzer wishes to advocate '... the politics of difference and, at the same time, to describe and defend a certain sort of universalism'.[52] Walzer is clearly aware of the inadequacy of certain forms of communitarianism and, while he does not want to argue that we have Kantian obligations to those concrete others, he does suggest that '... the members of all the different societies, because they are human can acknowledge each other's different ways, respond to each other's cries for help, learn from each other and march (sometimes) in each other's parades'.[53] Walzer, therefore, has argued for a 'thin' universalism. A thin morality is juxtaposed to a thick, contextualised and concrete morality occurring within a community. What is possible outside this type of community is a thin or minimal morality. A moral minimalism '... makes for a certain limited, though important and heartening solidarity. It doesn't make for a full-blooded universal doctrine.'[54] It refers to the ability to empathise and think morally about the other and depends '... most simply, perhaps, on the fact that we have moral expectations about the behaviour not only of our fellows but of strangers too'.[55] So moral minimalism means, for example, that we can empathise with what is meant when marchers in Prague use the terms 'freedom' or 'justice', without necessarily sharing the concrete particular meanings of the marchers.

Walzer's minimalism is nonetheless insufficient because, as he articulates it, it is not a principle of conversation but of intuition. Minimalism, argues Walzer, '... is less the product of persuasion than of mutual recognition among the protagonists of different fully developed moral cultures'.[56] However, while this moral minimalism claims some universal status while seeking recognition of the other's identity, it does not do so through conversation, communication or dialogue. Walzer, like Las Casas, believes the other to be worthy of moral consideration and even solidarity but holds this to be best recognised by a position of coexistence.

Likewise Brown's version of international society is also an attempt to acknowledge that communitarian premises do not rule out the possibility of a thin universal agreement. For Brown this exists in the form

---

[52] *Ibid.*, p. x.   [53] *Ibid.*, p. 8.   [54] *Ibid.*, p. 11.   [55] *Ibid.*, p. 17.
[56] *Ibid.*, Walzer's use of the term 'fully developed' here lends further support to his aim to refute the charge of relativism as it suggests a greater commitment to the possibility of ranking different cultures according to their moral development and thereby to a substantially 'thicker' sense of universalism.

of the rules of coexistence which, while minimalist and 'practical', are nonetheless moral. For Brown coexistence is a thin moral solution to the problem of ethical and cultural pluralism and provides the most satisfactory form for the recognition of difference in the international realm.[57] Unlike Walzer, Brown does argue that coexistence requires some form of conversation, if only to establish the nature of the pluralist international society. Having done so he then limits conversation to that task alone and rules out the possibility of engaging in more substantive conversation that might, for instance, lead to the emergence of shared, common purposes and, therefore, of a purposive international society.

Walzer and Brown are unable to articulate a proper sense of communication because of their communitarian starting point. Communitarians argue that liberal theorists rely on, but do not acknowledge or theorise, presupposed levels of community. They assume a 'we' who all belong to shared historical continuity of meaning; they assume *Sittlichkeit*. Liberals ask '[W]hich formulation of principles is most in harmony with pre-existing liberal beliefs and values?', while at the same time couching their answers in universal formulations which go beyond merely liberal communities. The communitarian project aims in part to expose the situated bases of liberal thinking. In taking the givens of community as the starting point of their critique of liberalism, however, communitarians underestimate the possibility of moving beyond and enlarging that community.

Beyond the cosmopolitan/communitarian divide

So far, this chapter has argued that liberal–cosmopolitanism offers the possibility of a universal community of humankind, while at the same time running the risk of requiring the community to be populated by a particular conception of human agents, by modern western autonomous individuals. Liberal–cosmopolitan positions, therefore, privilege identity over difference. Communitarians on the other hand proffer an articulation of justice that stresses the defence of cultural difference in the face of homogenising tendencies. Communitarian positions privilege difference over identity, thus underestimating what humanity might have in common. This scenario suggests that cosmopolitanism necessarily denies difference and plurality and that communitarianism necessarily

[57] I have outlined the problems with Brown's solution in Shapcott, 'Conversation and Coexistence'.

48

Communitarian: justice stresses defense of cultural difference in face of homogenising (handwritten)

stands opposed to universal claims and to human unity. This debate suggests only two, necessarily oppositional, ways of approaching the question of international community. It offers only a choice between assimilation and coexistence, and offers little suggestion that these positions can be transcended.

At this point it is useful to turn again to O'Neill and the cosmopolitan critique of communitarianism.[58] O'Neill argues that while the question: '[W]hat level of agreement can we or do we presuppose?', is necessary, it is not enough. Communitarian thinkers make the mistake of thinking that an established community is the limit and sole basis for arriving at moral principles. In a situation of moral diversity such as characterises the present there is as much need to construct new shared agreements as there is to understand existing ones. For O'Neill, therefore, the issue 'need not be "what agreement can we presuppose?" but rather, "[w]hat understanding and what agreement can we construct?"'[59] The communitarian approach makes the mistake of focusing on the first and ignoring or down-playing the latter. The communitarian position, according to O'Neill, has too determinate a conception of the 'we' as a consequence of its focus on the first question rather than the second:

> If one is concerned with presupposable agreements, the 'we' must be taken rather strictly. If on the other hand, one is concerned with the agreement that can be achieved, 'we' may have no unique interpretation and need not be defined by reference to any (pre-existing) shared ideal or outlook.[60]

The problem with the communitarian position is that it suggests the stricter version of the 'we', or, in the case of Walzer, posits a wider but very much weaker, or second order, 'we'.[61]

Universalist and cosmopolitan projects in contrast do not succeed in separating the two definitions of who 'we' refers to. Thus certain liberal conceptions of justice 'can be made more widely accessible only

---

[58] O'Neill's position shows how cosmopolitans and communitarians ask different questions and how these influence their substantive positions. In this sense, the cosmopolitan and communitarian positions provide useful and enlightening critiques of each other.
[59] O'Neill, 'Ethical Reasoning and Ideological Pluralism', p. 717.
[60] *Ibid.*
[61] A further problem with communitarian positions is that the position of coexistence requires the establishment of some agreement whereby difference can be valued and tolerance established, such as an 'ethics of coexistence', otherwise they lapse into an incoherent relativism. Such an agreement must in some sense be universal. Therefore at the very least even an ethics of coexistence requires an expansion of the meaning of 'we' and the development of some sort of universal ethic.

by imposing a conception of justice that embodies that (liberal) ideal';[62] that is, they are assimilative. O'Neill's questions suggest that in order to do justice to 'otherness', the question '[w]hat agreement can be constructed?' needs to be asked anew with the concerns of the communitarians in mind. The question that those concerned with the possibility of universal moral community need to ask is 'what community can be constructed, not by abstract, idealised and impartial agents, but by particular, embedded, concrete and situated agents?' In other words, an adequate account of the possibilities for justice to difference needs to include elements of cosmopolitan and communitarian positions in an exploration of how both can contribute to the constructive project.

One of the tasks of this chapter has been to suggest that a communitarian path to cosmopolitanism exists. In order to do justice to the other's alterity and to their humanity, in order to recognise the other as equal but not identical; in order to do justice to what is different and what is held in common, it is necessary to go beyond, while incorporating the best of both, liberal–cosmopolitan and communitarian positions. Taking such a path requires the attempt to conceive of the 'we' as a potential community of concrete agents engaged in a search for understanding.

The argument of this book is that the construction of a wider or universal sense of the 'we' that resists the movement of assimilation, both requires and endorses a practice of communication. Such a practice suggests the possibility of developing more inclusive moral communities without annihilating or assimilating the 'other'. It suggests an encounter with the other that is premised on the possibility of mutual understanding and agreement. In attempting to communicate an effort is being made to engage the other's difference through what is common, and that, in the first instance, is language. To encounter the other as different we need to presuppose as little as possible regarding their identity, only that we are capable of communicating with them and they with us. Understanding and agreement are possible because the other is seen neither as absolutely 'other' nor as essentially identical. To achieve this the other and the self must be understood from both 'concrete' and 'generalised' standpoints. From the standpoint of the 'concrete' other, the 'other' is understood as embedded in particular socio/politico/cultural situations: from the standpoint of the 'generalised' other it is possible to assume the capacity for communication and understanding as abstract properties belonging to particular selves or as universally shared capacities. Both standpoints are required in order to facilitate and undertake conversation. To enable genuine communication, acknowledgement of the concrete other must take place. Likewise, both the desire and the belief in conversation must exist and this requires emphasis on the possibilities of the generalised other. It is the standpoint of the 'generalised' other that motivates the question: 'what type of agreement/understanding can be constructed?'

A practice of communication premised on these grounds attempts to work towards a cosmopolitan morality from communitarian premises. In so doing, it suggests that the standpoints of the concrete and generalised other are both necessary and mutually corrective positions. Likewise, cosmopolitanism and communitarianism can be understood as mutually corrective, rather than mutually exclusive, positions. An ethics of communication so formulated takes from the cosmopolitan/Kantian tradition the project of universal community, to treat all others in a moral fashion regardless of national or communal boundaries. From the communitarian position it takes the premise that treating others in a moral fashion requires paying attention to their particularity and that such particularity may place (flexible) limits on the possible 'thickness' of any larger community. In this way a practice of communication aims to incorporate, while at the same time transcending, the insights of both cosmopolitanism and communitarianism.

Conclusion

This chapter has pursued the idea that the meaning of justice should incorporate the idea of justice to difference, and that a relationship premised on communication suggests a possible way of achieving such an aim. It can be suggested here that an account of justice as communication remains universalist in aspiration, while at the same remaining attentive to particularity. Phrasing this slightly differently, a communicative morality is universally inclusive of particular, situated agents. In this regard, Young has suggested the possibility of distinguishing between two senses of universalism. She argues that '[U]niversality in the sense of the participation and inclusion of everyone in moral and social life does not imply universality in the sense of the adoption of a general point of view that leaves behind particular affiliations, feelings, commitments, and desires.'[63] A communicative morality aspires to the

---

[63] Young, *Justice and the Politics of Difference*, p. 105.

first but not the second dimension of universality. The development of accounts of moral life that emphasise this first 'thin' sense of universalism and attempt to transcend the cosmopolitan/communitarian divide is what provides the focus of the next chapter. The 'interpretive' approaches of constitutive theory, poststructuralism and critical theory can all be understood as attempts to incorporate a communicative dimension to the question of community while aspiring to universalism. Chapter 2 examines these accounts and begins to assess their communicative dimension.

2   Community and communication
     in interpretive theories
     of international relations

> To celebrate diversity is necessarily to refuse to treat others as 'other'.
> It is to be aware of a moral duty to be obligated to others . . . In One
> world/Many worlds, others cannot be 'other'. They may be different –
> but not cast as exclusion and inferiority . . . The challenge is . . . to work
> with the necessary reciprocity of connections between peoples able to
> speak on equal terms.[1]

Recent interpretive developments in IR theory have generated a variety
of alternative accounts of community to those witnessed in the cos-
mopolitan/communitarian divide. In their own ways, constitutive theory, poststructuralism and critical theory have all emerged to challenge
the framework with which moral debate in IR is discussed. Although
there are many differences between them common to these approaches
is a hermeneutic or interpretative understanding of the subject matter of
IR and of moral questions especially. It is this dimension which provides
the resources with which they are able to move beyond the deficiencies
of the cosmopolitan/communitarian divide and resist the 'devastating
choices' it presents 'between being human or being a national citizen
and between being an autonomous individual or a participant in a social community'.[2] It is the essentially hermeneutic dimension of these
approaches which encouraged them to develop accounts of community
emphasising the importance of recognising particular concrete others
and their communities while simultaneously developing universalist
approaches to moral life. What emerges out of these works is the common theme that justice as recognition is now as important a component

---

[1] R. B. J. Walker, *One World, Many Worlds: Struggles for a Just World Peace* (Boulder: Lynne Rienner, 1988), p. 166.
[2] *Ibid.*, p. 136.

of discussions of international justice as the distribution of economic and political goods. As such, interpretative approaches are all engaged in redefining and re-conceptualising the moral problematique of IR.

Furthermore, there appears to be a general consensus emerging that crucial to this project is an understanding of the possibility of dialogue. However, it also appears that these 'schools' offer different interpretations and articulations of the content of, and possibility for, dialogue. This chapter will introduce and outline the contributions of these accounts, and explain how they attempt to move beyond the problems of the cosmopolitan/communitarian divide. Chapter 5 will develop a critique of these positions and outline some of their drawbacks. It is intended that such critique will contribute to the development of the project of theorising a discursively based cosmopolitanism.

The discussion begins with the 'constitutive' approach of Mervyn Frost, proceeds to examine poststructural approaches and concludes with the critical theory of Andrew Linklater. This chapter suggests that critical theory, in particular the work of Linklater, has provided the most thorough account of conversation that is available in international relations theory in the form of discourse ethics but that this account is not without its limitations

Constitutive theory

This section provides a brief examination of the 'constitutive' approach to international ethics, developed by Mervyn Frost.[3] While Frost's constitutive theory bears much in common with the communitarian position, it can be understood as an attempt to develop a more coherent international application of it.[4] Frost shares the communitarian position that norms and ethical argument must occur within the language we have available in any given social context; norms must be understood within the particular embedded contexts that generate them. For Frost, however, a 'communitarian' understanding of the constitution of the ethical subject does not preclude the viability of international norms such as human rights. A communitarian starting point does not,

---

[3] M. Frost, *Ethics in International Relations: A Constitutive Theory* (Cambridge: Cambridge University Press, 1996). Originally published as *Towards a Normative Theory of International Relations* (Cambridge: Cambridge University Press, 1986).

[4] Molly Cochran for instance categorises Frost as communitarian, and not without justification. However, it is argued here that Frost's commitment to human rights places his analysis somewhere outside this category. See M. Cochran, *Normative Theory in International Relations* (Cambridge: Cambridge University Press, 1999).

therefore, necessarily entail a particularist understanding of morality. However, Frost does not wish to advocate a full-blown cosmopolitanism that replaces the national community. Instead he argues that concepts such as human rights and sovereignty should be understood as part of a universal 'state domain of discourse' and that both are amongst what he calls, following Dworkin, the 'settled norms' of international society. In other words, Frost does not see human (or individual) rights and sovereignty as necessarily oppositional categories; instead, they are integral parts of a universal state-based domain of discourse that includes the individual and the state.

Frost's argument consists of several parts: first, individuality and subjectivity are understood to be constructed intersubjectively. In this he adheres to a broadly hermeneutic and communitarian understanding of subjectivity. Included in this is an understanding of political discourse as inherently normative. Frost refutes positivist and objectivist accounts of the social sciences that reject or deny the essential normativity of human social life. The next part of his argument is that moral/ethical argumentation and reasoning is carried out within communities of discourse and in terms of 'settled norms'. Again, he adheres to a communitarian account of norms and moral reasoning. Rejecting any transcendental or Archimedean understanding of morality, Frost accepts that discussion concerning right conduct and action can only take place within an already commonly held language and understandings: 'A problem cannot be formulated as a normative issue except within the context of given practice of normative argument. Normative issues only arise as such within the context of certain shared understandings.'[5] Frost follows Dworkin in arguing that these shared understandings for all intents and purposes can be understood as 'settled' in the sense that they are taken for granted as constituting the domain of discourse in which moral action and discussion occurs. Therefore, he argues, '... we who are seeking answers to pressing normative issues in international relations, must start by seeking an understanding of the area of normative agreement implied by our agreed list of pressing issues. Our task is to outline the relevant *domain* of discourse. A domain of discourse is an area of discussion within which the participants generally recognise (and recognise others as recognising) many rules as settled.'[6]

---

[5] Frost, *Ethics in International Relations*, p. 77.   [6] *Ibid.*, p. 78.

Frost's third point is that discussion on normative issues in world politics is and should be undertaken in terms of the settled norms of international society or what he refers to as the 'state domain of discourse'. Any and all attempts to talk about normative issues in world politics must necessarily refer to the norms associated with the state domain of discourse.[7] In this argument, in order to be comprehensible as a normative issue all normative discussion must refer to the state in at least three ways:

> ... all normative issues in world politics today refer, either directly or indirectly, to the state, inter-state relations and the role of individuals as citizens of states ... it is then possible to encapsulate all the several normative questions in the one central question: 'what, in general, is a good reason for action by or with regard to states?'[8]

This is what he means by the state domain of discourse.

In referring to the 'settled norms of discourse', Frost is also making a correlative claim here, not unlike that made by Bull in his Hagey lectures,[9] that the state and its domain of discourse, including the discourse of modernisation, has been universalised. In other words, no population or territory can any longer be understood as 'exterior' to this discourse in any meaningful way. Frost argues that: 'There are no significant groupings of people who fall totally outside it. Previously there were such outside groupings, in earlier times it was as plausible to characterise the world as consisting of the civilised groups and the barbarians.'[10] Today such divisions no longer exist. The ideological division between east and west, between Christianity and Islam for example,

---

[7] 'All the debates about normative issues in international relations take place *within* a common tradition of political theory – within what I have called the modern state domain of discourse. *Ibid.*, p. 83. Within this domain 'there is widespread agreement on what could be called the goals of modernisation. This includes the goals of technical advance, industrialisation and the education of the populace which is necessary to support the former two goals'. *Ibid.*, p. 84.

[8] *Ibid.*, p. 79. According to Frost there are at least eighteen settled norms of the state domain of discourse. They are: (1) preservation of society of states, (2) sovereignty, (3) peace, i.e. war requires special justification, (4) the anti imperialism norm, (5) action against imperialism is considered good, (6) balance of power, (7) modernization, (8) patriotism, (9) collective security, e.g. United Nations,(10) institutions of diplomacy, (11) international law, (12) citizens, domestic priority, (13) democratic institutions are good, (14) human rights, (15) non-intervention, (16) economic sanctions, (17) *jus in bello*, (18) economic cooperation. See *ibid.*, chapter 4.

[9] See H. Bull, *Justice in International Relations* (The Hagey Lectures), (Waterloo: University of Waterloo, 1983).

[10] Frost, *Ethics in International Relations*, p. 84.

while exhibiting a high degree of disagreement about substantive normative issues nonetheless remains embedded in and takes place in the context of the state and its domain of discourse.[11]

Frost argues that discussion of the ethical and moral issues of international relations must, therefore, take place in the context of the settled norms of international society. Thus Frost uses the communitarian insight in two ways: the local or national society is the most important community for the individual's realisation; the state, the highest form of community in which individual realisation occurs, is also constituted intersubjectively within a society of states and that as normative discussion within the state is constituted by the particular community, so normative discussion between states is conducted by that community, i.e. the community of states. However, Frost does not intend to argue that there exists a separate realm of the international that is wholly distinct from the domestic. Instead he argues that there is a hierarchy of institutions and that all levels play their part in the constitution of the individual. In this, he differs from the 'pluralist' account of international society provided by Brown. Frost's interpretation of international society sees it as a much thicker community that has moved well beyond a practical association to issues of purpose. This leads to the next and most interesting part of Frost's account.

Having outlined his understanding of the nature of normative issues in international relations, Frost outlines two more tasks of a constitutive theory. The first of these is to develop a justificatory background thesis for these settled norms; the second, is to examine certain 'hard cases' in world politics in order to understand how they may be addressed in terms of the settled norms outlined above. The remainder of this discussion examines Frost's account of constitutive theory as a background theory justifying the settled norms of the state domain of discourse.

Frost's list of the settled norms of international society includes both sovereignty and human rights. In both Bull's and Brown's accounts these two norms are in conflict, because the principle of individual human rights is seen to oppose and undermine the pact of coexistence between

[11] 'The language of this domain is the ordinary language of international relations. This language is a functioning whole – not a completely coherent one – which includes within it a mix of the following terms: state, sovereignty, self determination, citizen, democracy, human rights (individual rights and group rights), and a set of terms connected to the notion of modernisation . . . I simply contend that any discussion about what ought to be done in world politics . . . must be conducted in the language of the modern state.' *Ibid.*, pp. 89–90.

states that establishes their sovereignty, that is, their right to an exclusionary realm. Frost argues that Bull, for instance, is, therefore, unable to account for the importance of both of these norms. Frost also argues that contractarian, order based, and utilitarian approaches are similarly inadequate. He asserts, contra Bull, that there is no such opposition between the two norms of sovereignty and human rights. According to Frost, Bull and others have misunderstood not only the nature of sovereignty but also the nature of rights and the state discourse. He argues that a constitutive understanding of the individual and the state, drawing on Hegel's philosophy of Right, effects the necessary reconciliation.

According to Frost the modern state should be understood as constitutive of its citizens as rights holders and as free and equal citizens. Individuality should be understood as something that is constitutive and realised in the community in the form of the sovereign state, not against it. Frost argues, against liberals, that the state is not just an instrumental means of allowing individuals to compete and to realise their rights and ends. It is instead constitutive of their individuality. He, therefore, takes a Hegelian view of the state as the highest form of community in which individuality is realised. The state surpasses the family and civil society as an institution in which individuals are recognised and constituted. However, Frost does not posit a strict division between inside the state and outside it. He understands the state and the individual to be constituted in turn by embeddedness in an international society of states '... within the autonomous state all individuals are constituted as free citizens, but for their citizenship to be fully actualised their state needs to be recognised by other states as autonomous.'[12] The realisation of the individual can only occur within a state which is a member of an international society of states. The society of states itself rests on certain norms regarding the legitimacy of states and their internal and external obligations. Thus an ethically defensible state must guarantee the liberty of its citizens. It must be a state in which individuality and freedom are realised:

> [I]n order to be recognised as a state, a polity must be one in which the people recognise each other as citizens in terms of the law which they in turn recognise as being both constituted by them and as constitutive of them as citizens ... An autonomous state is one in which the citizens

---

[12] *Ibid.*, p. 151.

experience the well-being of the state as fundamental to their own well-being . . .[13]

In this way he argues that a constitutive theory is able to effect a reconciliation between the principles of sovereignty and human rights.[14] The two principles are, in effect, mutually constitutive, in that recognition of sovereignty, of state autonomy, is dependent on the state being one in which individual autonomy is recognised.

Thus it seems that the settled norms of international society, as understood by constitutive theory, are to be accepted because they provide the context in which individuals can be realised. The settled norms of international society allow for the development of domestic political orders in which individuals come to know themselves as rights-bearers.

However, Frost is not just attempting to reconcile the two norms of sovereignty and human rights in terms of a constitutive theory. He has another agenda which is to develop a normative justification, not only for the settled norms but also for the state and the states system. Constitutive theory supplies not only a descriptive account of international norms but also a normative defence of them.

By demonstrating the way in which both individuality and state autonomy are constituted, Frost attempts a resolution of the cosmopolitan/communitarian divide from an essentially communitarian starting point. His argument contributes an understanding of the way in which the rights discourse is developed and embedded in real concrete situations and institutions, and the way in which those institutions are similarly embedded in international institutions. Frost's account of individuality allows the particularity of concrete others by acknowledging context of their constitution as subjects. It could be argued that he uses this starting point to develop a communitarian defence of certain universal principles. Furthermore, in his attempt to reconcile sovereignty and human rights, Frost takes individuals as his moral starting point but situates them in a particular community, the state. In so doing he can be seen as attempting to reconcile cosmopolitan and communitarian positions and developing a communitarian path to cosmopolitanism. Frost suggests that belonging to a particular community is not exclusive of certain universal principles

---

[13] *Ibid.*, p. 152.

[14] For a more detailed discussion of this dimension see P. Such, 'Human Rights as Settled Norms: Mervyn Frost and the Limits of Hegelian Human Rights Theory', *Review of International Studies*, 26 (2000), 215–31.

which target the individual.[15] In this manner he attempts to reconcile the tension between community and difference. For Frost, a constitutive theory that mediates between and recognises the different levels in which subjects are constituted is able to surpass the cosmopolitan/communitarian divide and to do justice to individuality and difference without settling for a norm of strict coexistence. Frost has a thicker understanding of coexistence than that provided by either Walzer or Brown.

Where Frost's account fits the category of communication, is in the central concepts of a domain of discourse and the idea of settled norms. At the heart of Frost's theory is the notion of normative discussion and agreement because a domain of discourse is 'an area of discussion within which the participants generally recognise (and recognise others as recognising) many rules as settled'.[16] Furthermore, although he provides no account of how these rules have come to be 'settled', that is, the historical processes in which they were generated and came to be understood, the settled norms he describes have status and authority because they are *agreed* upon. Frost's account suggests that the development of these norms is historical and contextual, and most importantly, discursive.

However, Frost's account presents some problems that prevent it from fitting neatly into the category of communication. First, while Frost's account does attempt to mediate and reconcile both cosmopolitan/communitarian positions and gives evidence of the standpoints of both concrete and generalised others, it nonetheless relies on a universalised account of agency and subjectivity. In particular, the resort to a Hegelian account of individuality and the state provides a 'thick' conception of subjectivity that is rooted to a particular social formation and institution. The hope for ethical international politics, in Frost's account, is couched in terms of the individual, the state, modernisation and rights discourses. These provide the only vocabularies in which we

---

[15] However, it is important to note that Frost doesn't endorse or subscribe to cosmopolitanism as he understands it. He remains committed to the state as the highest form of institution necessary for the recognition of individuality and furthermore he is sceptical regarding the possibility of the development of a world order in which individuals feel the same attachment to the species as they do to their particular, national, communities. Cosmopolitanism 'claims that there is a moral community of mankind which it conceives to be in some way independent of the modernizing inter state practice, whereas I consider just that modernizing state system as providing the idiom within which normative argument takes place.' Frost, *Ethics in International Relations*, p. 85.

[16] *Ibid.*, p. 78.

can meaningfully speak of international or universal norms. However, constitutive theory displays little understanding or recognition of the many ways in which the state, even the democratic state, frustrates the aspirations and the realisation of the identities of some individuals and communities. For these reasons, Frost's account remains substantially within the category of assimilation, in that normative discourse requires the universalisation of one conception of subjectivity and one social institution, in the form of the state. While this understanding of agency is not idealised, in O'Neill's sense, and is accounted for contextually, it nonetheless requires the assimilation of alternative subjectivities in order to have the universal status it claims.

Frost's constitutive account holds open the possibility of the construction of substantive normative agreement in the international realm. It suggests not only the possibility, but the reality, of a communitarian path to cosmopolitanism. It attempts to demonstrate how community can be constructed, not by abstract universal and impartial agents, but by particular embedded and situated agents. Frost provides one answer to O'Neill's question: 'What understanding and what agreement can we construct?', based on an answer to the question: 'What agreement can we presuppose?' He argues that 'we' have already agreed upon substantive international norms and these can be used as the basis of ethical reasoning. In this regard Frost provides an advance upon the cosmopolitan and communitarian positions. However, for the reasons outlined above, the constitutive theory remains within an assimilationist logic at the level of agency.

Poststructuralist international relations theory

Postmodern and poststructural approaches have been amongst the most important developments in recent IR theory.[17] While remaining

---

[17] For the purposes of clarity I will use the term poststructuralist to denote a broad range of thinkers also sometimes referred to as postmodernist. There exists a great deal of disagreement and dispute about the use of these terms in themselves and as applied to particular writers both in the field of international relations and more widely. In particular whether the works of Foucault and Derrida can be placed together under the name poststructuralism without doing significant violence to either of them is at issue. My usage follows what I perceive as the dominant usage of these terms in IR. Thus Richard Ashley, R. B. J. Walker, William Connolly and David Campbell are more likely to refer to themselves as practising poststructuralist rather than postmodern IR (though Campbell himself resists this categorisation). In following this usage I am also distinguishing between poststructuralism as a strategy of reading and postmodernism as a term that delineates a particular historical epoch or movement, as has been suggested by Jean-François Lyotard. See

on the margins in terms of the discipline as a whole they have made a significant contribution towards bringing normative issues to the forefront of inquiry. The principal normative achievement of poststructuralism has been to highlight the centrality of questions of otherness and alterity to the issue of community in IR. Poststructuralists pursue this interest by conducting critique aimed to destabilise those projects engaged in establishing realms, discourses, identities or territories where difference is excluded, assimilated or denied. Poststructuralist accounts are motivated by a concern to envisage or allow the creation of new spaces where difference and heterogeneity can flourish. Within the domain of IR this concern has manifested itself in a critique of the principle and practice of sovereignty and the advocacy of moves towards a deterritorialisation of ethics and community. While poststructuralists are concerned to critique the sovereign state as an exclusionary form of community they are less inclined to articulate alternative forms of community, and, especially, wish to eschew the project of defining the parameters of a 'thick' community or morality. They do, however, have more to say about what a poststructuralist ethic might look like.[18] This ethic is informed by particular emphases on freedom, on one hand, and responsibility on the other. This section discusses two streams of poststructuralist ethics and attempts to determine from them the most important dimensions of poststructuralist accounts of community. It is argued that poststructuralists provide an ethic which, in principle, excludes no member of the species from moral consideration, and dialogue and, therefore, shares common ground with critical theory. It is also argued that poststructuralist accounts of dialogue, freedom and responsibility are motivated by a concern to overcome the dichotomies of the cosmopolitan/communitarian divide. In particular, poststructuralist approaches suggest an understanding of freedom and responsibility that is explicitly linked to the possibility of communication between 'concrete' others. Poststructuralism, therefore, provides a significant contribution to the search for an ethics of communication.

This section begins with a brief outline of the poststructuralist project in IR and then moves on to outline poststructuralist ethics and the relation of these ethics to the issues of freedom, enlightenment and democracy.

J-F. Lyotard, *The Post-Modern Condition: A Report on Knowledge* (University of Minnesota Press, 1984).

[18] Poststructuralists appear to resist the metanarratives of 'morality' and 'justice' preferring to restrict themselves to the apparently less determinate discourse of 'ethics'.

truth/power symbiosis post structuralists

Poststructuralist international relations and the problem of community.

Poststructural approaches to IR follow the lead of Foucault and Nietzsche in theorising about truth and power. For the most part, post-structuralist inquiries into IR have concerned investigations into the relationship between truth and power in international relations the-ory and in international practices and foreign policy. Rather than ad-vocating a hermeneutics of suspicion[19] involving a deep uncovering of truth, a truth hidden by or suppressed by power, as critical theorists do, poststructuralists argue that truth and power are mutually impli-cated. As Foucault argued '. . . there is no power relation without the correlative constitution of a field of knowledge, nor any knowledge that does not presuppose and constitute at the same time power relations'.[20] Therefore, Campbell and George state, poststructuralism 'looks for no distinction between "truth" and power, for it expects none'.[21] Poststruc-turalists are concerned to analyse the way in which truth works as a discourse and as an effect of power. The upshot of this position is that poststructuralism focuses on offering readings of the way in which his-torically and culturally contingent interpretations and practices come to be taken as given, sovereign, ahistorical, true or natural.[22] This line of thinking leads poststructuralists to ask questions, not of the type 'is this true?' but instead 'How has this come to be/act/function as truth?' According to Devetak, poststructuralists follow Nietzsche's assertion that 'it is more important to determine the forces that give shape to an event or a thing than to attempt to identify its hidden, fixed essence'.[23]

[19] For a discussion of the terms hermeneutics of recovery and suspicion, see M. Gibbons (ed.), *Interpreting Politics* (New York University Press, 1987). See also the discussion of philosophical hermeneutics in chapter 4.
[20] M. Foucault, *Discipline and Punish: The Birth of the Prison* (London: Penguin, 1977), p. 27.
[21] J. George and Campbell, D, 'Patterns of Dissent and the Celebration of Difference: Crit-ical Social Theory and International Relations', *International Studies Quarterly*, 34 (1990), 269–93, p. 281.
[22] Poststructuralist readings of IR, therefore, have a concern with revealing the historicity of the human world and in particular with challenging interpretations that deny that historicity and claim an ahistorical or transcendent source. They share with critical theory a concern with the relationship between knowledge and power and with the way in which humans make their own social world and then attribute a 'natural' status to it. They have often followed the work of Michel Foucault in providing a reading of how the modern subject as 'sovereign man' has come to be constructed as part of the larger historical project of modernity. They have provided readings of international relations that examine how the idea of sovereign man has entered and helped to constitute that discourse.
[23] R. Devetak, 'Critical Theory', in S. Burchill and A. Linklater (eds.), *Theories of Interna-tional Relations* (London: Macmillan, 1996), p. 186.

This type of genealogical approach has been applied most thoroughly to the question of subjectivity. Amongst the most important contributions of poststructuralism has been an account of how the modern notion of subjectivity has come about. Poststructuralist accounts have been concerned to identify the historicity of the modern subject, rather than identify and define its rational essence.

An important part of the broader poststructuralist project is to understand how and in what ways dominant categories of truth, reason, subjectivity, identity, community, and sovereignty establish themselves as totalities, or, in Frost's terms, as settled, by excluding or marginalising that which is different or other. The rationale behind this project stems from a concern to include that which has been excluded or denied. As George and Campbell put it:

> The (poststructuralist) project is a search for thinking space within the modern categories of unity, identity, and homogeneity; the search for a broader and more complex understanding of modern society which accounts for that which is left out – the other, the marginalised, the excluded.[24]

Following Derrida, poststructuralists argue that any claim to represent or establish a truth, text or thing 'in itself' is always premised on, or implicates, that which it is not. Thus any truth claim, or claim to pure presence, is always constituted by its opposite. The outcome of this insight is a reading that suggests that 'totalities, whether conceptual or social are never fully present and properly established'.[25] The aim of poststructural readings, therefore, is to disturb and unsettle totalising truth claims and discourses, in order to reveal and disestablish the hierarchies and dichotomies and exclusions they contain.[26] Within the field of IR this project has taken the form of a preoccupation with the practices associated with the concept of state sovereignty.[27]

---

[24] George and Campbell, 'Patterns of Dissent', p. 280.

[25] Devetak, 'Critical Theory', p. 189.

[26] According to Devetak poststructural strategies of deconstruction aim, 'to disclose the parasitical relationship between opposed terms, and to attempt a displacement of them'. *Ibid.*, p. 189. Deconstruction, therefore, claims that the supposed opposition between two parts of a pair is misleading and instead opposites should be understood as contaminating each other, neither able to establish a pure presence independent of the other.

[27] Poststructuralist readings of international relations have, in particular, been concerned with analysing the way in which the discourse of sovereignty has not only come to be constructed, but also how it has come to be constructed as, in effect, an ahistorical phenomenon. They offer alternative readings of sovereignty that stress the historicity of both sovereignty and the concepts of state, anarchy and reasoning man in which it is embedded.

Poststructuralist readings of IR have been concerned to identify the historicity of the principle of sovereignty as the 'dominant mode of subjectivity in IR' and reveal how it has come to function as a naturalised and given effect of power. Poststructuralists have questioned the principle of sovereignty as the universal form of social and political life, and in particular they have questioned the practices of exclusion that constitute it.

According to poststructuralists, the principle of state sovereignty asserts a political and ethical monopoly over a territory and population. The sovereign state represents a clear boundary between inside and outside and presents itself, and is represented by others, as a stable, fixed and naturalised boundary. The link between territory, identity and community encapsulated by the principle of state sovereignty is exclusionary of those outside its boundaries. The central plank of the critique of sovereignty, therefore, revolves around the question of exclusion and of boundaries and, in particular, the way in which 'framed within a spatial metaphysics of same and other, citizen and enemy, identity and difference . . . [sovereignty] expresses an ethics of absolute exclusion.'[28] Inside the state is community, morality, politics, freedom etc., and outside is anarchy, power, war, danger, difference and insecurity. In particular, the principle of sovereignty underscores and buttresses rigid, hierarchical and closed forms of political practice, subjectivity, identity and community. Poststructuralist writers suggest that for ethical and practical reasons the state's claim to a sovereign jurisdiction over a population and territory is no longer able to provide a satisfactory resolution of questions about the nature and location of political community.[29]

William Connolly, for example, argues that democratic practices should no longer be constrained by the principle of sovereignty and the connection with a clearly demarcated territory. Connolly argues that the sovereign state has both helped and hindered the practice of

---

[28] R. B. J. Walker, *Inside/Outside, International Relations as Political Theory* (Cambridge: Cambridge University Press, 1993), p. 66. According to Walker ' . . . the principle of state sovereignty already expresses a theory of ethics, one in which ontological and political puzzles are resolved simultaneously, it affirms that the good life, guided by universal principles, can only occur within particularistic political communities'. *Ibid.*, p. 64.

[29] According to David Campbell 'the extent and nature of the vast network of relations within which states are sequestered as subjects disturb the efficaciousness of any one-dimensional representation of agency, power, responsibility or sovereignty. Accordingly security cannot only (or even primarily) be about territorial boundaries and the ethical borders that instantiate them.' D. Campbell, *Politics Without Principle: Sovereignty, Ethics and the Narratives of the Gulf War* (Boulder: Lynne Rienner, 1996), p. 84.

morality of exclusion, ethics/responsibility NOT linked to

democracy, but that conditions in the world today require a rearticulation of the democratic ethos that exceeds the state. He argues that '[S]ome elements of a democratic ethos can extend beyond the walls of the state.'[30] In other words, he argues that the democratic ethos should not be exclusive of those outside the state.

The sovereign state is problematic because it arbitrarily and contingently sets the limits of ethical responsibility and political action. Poststructuralist accounts argue that the possibilities for ethical and political life need not necessarily be constrained by the oppositions between self and other, inside and outside that the principle of sovereignty keeps in place. They are directed towards a reading of sovereignty that 'deconstructs' the sovereignty/anarchy dichotomy and the modes of identification, ethics and community that correspond to it.[31] This would include the so-called settled norms of the state domain of discourse identified by Frost.

The most significant ethical impact of this reading of sovereignty and the concern to question the ethics of exclusion is the move to, what Campbell calls, 'a deterritorialisation of responsibility'.[32] The major argument here is simply that notions of ethics and responsibility should not necessarily be linked to those who happen to share the arbitrarily demarcated boundaries of the territory of the sovereign state. Poststructuralist accounts, therefore, should be understood as concerned with questioning the morality of exclusion, and included in this concern is the project of beginning to think of new ways of relating to others and of envisaging community.[33] They are concerned to articulate conceptions of ethics and community that are not bound by

[30] W. Connolly, *The Ethos of Pluralization* (University of Minnesota Press, 1995), p. 155. In this Connolly sounds not unlike Frost, who likewise extends the principles of democracy beyond the state. However, Frost remains committed to the state and its domain of discourse in a way in which Connolly and other poststructuralists are not.

[31] For Devetak 'The consequence of taking a postmodern stance is that central political concepts such as community, identity, democracy and the state are rethought without being anchored in "ultimate markers of certainty" like sovereignty'. Devetak, R. 'Postmodernism', in Burchill and Linklater, *Theories of International Relations*, p. 203. For poststructuralists such as Walker the most important examples of this are new social movements which stress the connections between peoples across national boundaries.

[32] 'Levinas' thought is appealing for rethinking the question of responsibility, especially with respect to situations like the Balkan crisis, because it maintains that there is no circumstance under which we could declare that it was not our concern.' D. Campbell, 'The Deterritorialisation of Responsibility: Levinas, Derrida, and Ethics After the End of Philosophy', *Alternatives*, 19 (1994), 455–84, p. 463. See also D. Campbell, *National Deconstruction* (University of Minnesota Press, 1998).

[33] As Devetak argues 'the practical political task is to move towards forms of state which do without the claims of territorial exclusion and supremacy as necessary constitutive

the sovereign state nor by its opposite, of a universally homogenous state/community and that resist the strict dichotomies of self/other and identity/difference that accompany these categories. Thus, rather than surrendering the normative project altogether poststructuralism is concerned to deconstruct and rethink the framing of moral questions.[34]

Deterritorialised ethics: freedom, democracy and responsibility

Rather than attempting to delineate the boundaries of some new form of human community or to articulate the content of a 'thick' community, poststructuralist writers have, instead, been more concerned with the articulation of a poststructural ethical disposition. However, it is possible to draw the following conclusions regarding community from poststructural discussions of ethics and the critique of sovereignty. To date, poststructuralist accounts of ethics have tended to fall into two streams: an ethics of freedom/democracy and an ethics of responsibility.[35] However, an important, though under-theorised, shared attribute is a concern with dialogue and an ethical engagement with difference.

The first of these streams is related most closely to the critique of sovereignty and has most forcefully been put by Ashley and Walker, with more recent contributions from Connolly. According to Ashley and Walker, the critique of exclusionary practices of the sovereign state is carried out in what they call a 'register of freedom'. In their work freedom is associated with the critique of boundaries and the register of freedom is a 'register that affirms and exploits ambiguity, uncertainty

---

features of modern politics'. Devetak, 'Postmodernism', p. 202. Included in this task is a question of how those who are seen to be different come to be treated as unequal or excluded from moral consideration.

[34] Thus, for example, Devetak argues that 'poststructuralism is only critical of community to the extent that it attempts to inscribe fixed, rigid boundaries of enclosure; that is to the extent that it claims or institutes sovereignty'. R. Devetak, 'The Project of Modernity in International Relations Theory', *Millennium*, 24. 1 (1995), p. 44.

[35] Devetak argues that the two streams can be distinguished thus: 'One strand challenges the ontological description on which traditional ethical arguments are grounded. It advances a notion of ethics which is not predicated on a rigid, fixed boundary between inside and outside. The other strand focuses on the relation between ontological grounds and ethical arguments. It questions whether ethics ought to begin with ontology before moving to ethics.' Devetak, 'Postmodernism', p. 204. He also notes that the ethical dimension of poststructuralist thinking in IR remains the most underdeveloped component. There are perhaps good reasons, consistent with the poststructuralist approach, for this being the case. In particular poststructuralists do not attempt to develop universal accounts of the good life and, therefore, are not necessarily concerned to develop universal accounts of morality.

and the trangressability of institutional boundaries ...'[36] To privilege any particular line, community or identity is to give that line sovereign authority and to create a boundary limiting the space for the exercise of freedom and 'with the hardening of boundaries, one's own domain of freedom is now more limited'.[37] The central premise here is that freedom lies in the ability to transgress boundaries. Understood in this way, freedom necessarily requires a particular orientation and labour and '... a readiness to question supposedly fixed standards of sovereign judgement and to transgress institutional limitations ...'[38] The concern with questioning boundaries and limits underpins the entire poststructural project. Poststructuralism finds freedom in the very refusal '... to privilege any partisan political line. It is in the act of not privileging that it offers emancipation and liberation.'[39] Freedom is understood as freedom from totalisation.

William Connolly sees the democratic ethos as consistent with the problematisation of boundaries and 'final markers' in a register of freedom. He argues that such an ethos is about more than just electoral accountability; it embodies a certain disposition, a disposition that contests settled discourses and is involved in a project of denaturalisation of boundaries (and identities). The democratic ethos

> treats the contestation of final markers as a contribution to freedom, self formation and self governance among constituencies no longer required to believe that how they have been constituted historically is what nature requires them to be ... A democratic ethos balances the desirability of governance through democratic means with a corollary politics of democratic disturbance through which any particular pattern of previous settlements might be tossed up for grabs again.[40]

Such an ethos counters the tendency of democracy towards institutionalisation and naturalisation of itself in territorialised practices. Democracy must therefore, like freedom, be forever questioning itself and the boundaries it invokes.

The register of freedom Ashley and Walker describe is a response to what they call a crisis of representation in modern subjectivity (linked to

---

[36] R. K. Ashley and R. B. J. Walker, 'Reading Dissidence / Writing the Discipline: Crisis and the Question of Sovereignty in International Studies', *International Studies Quarterly*, 34 (1990), 367–426, p. 389.
[37] *Ibid.*, p. 394.   [38] *Ibid.*, p. 389.
[39] George and Campbell, 'Patterns of Dissent and the Celebration of Difference', p. 284.
[40] Connolly, *The Ethos of Pluralization*, p. 154.

a disciplinary crisis). As was noted above, poststructuralists have been engaged in a reading of western notions of subjectivity that reveal their historicity and hence their contestedness. For Ashley and Walker, this historicity is revealed in crisis. For them, subjectivity is always in crisis, contested, contingent and delimited. Crisis in an identity, truth or representation is revealed when it becomes impossible 'to exclude the contesting interpretations of subjective being that must be absent if this presence is simply to be'.[41] In other words, all subjectivities, indeed all representations that attempt to establish themselves as purely present and uncontested, are always in crisis. Thus the dominant notions of freedom in modern western discourse which rely on such essentialised accounts of human agency as reasoning, rational, western male egos are also in crisis. The crux of the critique of western or modern subjectivity is not that it is western or modern but that it attempts to connote 'an absolute origin of truth and meaning in itself'[42] that excludes other representations. Ashley and Walker argue that the revelation that the establishment of any identity, agency, subjectivity, truth claim, must rest upon the creation of the other, and that the other must 'infect' that identity, thereby undermining its claim to a pure presence, has significant ethical fallout. Any claim to a totalising sovereign identity must necessarily do injustice by excluding or marginalising others. Concerned to critique any notion of 'sovereign' subjectivity that claims to represent a pure presence, instead subjects and objects are understood as 'ever in the process of being inscribed through a hazardous contest of representations (and)... deprived of a self-evident reality'.[43] Poststructuralists are concerned to demonstrate not only how this conception has come to be, but also its relativity and contingency.

The ethical motivation of this critique of subjectivity is a concern to do justice to, or at least, not to exclude through totalisation, other modes of subjectivity.[44] This reading of subjectivity, therefore, shares the critique of the 'abstract' other by Benhabib. Privileging the abstract other

---

[41] Ashley and Walker, 'Reading Dissidence / Writing the Discipline', p. 378.
[42] *Ibid.*, p. 378. [43] *Ibid.*, p. 379.
[44] Poststructuralists argue that the marriage of freedom to one particular (though universalised) account of subjectivity and agency manifests a denial of other subjectivities and consequently a restriction of freedom. Poststructuralists attempt to rearticulate the meaning of freedom without tying it to a particular formulation of subjectivity and the hegemonic and exclusionary practices associated with it. If Poststructuralists provide readings of IR that unsettle and question totalising discourses motivated by a concern with human freedom and enlightenment, then it also stands that poststructuralism is concerned to problematise these discourses themselves. They understand enlightenment and

involves a problematic universalisation of a particular sense of agency or subjectivity and is exclusive of other accounts that would contest it. Ashley and Walker attempt to develop an account of freedom that does not presuppose privileging the abstract other, in the form of a universal account of a sovereign subject.

A freedom that does not attempt to claim an exclusive monopoly over human identity or to privilege any particular account, or establish a sovereign claim to truth, is a freedom that permits the largest possible space for diverse articulations of being, doing and belonging, and is a freedom that allows a more diverse flourishing of different 'concrete' subjectivities. Freedom in this sense is about creating a space in which 'concrete' others can express and realise their differing subjectivities and 'that sustains and expands the cultural spaces and resources enabling one to conduct one's labors of self making . . . '[45]

The emphasis on questioning boundaries, and resistance to totalisation, in this strand of poststructuralist thought can be understood also as an ethics of Foucauldian resistance. An ethics of Foucauldian resistance is an ethics of radical autonomy. Thus, the testing of limitations is conducted in order to pursue freedom in such a way that allows the greatest scope for freedom for all concerned to pursue it while recognising that not only does this amount to different things in different times and places but that it cannot be carried out in isolation.[46] Rather than advocating a nihilism or relativism poststructuralism can be understood as being motivated by a concern for freedom, democracy and autonomy.[47]

Again, Ashley and Walker's treatment of freedom shares much with Connolly's understanding of the democratic ethos. Connolly is involved

freedom not as fixed endpoints, universally and transcendentally defined, outside of time or place but as continuing processes with flexible, contingent and particular meanings in particular locations.

[45] *Ibid.*, p. 139.

[46] It is important to note here that this 'labor of self-making' is not conceived of as a project undertaken by individuals in isolation: '. . . Self making is not a private matter; . . . the expansion of freedom cannot be equated with the expansion of sovereign powers'. *Ibid.*, p. 392. Indeed the very ethicality of this notion of freedom lies in the recognition that one's own 'labor of self making' is carried out in the context of others attempting to do the same, that 'it is just at this point – where the differences between the 'she' of a locality and the 'ourselves' who span localities are tested – that ethical considerations . . . arise'. *Ibid.*, p. 393.

[47] Walker, for example, argues that '[M]uch of the postmodern turn can be understood as a series of attempts to reclaim or reconstruct or even finally to create some practical space for, say, a Kantian concern with the conditions of the possibility of knowledge or the meaning of autonomy in a world in which the secular guarantees of Reason and History can no longer console us for the death of God'. Walker, *Inside/Outside*, p. 20.

in an attempt to provide an account of democracy that does not privilege the 'abstract' other and a universal subjectivity or the territorial restrictions of the nation-state. For Connolly, a democratic ethos is the best way of approaching the identity/difference paradox; that paradox in which identity and, therefore, autonomy cannot be posited without positing difference. A democratic ethos of questioning final markers is also an appropriate response to the crisis of representation. Such a questioning applies to the markers of identity and subjectivity as it does to the boundaries of any social formation. A democratic ethos is an ethos of pluralisation, it is an ethos that '... strives to create more room for difference by calling attention to the contingent, relational character of established identities'.[48] According to Connolly, a democratic ethos allows for the flourishing of different subjectivities, while at the same time recognising that these subjectivities are contingent, interdependent and contending. In a similar vein to Ashley and Walker, Connolly's agonistic democratic ethos is concerned with the creation of a space in which different subjects can engage in labours of self-making. An agonistic democratic ethos '... opens up a cultural space through which the other might consolidate itself into something that is unafflicted by negative cultural markings'.[49] Thus, for Connolly, a democratic ethos is the most appropriate ethos for fostering pluralism and giving due recognition to identity and difference. Connolly's emphasis on the recognition of contingency and on an agonistic conception of democracy attempts to articulate a conception of democracy that incorporates 'concrete' others.

The question remains, how does 'one' act or proceed in a register of freedom, knowing one's own and the other's identity to be in flux and knowing that one's own 'labours of self-making' cannot be unproblematically universalised or exported? Ashley and Walker answer that to proceed in a register of freedom one must 'be disposed to undertake a patient work of questioning and listening...'[50] Undertaking one's labours of self-making in a world without sovereign centres requires an ethics where 'the democratic practices of listening, questioning and speaking are encouraged to traverse... institutional limitations...'[51] Freedom comes to be seen as freedom to be heard and to speak and not to be excluded from communication and conversation. Furthermore,

---

[48] W. Connolly, *Identity/Difference: Democratic Negotiations of Political Paradox* (Cornell University Press, 1991), p. 33.
[49] Connolly, *Ethos of Pluralization*, p. xvii.
[50] Ashley and Walker, 'Reading Dissidence / Writing the Discipline', p. 395.
[51] *Ibid.*

deterritorialised ethic

freedom means that no single voice can come to dominate or 'stand heroically upon some exclusionary ground, offering this ground as a source of a necessary truth...'[52] A deterritorialised ethic is, therefore, an ethic that subjects institutional boundaries and limitations to radical critique in the pursuit of greater freedom and communication between radically different subjectivities.

A democratic ethos is, according to Connolly, an ethos of agonistic respect and care. It is a 'politics in which one of the ways of belonging together involves strife and in which one of the democratising ingredients in strife is the cultivation of care for the ways opponents respond to mysteries of existence'.[53] The cultivation of care itself stems from the recognition of contingency in oneself and in others. A recognition of contingency '... cultivates a politics of agonistic respect among multiple constituencies who respond differentially to mysteries of being while acknowledging each other to be worthy of respect partly because they are implicated in *this* common condition'.[54] No constituency, knowing itself to be contingent, can assert or know itself to be grounded or to be the model for all. For Connolly exactly how this agonal ethos of critical responsiveness is undertaken remains unclear. He talks of an agonism in which strife, care and respect are mixed and in which different subjects contest, but he says little of the actual manner of this contest. The overall thrust of Connolly's work is to move beyond the options of annihilation, assimilation and coexistence, towards an ethics of engagement with otherness in all its alterity. However, at least part of this agonism is based on the possibilities of communication in the sense that an ethos of democratisation involves an 'agonistic dialogue in interpreting actuality, projecting future possibilities and identifying present dangers'.[55] Beyond this, however, Connolly does not develop the qualities and characteristics of conversation itself and of what exactly is involved in an agonistic dialogue.

Poststructuralists therefore, as their critique of subjectivity suggests, place particular emphasis on the 'concrete other' labouring in particular sites under particular conditions.[56] Most importantly the substantive ethical thrust of this approach is that conversation, the patient labour

---

[52] *Ibid.*   [53] Connolly, *Identity/Difference*, p. 33.   [54] *Ibid.*   [55] *Ibid.*, p. 33.
[56] 'The problem is not one of how to impose this ethics from on high or how to make doubters believe in it – a problem whose very posing can only seem strange to people of marginal sites who would practice this ethics of freedom. It is a problem of how working from local sites and according to this ethics of freedom, to enable the rigorous practice of this ethics in the widest possible compass.' Ashley and Walker, 'Reading Dissidence / Writing the Discipline', p. 395.

72

of listening and questioning, is oriented to allowing the voice of particular 'others' to speak and be heard. For Ashley and Walker, inspired by Foucault, this is very much an ethics of resistance to totalisation, rather than say, an ethics oriented towards the creation of substantive agreement on normative principles. But it is nonetheless an ethics that implies, without theorising, that justice is pursued or realised in conversation, or more correctly by allowing different voices to be heard and engaged with.

The ethics of responsibility

If the major ethical thrust of the first stream of poststructuralist thought is resistance to totalisation and towards the freedom of radically autonomous subjectivities, then the second stream of poststructuralist ethics provides an emphasis on responsibility. Where the first stream draws on a largely Foucauldian reading of the relationship between ethics and subjectivity the second stream draws on a Levinasian/Derridaean reading. While David Campbell is equally concerned to question the exclusionary practices of the sovereign state and in particular to disconnect ethics from territory, his ethical motivation comes from what he sees as the primacy of ethical responsibility to otherness as 'first philosophy'.[57] However, where the ethics of freedom and responsibility concur is in the recognition that an ethical relationship between self and other requires contestation and negotiation; in other words, communication.

The central insight of Levinas' philosophy, according to Campbell, is that there is no being, no subjectivity, without a responsibility to the 'other' because 'being is a radically interdependent condition'.[58] Subjectivity, in this account, is actually more like intersubjectivity. Furthermore, there is, he argues, a real sense in which our subjectivity is constituted by ethicality: 'ethics can be appreciated for its indispensability to the very being of the subject'.[59] Campbell argues that Levinas' articulation of a radical interdependence of subjectivity means that all ethics is constituted by our relationship to otherness. The ethical outcome of this is that the 'other' has an ethical hold on the self from the beginning by way of its part in the constitution of the self but also because the self 'is called into question by the prior existence of the other'.[60]

---

[57] Campbell, 'The Deterritorialisation of Responsibility', p. 461.
[58] *Ibid.*, p. 460.   [59] *Ibid.*, p. 463.   [60] *Ibid.*, p. 460.

The larger ethical implication of this, however, is that the self is in effect constituted by its *responsibility* to the other and, further, 'one's being has to be affirmed in terms of *a right to be* in relation to the "other".[61] Ethics, then, is a response to the 'call of the other' and involves not a struggle for one's own freedom but a decentering of self in the face of one's responsibility to the 'other'.[62]

According to Campbell, an understanding of Levinas' ethics of responsibility undermines the principle of sovereignty, and indeed all exclusionary practices, because such practices place limits on the extent of responsibility, by restricting it to the nation-state or the particular community, gender, race or other grouping. Thus, for example, Campbell argues 'there is no circumstance under which we could declare that (the war in the Former Yugoslavia) . . . was not our concern'.[63] To take this ethics seriously is to deterritorialise ethics completely.[64] This condition means that we cannot stop our moral duties at the water's edge. Furthermore, it is an ethics that in acknowledging interdependence suggests we have to resist assimilating the other into our world; and at the same time we have to live for the other in all their alterity.

This transcendent and universal responsibility to 'others', according to Campbell, suggests (at least) two further responsibilities. The first is shared with the Foucauldian stream and consists of the project of permanent critique of totalisation in the name of a single identity, and thus is an act of resistance. The second suggests that the responsibility to the other requires a politics and ethics that is oriented positively towards otherness; '. . . one in which its purpose is the struggle

---

[61] *Ibid.*, p. 460.

[62] 'Ethics redefines subjectivity as this heteronomous responsibility, in contrast to autonomous freedom.' Levinas quoted in Campbell, *ibid.*, p. 463. Where Ashley and Walker are concerned to foster, celebrate and respect difference, their ethical starting point is a radical understanding of autonomy as resistance. For Campbell on the other hand, following Levinas, ethics begins with recognition of radical human inter-subjectivity which requires a further recognition of responsibility.

[63] *Ibid.*, p. 462.

[64] While Campbell is concerned to critique the exclusionary practices associated with sovereignty he is also aware that sovereignty under certain circumstances provides the best resource. Sovereignty might help the defence of pluralistic communities in Bosnia for example. He argues '[W]e cannot be for or against sovereignty in such a circumstance; instead, we have to be alert to sovereignty's investments and effects in the light of our responsibility to the Other. Only a critical attitude which enables flexible strategies which are governed neither by abstract universals (and thus likely to further the conditions they are responding to) nor by purely ad hoc ones (and thus unaffected by the ethical imperative of responsibility), can hope to respond to our responsibility to the Other.' Campbell, D. 'The Politics of Radical Interdependence: A Rejoinder to Daniel Warner', *Millennium*, 25. 1 (1996), pp. 129–41, p. 141.

for-or *on behalf of*-alterity, and not a struggle to efface, erase, or erad-icate alterity'.[65] It is an ethics that celebrates and respects proliferate differences.

What then does this mean in terms of conduct and practice in an ethi-cal realm? For Campbell, the answer seems to lie in something not unlike Connolly's agonistic democracy. The substantive ethical outcome of this position is that Campbell sees politics and ethics as a matter of delib-eration between contesting selves and others. According to him, this is a different understanding of ethics from that of traditional approaches in IR which 'have sought to specify in the abstract what good and right conduct consists of . . . '[66] In contrast, Campbell argues, an approach in-formed by Levinasian and Derridaean readings amounts to more of an ethical disposition towards others, a disposition 'attuned to the politi-cal nature of agency and identity',[67] which nonetheless acknowledges and stems from a recognition of the radical intersubjectivity of diverse agents.

To get to this end, Campbell's reading of Levinas is concluded with a supplementary reading of Derrida. Campbell argues that Levinas' ethics require a supplementation with Derridaean deconstruction in order to take account of the plurality of others. According to Campbell, the plu-rality of others to whom one might be responsible means that the lines of responsibility are not clear cut. As a result it becomes necessary to prioritise one's ethical responses but doing so is itself morally prob-lematic and Levinas' work provides no guidance for such prioritising. Campbell argues that one way of coming to grips with this dilemma is via Derrida's notion of undecidability. Confronted with a plurality of others to whom one is responsible Campbell argues there remains a responsibility to act, to make a decision. Derrida's account of unde-cidability, of the madness of the decision, acknowledges this dilemma and suggests the need for a 'double gesturing' wherein one acknow-ledges that in making a decision one is simultaneously doing justice and injustice to others, by giving priority to some or one and not oth-ers or another. What the need for a double gesture demonstrates is that questions of responsibility are not clear cut and cannot be decided in advance or in a programmatic way. Instead they require the making of decisions and a knowledge that the decision will necessarily be unjust.

---

[65] Campbell, 'The Deterritorialisation of Responsibility', p. 477.
[66] Campbell, *Politics Without Principle*, p. 99.
[67] *Ibid.*

To be aware of this dilemma and yet at the same time to have to act requires a 'double contradictory imperative 'an imperative that requires an "interminable" experience and experiment of the impossible'.[68] What such a double gesturing, what an acknowledgement of the complex lines of responsibility to otherness that exist in a condition of radical intersubjectivity, raises is the necessity of keeping lines of communication and political action open and in continual flux. This reading of Derrida, for Campbell, suggests that to do justice to the other, and to others, requires a realm of contestation and negotiation in which differences flourish and totalisation is resisted. It suggests that one's duties can only be decided through contestation and negotiation and the meaning and practices of concepts such as democracy, identity, freedom, must also be continually re-negotiated and questioned. Were there no need for decisions, there would only be the implementation of programmes. However, the 'heteronomous responsibility to the other' requires that politics and ethics cannot be reduced to a programme.

Campbell calls for an understanding of ethics and politics as a field of contestation motivated by responsibility to otherness. The ethical disposition he endorses rejects the traditional modern 'preference for deriving norms epistemologically over deciding them politically'.[69] Thus, our ethical responsibility to otherness must not be derived or decided in advance of our engagement with the 'other'. Instead the 'way in which our ethical responsibility has to be acted upon has to be contested and negotiated'.[70] In this, Campbell's approach seems to resemble the agonistic democratic ethics of Connolly: an ethos in which the responsibility to otherness requires the critique of fixed standards of exclusion and of judgement, the proliferation of multiple discourses and agents, and the engagement with the 'other's' particular alterity in some form of dialogue or communication.

Thus, Campbell's approach contributes to a critique of the sovereign state and, most importantly, the development of an ethical disposition in which individual subjectivity is understood as ethically constituted in its relationship to otherness. What this ethicality suggests is that, if one understands oneself to be so constituted then, one's relationship to otherness cannot be premised on practices of superiority or indifference but on respect and engagement. Respect and engagement suggests a

---

[68] Campbell, 'The Deterritorialisation of Responsibility', p. 477.
[69] Campbell, *Politics Without Principle*, p. 99.
[70] *Ibid.*

practice of communication and dialogue rather than the alternatives of assimilation or coexistence.

Poststructuralism and the cosmopolitan/communitarian divide

The question of the other, of the excluded and marginalised, is central to poststructuralist writings on IR. The critique of sovereignty and the reading strategies of deconstruction and double reading have been motivated by a concern to articulate that which has been excluded. Most importantly poststructural accounts of ethics and community can be understood as being concerned with articulating and investigating new possibilities of conceiving ethical relationships to difference. This focus on the excluded, the marginal and different and the critique of to- talising and universal discourses, has led some to suggest or imply that poststructuralists are concerned exclusively with the particular and the local, that poststructuralism stands opposed to cosmopolitan, universal projects and global discourses and, therefore, should seem to be the natural ally of communitarianism.[71] Alternatively, poststructuralism has stood accused of surrendering the possibility of moral judgement altogether, and advocating nihilism and relativism instead. If the will to truth is replaced by the will to power and if all understandings of truth are to be understood as particular and contingent rather than universal and grounded, then how is it possible to judge between them?

Such characterisations, however, rest on a misreading of the post- structuralist project. From a poststructuralist perspective, the charge of nihilism is misdirected because freedom is seen to lie in the very pro- liferation of perspectives and transgression of boundaries:

> If conduct in the margins proceeds in a celebratory register of free- dom, it certainly will not announce that 'anything goes' precisely be- cause freedom is valued under circumstances like these, no maxim could be considered less efficacious. Here especially one must always be prepared to understand that some ways of acting, speaking and

---

[71] Indeed on another occasion I have suggested, following Taylor and Rengger, that the poststructuralist emphasis on difference endorses the concept of 'radical value incommen- surability' between inhabitants of different traditions and communities. See R. Shapcott, 'Conversation and Coexistence, Gadamer and the Interpretation of International Society', *Millennium*, 23, 1, Spring (1994). The argument on that occasion suffered from a too-close adherence to Taylor's reading of Foucault. The present discussion can be understood as a correction to that earlier suggestion.

writing are better or worse, more or less effective, and more or less dangerous.[72]

What is 'good', therefore, is that which stands opposed to or resists totalisation, that encourages freedom or alternatively, in Levinasian terms, acts out of responsibility to otherness.

Poststructuralists, this section has argued, advocate an ethics defined by or involving practices of freedom, democracy and responsibility. The next question to be addressed is where does poststructuralism stand in relation to cosmopolitan/communitarian perspectives and, perhaps even more importantly still, the issue of universalism?

As Cochran points out, poststructuralists share certain elements of the communitarian position, namely the critique of Liberalism and an understanding '... that subjectivity, is integrally tied to objectivity ... any understanding of the individual as subject is linked to the historical practices of the social matrix, and similarly, the understanding of those practices is reinforced by subjective consciousness'.[73] However, poststructuralists are critical of communitarianism in so far as they argue that the 'community' does not exhaust the possibilities of subjectivity. Poststructuralists see the practices of the 'historical matrix' as both simultaneously constitutive of individuals *and* exercising a power and discipline over them. Poststructuralists adopt a different ethical orientation to this social matrix in that they are concerned to question, disturb and unsettle and to push the boundaries and understandings in which the subject is enmeshed. In keeping with the poststructuralist critique of sovereignty, communitarian accounts of community are seen to endorse contingent acts of closure and exclusion and to provide support for the naturalised, bounded, sovereign community.

Poststructuralism is, however, critical of cosmopolitanism, especially in its liberal form. It shares with the communitarians a refusal to privilege the abstract other. It is sceptical towards cosmopolitan attempts to define universal accounts of the good life based on particular interpretations of human agency, reason and community. Similarly, poststructuralism is critical of universalism, especially that which presents itself as transcendent, or outside history, representing a sovereign centre and exclusionary domain. Universalism is linked with totalisation in most instances.

---

[72] Ashley and Walker, 'Reading Dissidence / Writing the Discipline', p. 391.
[73] M. Cochran, 'Postmodernism, Ethics and International Political Theory', *Review of International Studies*, 21 (1995), 237–50, p. 244.

Despite this emphasis, it is possible to detect a significant universalist, if not cosmopolitan, dimension in poststructuralism, that is comprised of three elements. First, it seems that while poststructuralists question and disturb universal accounts of subjectivity they simultaneously offer an alternative. In particular, they suggest that all subjectivity should be understood as contingent, contested, in doubt and negotiated. Second, poststructuralists accompany their accounts of subjectivity with what appears to be an advocacy of the universalisation of an ethics of freedom and responsibility, even if simultaneously problematising that universalisation. Third, the emphasis on deterritorialisation and the critique of closure also represents a refusal to delimit the scope of poststructuralist ethics. Therefore it is reasonable to assume that these ethics are applicable to the species, or the globe as a whole and indeed Campbell is most explicit about this. [74]

However, it is easier to comprehend these instances of universalism if it is recalled that poststructuralism problematises not just totalisation but also binary oppositions. Poststructuralist readings of IR are concerned to 'deconstruct' the established discourses revolving around the binary oppositions of 'Man and Citizen', and cosmopolitanism/communitarianism, and to attempt to think alternative formulations of identity, community and ethical responsibility. That is to say, they do not aim to replace one sovereign totalising centre with another. The problem therefore, according to Walker, '. . . is not the claims of universalism as such. It is rather, the way in which universalism has come to be framed as both the opposite of and the superior to pluralism and difference'. [75] What a poststructuralist reading of IR suggests is the 'possibility of forging a language in which to speak of those things that human beings share in common: a language in which to explore universals while recognising the arrogances of existing claims to universality'. [76] Thus, the move beyond state sovereignty requires at least some minimal universalism, at the same time as a never-ending project of problematising and questioning that universalism. Thus, Walker

---

[74] 'Indeed, because engagement with the world is necessarily "global" in its scope, but the world is characterised by a multiplicity of agents, none of whom can single-handedly bear the burden of global responsibility, the way in which our ethical responsibility is to be acted upon has to be contested and negotiated.' Campbell, *Politics Without Principle*, p. 98.

[75] Walker, *One World, Many Worlds*, p. 136.

[76] *Ibid.*, p. 134. Campbell likewise appears to endorse such a project, see his quote from Derrida in Campbell, 'The Deterritorialisation of Responsibility', p. 476.

argues, '[U]niversalism has to be sought and resisted at the same time'.[77] Again, what is required is a double gesture both affirming and questioning the necessity of universals. What a deterritorialisation of ethics and community amounts to is not a rejection of universalism in favour of particularism, or cosmopolitanism in favour of communitarianism but instead, according to poststructuralists, new resolutions and balances between them. Thus while poststructuralists are not concerned to establish or define a universal account of the good life or the good community they attempt instead to find some way of living with the *dilemmas* of universalism and particularism. It can be argued that the most important element of their response to these dilemmas involves a recognition of the need for communication and dialogue between concrete agents originating from particular, though, problematic places, times and social matrices. In particular, it is the poststructuralist concern to be *engaged* with the other in all their alterity, stemming from the problematisation of boundaries, that gives the greatest support to an ethic of communication.

Thus, as suggested above, poststructural accounts can be understood as wishing to privilege neither side of the cosmopolitan/communitarian divide. In particular, by attempting to deconstruct traditional accounts of community and morality in IR poststructuralists are engaged in an attempt to rethink and articulate new balances between universalism and particularism similar to that undertaken by critical theorists.

Critical theory

The 1980s saw the emergence of a critical theory of IR in part, and, like poststructuralism, as a response to the re-articulation of Realism in the work of Kenneth Waltz.[78] Critical theorists such as Robert Cox, Richard Ashley, Mark Hoffman, Andrew Linklater and Mark Neufeld have all taken issue with Neo-Realism and its agenda.[79] In particular, they have argued that Neo-Realism provides an ahistorical account of

---

[77] Walker, *One World, Many Worlds*, p. 135.

[78] See K. Waltz, *Theory of International Politics* (Reading: Addison Wesley, 1979).

[79] See R. W. Cox, 'Social Forces, States and World Orders: Beyond International Relations Theory', in R. O. Keohane (ed.), *NeoRealism and Its Critics* (Columbia University Press, 1986); A. Linklater, *Beyond Realism and Marxism: Critical Theory and International Relations* (London: Macmillan, 1990); A. Linklater, *The Transformation of Political Community: Ethical Foundations of the Post-Westphalian Era* (Cambridge: Polity Press, 1997); A. Linklater, *Men and Citizens in the Theory of International Relations*, 2nd edn (London: Macmillan, 1990); M. Hoffmann, 'Critical Theory and the Interparadigm Debate', *Millennium*, 16. 2, Summer, 1987; R. K. Ashley, 'Political Realism and Human Interests', *International Studies*

the state and the states-system that was blind to the possibilities and likelihood of change in the structure of international system. By focusing on the reproduction of the states-system Neo-Realism ignored those developments at work in the realms of class, production, and what Cox called 'social forces' that would serve to generate structural transformation. Critical theorists, therefore, were concerned to develop a theory that could investigate the possibilities for the transformation of world politics.

Critical theorists have a particular normative concern with investigating the possibilities for change that may bring about reductions in systematic violence, inequalities of wealth and power and improvement in the conditions of human existence. They are concerned both to understand the present world order and to provide a normative critique of it. Critical theory is informed by Marx's 11th thesis on Feuerbach: 'philosophers have only interpreted the world in various ways; the point is to change it'.[80] Most importantly, critical theory is understood to be constituted by an interest in human emancipation, in expanding the realm of human freedom. This commitment requires subjecting the social world to rational scrutiny and in particular 'to promote emancipation by providing enlightenment about the constraints upon human autonomy'.[81] It is this interest that differentiates it from 'traditional', problem solving or technical theories, like Neo-Realism and Rationalism, which seek to merely understand and contribute to the maintenance of the status quo.[82]

Quarterly, 25. 2, June (1981) 204–36. M. Neufeld, *The Restructuring of International Relations Theory* (Cambridge: Cambridge University Press, 1994).

[80] Quoted in Devetak, 'Critical Theory', p. 146. As Cox argues critical theory '. . . allows for a normative choice in favour of a social and political order different from the prevailing order. But it limits the range of choice to alternative orders which are feasible transformations of the existing world.' Cox, 'Social Forces, States and World Orders', p. 210. Critical theory, therefore, is an immanent theory, it focuses on the tensions, contradictions and possibilities within existing arrangements that may allow for or lead to transformation.

[81] A. Linklater, 'The Question of the Next Stage in International Relations: a Critical Theoretical Point of View', *Millennium*, 21.1 Spring (1992), 87.

[82] Following Max Horkheimer, Robert Cox made a distinction between technical, problem solving theory and critical or emancipatory theory. Realism Cox argued is a technical or problem solving theory while critical theory is emancipatory. See Cox, 'Social Forces, States and World Orders'. Linklater follows Habermas in making a threefold distinction between technical, practical and critical theory. According to Habermas the type of knowledge acquired in any investigation is conditioned by the meaning contexts of the type of enquiry, by the purpose, or interest, of the investigation: 'The approach of the empirical–analytic sciences incorporates a technical cognitive interest: that of the historical hermeneutic sciences incorporates a practical one; and the approach of critically oriented sciences incorporates the emancipatory cognitive interest . . . ' J. Habermas, *Knowledge and*

One strand of critical theory, influenced by the Frankfurt school, argues that this concern necessarily leads to an investigation into the possibilities for realising a cosmopolitan community of humankind. These critical theorists argue that freedom and equality cannot be fully realised in a world of sovereign states but only in a world based on cosmopolitan principles; a critical theory of international relations should identify 'the prospects for realising higher levels of human freedom across the world society as a whole'.[83] Thus Linklater, for example, disputes Frost's reading of Hegel, in which individual recognition is tied to the sovereign state, and argues instead that complete individual recognition can only come about with the emancipation of the species and the realisation of a form of community that transcends the state.

For Mark Neufeld, the projects of universal freedom and community are united in terms of what he refers to as the 'Aristotelian project'. The task of a critical theory of IR is to direct this project to the international realm. According to Neufeld the Aristotelian project was centred around the *polis* and the question of how to lead a 'good and just life' in it. The central achievements of the *polis* rested on two qualities: 'the understanding that to live in a *polis* meant that everything was decided through words and persuasion';[84] and, that to do so requires upholding the values of liberty and equality. Neufeld stresses (following Arendt) that the *polis* was not a physical space but a political one created by those who partook of it and adhered to these two chief characteristics. The task of international relations theory in a globalised age, he argues, must be to expand or recreate the *polis* on a planetary scale. Accordingly, what is required is a theory directed towards human emancipation and the creation of a universal *polis* in which 'everything is decided through words

Human Interests (London: Heinemann, 1972), (trans. Jeremy Shapiro), p. 308. Linklater argues that these interests have their representatives in IR theory: Realism, Rationalism and Revolutionism (which he renames critical theory) correspond respectively to the Technical, Practical and Emancipatory cognitive interests. Furthermore Linklater argues they ' . . . form a sequence of progressively more adequate approaches to world politics . . . a theory which analyses the language and culture of diplomatic interaction in order to promote international consensus is an advance beyond a theory of recurrent forces constituted by an interest in manipulation and control. And an account of world politics which seeks to understand the prospects for extending the human capacity for self-determination is an even greater advance in this sequence of approaches.' Linklater, *Beyond Realism and Marxism.* p. 10.

[83] *Ibid.*, p. 7. Neufeld's inclusion of the search for 'the good and just life' into the definition of the polis needs to be contrasted with Linklater's acceptance of Habermas' distinction between matters of the good life and matters of justice.

[84] Neufeld, *The Restructuring of International Relations*, p. 10.

and persuasion'.[85] Such a theory is attempted by Andrew Linklater. According to Linklater a critical theory of this sort needs to embrace 'normative, sociological and praxeological analysis'[86] of the practices and values of inclusion and exclusion which stand in the way of achieving this goal.

For Linklater, emancipation requires that the cosmopolitan community be constituted discursively as one in which all humans have the opportunity for equal participation in a conversation, and thereby of determining their own lives. A cosmopolitanism informed by critical theory must strike a balance between the claims of universalism and particularism or, using the vocabulary of previous chapters, the claims of cosmopolitanism and communitarianism. Linklater pursues this balance by way of utilising a discursive account of moral reasoning drawing on the discourse ethics of Jürgen Habermas. Linklater's work also provides the most comprehensive attempt to incorporate the concerns of communitarians, and the position of the concrete other, into a cosmopolitan account: critical theory, therefore, aspires to unite the project of human emancipation, universal community and human conversation and to expand the values of the *polis* into the international realm.

Discourse ethics and the cosmopolitan project

Linklater argues that the pursuit of universal freedom and equality should be understood as a project of maximising inclusion in a discursive community. The aim is to pursue freedom and equality while at the same time striking a balance between universalism and particularism. In this, he takes his lead from the later Frankfurt school theorist Jürgen Habermas. Linklater draws on Habermas for three major purposes: to help articulate and differentiate the purpose and constitution of a critical theory; to contribute to the philosophical defence of moral universalism; and to articulate a conception of cosmopolitan community informed by discourse ethics.[87] Discourse ethics in turn provides two things: a philosophical account of why community should be understood as a discursive community and a model of dialogue or conversation. Discourse ethics provides the basis for the development of a 'thin' universality which 'defends the

---

[85] *Ibid.*   [86] Linklater, *The Transformation of Political Community*, p 11.
[87] See note 82.

ideal that every human being has an equal right to participate in dialogue . . . '[88]

According to Linklater, the principal argument of discourse ethics is that moral and political arrangements only gain legitimacy if they have secured the consent of all those affected by them. Habermas' defence of universalism emphasises

> the importance of answerability of all others; what it highlights is the need for the destruction of all systematic forms of exclusion and the pre-eminence of the obligation to develop global arrangements that can secure nothing less than the consent of each and every member of the human race . . . *this notion of universal consent is the essence of ethical universalism.*[89]

For Linklater the principle of consent is the best means for both achieving and defending the aspiration to universalism.

Discourse ethics is premised on Habermas' reworking of Kant's categorical imperative. Habermas argues, after Kant, that for morals to be valid they must be universalisable: '. . . only those norms are accepted as valid that express a *general will*. As Kant noted time and time again, Moral norms must be suitable for expression as "universal laws" . . . Kant wants to eliminate as invalid all those norms that "contradict" this requirement.'[90] For this reason discourse ethics is classified as a deontological theory which describes the 'moral point of view'. It provides the procedures by which the validity of moral claims, understood in the strict Kantian sense as those norms which are applicable to all, or 'what everybody ought to do', can be ascertained. Thus, Habermas sees discourse ethics, resting on a principle of universalisation (U), as the correct re-working of Kant's principle. Where discourse ethics differs from Kant's formulation is that, for Kant, universal applicability was the result of private reasoning on the part of the philosopher. Discourse ethics on the other hand ascertains the validity of norms in a process of discourse and argumentation between genuine, concrete, situated agents. Discourse ethics reworks the categorical imperative from a monological

---

[88] Linklater, *The Transformation of Political Community*, p. 107. The 'thin cosmopolitanism' developed here is obviously to be distinguished from that offered by Michael Walzer and discussed in chapter 1. The principal difference being the lack of any discursive dimension in Walzer's account.

[89] A. Linklater, 'The Problem of Community in International Relations', *Alternatives*, 15 (1990), 135–53, p. 142. Emphasis added.

[90] J. Habermas, *Moral Consciousness and Communicative Action* (Cambridge: Polity, 1990), p. 64.

exercise in abstract reason into a principle of actual intersubjective dia-logical consent: 'rather than ascribing as valid to all others any maxim that I can will to be universal law, I must submit my maxim to all oth-ers for purposes of discursively testing its claim to universality'.[91] Dis-course ethics, then, provides a procedure for determining the universal validity of norms, based on a presupposition that norms are only valid if capable of commanding universal consent: 'Only those norms can claim to be valid that meet (or could meet) with the approval of all affected in their capacity as participants in a practical discourse.'[92] Discourse ethics does not in itself provide or contain substantive moral content, it merely provides the correct procedures for determining which norms can be said to hold universal validity, or rather which norms can be said to be legitimately moral in that they can apply to all.

The principle of discourse ethics supports the cosmopolitan project, according to Linklater, because a commitment to securing the consent, in principle, of every member of the species entails that any form of exclusion from moral or political community can only be justified if it has the consent of those excluded as well as those included. Discourse ethics suggests that

> there are no valid grounds for excluding any human being from dia-logue in advance. No system of exclusion passes this moral test unless its constitutive principles can command the consent of all, in particular those to be excluded from the social arrangement in question.[93]

A critical theory of international relations, therefore, requires an exami-nation of the principles underlying state exclusivity and the arguments for the state's exclusion of non-citizens from its moral consideration: '[S]ince Critical Theory begins with a prima facie commitment to hu-man equality, the first question to ask concerning the normative ques-tion of the state concerns the justification for excluding any human being from any social arrangement.'[94] Linklater argues that the sovereign state maintains strict practices of exclusion based only on the consent of its domestic population and not of those excluded. Accordingly, Linklater argues, the state can no longer defend its claim to a sovereign realm, that is, to a realm of purely internal affairs resistant to and dissuasive of the claims of outsiders. The logical outcome of the principle of consent is

---

[91] McCarthy quoted by Habermas. *Ibid.*, p. 67.   [92] *Ibid.*, p. 66.
[93] Linklater, 'The Question of the Next Stage', p. 92.   [94] *Ibid.*

that discourse ethics requires the establishment of a cosmopolitan community in which the issue of moral boundaries, amongst others, can be discussed.

If the first principle of discourse ethics, that of consent, requires the creation of a cosmopolitan community (in Linklater's reading), the second principle (D) is that the community should be a discursive community. Linklater follows Habermas in arguing that consent can only be achieved by establishing a realm that allows a universal and 'unconstrained' dialogue of equals. Linklater envisions a cosmopolitan community in which all humans can participate in discussion concerning matters that affect them, including the drawing of moral boundaries, a community in which 'no person and no moral position can be excluded from dialogue in advance'.[95] This aspect of discourse ethics can, Linklater suggests, be understood as a continuation of the Kantian tradition of enlightenment.[96] If the normative purpose of critical theory is the realisation of universal human community, then the quality, character and nature of the community must be consistent with the principles of freedom and equality. According to Linklater, it is only in such a world that human freedom and equality can be realised: a community embodying the principle of human autonomy and universality needs to be a dialogic and discursive community. Linklater agrees with Habermas that discourse ethics realises the spirit of Kant's categorical imperative by incorporating the argument that '... every human being (has) an equal right to participate in open dialogue about the configuration of society and politics'.[97] The realisation of a discursively based cosmopolitan human community is the end point of a project of emancipation. Emancipation then comes to mean freedom from unjustifiable forms of exclusion.[98]

[95] A. Linklater, 'Citizenship and Sovereignty in the Post-Westphalian State', *European Journal of International Relations*, 2. 1, March (1996), 77–103, p. 86.

[96] Linklater, 'The Question of the Next Stage', p. 92. '.. class particularism exists alongside forms of national particularism for most of human history, and, therefore, the state and the states-system must also be regarded as obstacles to the universal recognition of men as species-beings. Marx's theory shares with Kant's the desire for a universal society of free individuals, a universal kingdom of ends'. Linklater, *Men and Citizens*, p. 159.

[97] Linklater, 'The Question of the Next Stage', p. 92.

[98] Discourse ethics rests on the argument that the unforced force of the better argument favours inclusion over exclusion. The force of the better argument is in favour of universal ethics and the principle that the highest forms of ethics consistent with the species capacities for self-determination involve recognising the equal rights of all humans to participate in dialogue. For Linklater the question of community formulated in this way suggests that the study of international relations should expand its attention on the study of the competition for power to include a study of how certain practices of exclusion

In addition to justifying universalism in terms of a principle of consent discourse ethics also outlines the mode of conversation that is appropriate to an unconstrained dialogue. The means for pursuing consent is through 'a mode of dialogue in which human beings strive to reach agreement'.[99] This mode of dialogue has several prerequisites. The first is that no position can be excluded in advance. Another is that agents must be willing to enter into dialogue and to strive towards agreement. This, in turn, requires a particular moral psychology in keeping with a principle of unconstrained dialogue. Conversation is to be understood not as a competition nor a 'trial of strength between adversaries bent on converting others to their cause...'[100] Instead, Linklater suggests that an authentic dialogue should be motivated and guided by a willingness to be persuaded by the 'unforced force of the better argument'. A commitment to the unforced force of the better argument suggests that 'agents suspend their own truth claims, respect the claims of others and anticipate that their initial points of departure will be modified in the course of dialogue'.[101] The process of coming to an agreement requires that agents be able to reflect upon their own starting points and positions and, in principle, change them, or come to see how these positions 'reflect personal biases and local cultural influences which others may not share'.[102] A commitment to dialogue requires a degree of openness and reflexivity between agents who are willing to engage in a conversation involving reciprocal critique and in which 'there is no certainty about who will learn from whom'.[103] Linklater follows Habermas in referring to this standpoint as a postconventional morality.[104] A postconventional morality allows reflection and critique and more importantly it is only from this point that actors can 'ask whether they are complying with principles which have universal applicability'.[105] In other words,

---

have worked over time and how they have been replaced by the adoption of ever more universalistic perspectives.

[99] A. Linklater, 'The Achievements of Critical Theory', in S. Smith, K. Booth and M. Zalewski (eds.), *International Theory: Positivism and Beyond* (Cambridge: Cambridge University Press, 1996), p. 286.

[100] Linklater, 'Citizenship and Sovereignty', p. 86.   [101] *Ibid.*, p. 86.

[102] Linklater, 'The Achievements of Critical Theory', p. 286.

[103] Linklater, 'Citizenship and Sovereignty', p. 86.

[104] The topic of the postconventional agent is dealt with in more depth in the following chapters. For Linklater 'the widening of the sense of who counts as amoral person or moral equal and the willingness to be bound by universalisable norms are, arguably, the two main features of the more advanced moral codes'. Linklater, 'The Problem of Community', p. 142.

[105] Linklater, 'The Achievements of Critical Theory', p. 285.

postconventional morality is necessary in order to learn how to conduct social life consensually.

Linklater is also keen to assert that learning how to conduct social life consensually does not require the creation of universal agreement as to the good life, as, for instance, is the case in Rawls's original position.[106] While the search for consensus suggests that agents are involved in a search for agreement on 'thick' universals it may also involve merely attempting to 'reach agreement about the principles of inclusion and exclusion and [the] attempt to understand the rules of coexistence which agents could accept where they fail to reach consensus'.[107] In other words, discourse ethics accepts that a position of coexistence may be the best available option and that agents may agree to disagree. The important point here is that a practice of coexistence be consented to by all parties and is itself the outcome of dialogue. Again, discourse ethics does not attempt to determine the outcome of conversation in advance; it does, however, begin with certain assumptions about how dialogue should be conducted and with certain formal principles which need to be established before dialogue can commence. In discourse ethics dialogue is constituted as a genuine dialogue between real agents and not as an exercise in monological reasoning, as in the case of Rawls's original position. It involves the opposite principle to the 'veil of ignorance'. Conversation is an avenue for the pursuit of genuine knowledge of the other and the self, and the agreements it pursues are the outcome of deliberations concerning genuine, situated, and not hypothetical, positions. Discourse ethics, Linklater argues, is commensurate with Benhabib's concern to engage with concrete others, as well as with O'Neill's project to reduce the level of idealisation of agency involved in previous cosmopolitan projects. Conversation does not require a notion of individuals removed entirely from their social contexts but instead works on the premise that contextualised and embedded individuals are nonetheless capable of thinking in universalist terms and being persuaded by the unforced force of the better argument. Discourse ethics argues that real contextualised agents are capable of engaging in dialogue in order to understand each other, of transcending their own, particular, starting points and of coming to agreement as to how to conduct social life. Thus Linklater suggests, this vision of a discursive universalism

---

[106] In this his understanding of the Aristotelian project's application to international relations is different from Neufeld's.
[107] *Ibid.*, p. 292.

'imagine[s] a stronger universalism in which dialogue encounters difference ...'[108] Justice to difference, to diverse cultures and individuals, is obtained by inclusion in the discursive realm. In this sense, discourse ethics does not, it is claimed, require the universalisation of a particular idealised sense of agency. This claim is examined more closely in the next chapter.

On the other hand, what discourse ethics shares with the Rawlsian contract is the aspiration of universality and the belief that moral principles can be just only if they are universally applicable. In this way, both inhabit the Kantian deontological tradition. Neufeld, amongst others, has argued that Habermas' discourse ethics shares with Rawls's theory of justice the aim of developing a universal procedural account of the right as a means for mediating between different accounts of the good.[109] While the two share the aim of universality the emphasis in discourse ethics is less on the determination of substantive or specific universal principles than it is with the creation of a realm in which discussion as to what may be universalisable can take place.

The creation of a cosmopolitan community informed by discourse ethics, Linklater asserts, overcomes the weaknesses of liberal cosmopolitanism. It does not require the creation of a completely homogenous society that is dismissive of group and particularistic identities. It is not a requirement of discourse ethics that the interests of the particular group should simply 'lose out' as Beitz argued. For Linklater a cosmopolitanism that is commensurate with the principles of discourse ethics, is one that is able to coexist with, and is not exclusive of, minority or particularistic identities and obligations: 'The point is not to dissolve the obligations at the core of the concentric circles of human obligation but to modify them in response to the rights of those located in the penumbra.'[110] Linklater denies, therefore, that discourse ethics must necessarily involve a universal form of identity resting on the necessary subordination of cultural diversity and individual or group identities:

> The issue for the universalist is not to replace customary moral differences with a single universalised moral code but rather to find the right balance between the universal and the particular. The aim is to defend moral inclusion and equality without positing a single human identity

[108] Linklater, 'Citizenship and Sovereignty', p. 87.
[109] M. Neufeld, 'The Right and the Good in International Ethics'. Paper Presented for the ISA Annual Convention. San Diego, April, 1996.
[110] Linklater, 'The Problem of Community', p. 143.

and to value difference without subscribing to doctrines of innate superiority and inferiority and correlative forms of moral exclusion.[111]

This conception of community, he argues, is one that can include group rights, to land and cultural self determination, as well as universal rights of inclusion.[112] However, discourse ethics does not wish to privilege the local and particular either. According to Linklater, the universalism of discourse ethics '... does not entail the demise of inner circles of obligations ... but it does imply that the inner sanctum must be available for the scrutiny of outsiders if it has any impact at all upon their equal rights to promote their own ends'.[113] In this way one of the aims of discourse ethics is, according to Linklater, to strike a balance between universalism and particularism.

Linklater defends discourse ethics against the charge that it is merely formalistic and lacking in content and argues that it contains a specific politics. A cosmopolitanism informed by discourse ethics seeks to critique all forms of violence, oppression or systematic inequality that prevent active participation in dialogue and is, therefore, committed to 'the critique of structures and beliefs which obstruct open dialogue'.[114] One of the principal targets of a critical theory of international relations is the examination of systems of exclusion whereby those who are different are excluded from moral consideration.[115] This form of cosmopolitanism stands opposed to practices which exclude the 'other' from moral consideration and from being legitimate partners in conversation. In particular, discourse ethics requires the eradication of two forms of exclusion, those generated by economic inequality and those generated by the question of group difference. This conception of cosmopolitan democracy is concerned with creating the conditions that

[111] *Ibid.,* p. 141.
[112] 'The normative ideal of the extension of community does not simply involve bringing aliens or outsiders within one homogeneous, moral association. It also entails recognition of the rights of groups, such as indigenous people, which fall within the jurisdiction of the sovereign state, but which suffer exclusion from full participation in the national community ... it is a vision which argues for greater power for subnational and transnational loyalties, alongside older, but transformed, national identities and separate, but not sovereign, states.' Linklater, 'The Question of the Next Stage', p. 93.
[113] Linklater, 'The Problem of Community', p. 142.
[114] Linklater, 'Citizenship and Sovereignty', p. 87.
[115] Discourse ethics argues that '... human beings need to be reflective about the ways in which they include and exclude others from dialogue (and therefore) that they should be willing to problematize bounded communities ... and the legitimacy of practices of exclusion is questionable if they have failed to take account of the interests of outsiders'. *Ibid.,* p. 85.

allow the practice of a conversation amongst equals. Therefore what discourse ethics can be said to contribute to the project of a cosmopolitan community is an emphasis on creating a context in which competing understandings of the good life can be brought into communication. As noted above, discourse ethics is inconsistent with the maintenance of a system of sovereign states and instead endorses the pursuit of new forms of political community that take account of the limits to universalism and the limits of particularism.

Discourse ethics and post-Westphalian communities

In his most recent work, Linklater has suggested that the notion of 'post-Westphalian citizenship' may be one way of embodying discourse ethics in a cosmopolitan political structure that replaces the sovereign states-system.[116] Modern notions of citizenship, he argues, must be reformulated in order to become more inclusive. Previously citizenship has worked to define insiders from outsiders and to cement and confirm individual loyalty to the nation-state. Linklater argues that discourse ethics can contribute to an alternative universal and post-sovereign conception of citizenship. Such a conception might allow for overlapping multiple loyalties as well as universal ones. It is crucial that 'the politics of recognition be incorporated within post-sovereign conceptions of cosmopolitan democracy'.[117] Such a conception of political community and citizenship suggests that individuals and groups, including sub-national and transnational communities should have recourse to authorities both above and below the level of the nation-state.[118] The notion of post-Westphalian citizenship must transcend earlier formulations by including the commitment to consent through dialogue. In post-Westphalian citizenship legal and welfare rights are '... necessarily accompanied by rights to participate in dialogue as equals who can either grant or withhold their consent'.[119] Such developments allow for the creation of a political community

---

[116] *Ibid.*   [117] *Ibid.*, p. 94.

[118] Linklater identifies four means of pursuing this goal: '(1) devolving political power so that citizenship can be enjoyed through participation in subnational assemblies; (2) given their desire to reclaim lost rights though international recognition, ensuring that subnational groups are adequately represented in transnational institutions; (3) making it possible for subnational groups to appeal to international courts authorised to scrutinise claims of discrimination against minorities and (4) ensuring that subnational regions receive adequate resources to withstand the effects of de-industrialisation upon vulnerable economies and to ensure the survival of their various languages and cultures.' *Ibid.*, p. 96.

[119] *Ibid.*, p. 92.

wider than the state but which does not merely reproduce the practices of sovereignty at a larger level. Citizens of post-Westphalian states can have multiple loyalties and identities as well as being subject to a variety of authorities situated at a trans-and sub-state level. Again the aim of such developments is to strike a balance between the universal and the particular, between cosmopolitanism and communitarianism.

This section has attempted to outline the most important elements of the contribution to the project of community in international relations from a critical theoretical perspective. It argued that the constitutive interest of a critical theory of international relations in emancipation has resulted in a defence of universal community informed by discourse ethics and the development of post-Westphalian communities. This form of universal community is, according to Linklater, able to meet the communitarian criticism of cosmopolitanism and provide a universal defence of difference while at the same time developing a substantive conception of global community. Indeed, one of the goals of cosmopolitan democracy as understood by Linklater is the protection and inclusion of minority and sub-national groups in the global cosmopolis. The extent to which Linklater has been successful at this will be examined in the following chapters.

Conclusion

This chapter has provided an account of constitutive, poststructuralist and critical theoretical approaches to the problem of community in IR and has argued that in different fashions these perspectives provide an advance on liberal cosmopolitan and communitarian perspectives. The works presented here all contribute significant steps towards transcending the cosmopolitan/communitarian divide and in beginning to chart what might be called a communitarian path to cosmopolitanism. In a variety of ways these approaches address the cosmopolitan question: 'what kind of community can we construct?' In so doing, they can all be seen to be motivated, in different ways and to different degrees, by the standpoints of both concrete and generalised others. They are all concerned with articulating different possibilities of community that neither exclude those outside the boundaries of the sovereign state nor achieve inclusion at the price of a universal homogenous identity. The primary importance of these perspectives lies in their emphasis on the centrality of communication and dialogue in allowing a more ethical and equal relation to concrete others. All three perspectives appear to share the contention that a more satisfactory ethical relation to otherness can be achieved through recognition in conversation. The basis for this common understanding of the place of dialogue in normative thought stems in part from their shared hermeneutic position on knowledge and agency. Critical theory, poststructuralism and constitutive approaches are all premised on an interpretative account of social life and it is this element that makes for their appreciation of the communitarian position. This hermeneutic moment involves an appreciation that moral codes, community and human agency are all constituted by and in the constellation of meanings of particular humans and their communities. In turn, this means that any account of the right or the good and of what constitutes the community must be articulated and negotiated by particular, situated agents in dialogue, and cannot be delivered from outside any given social context nor found in some ahistorical or asocial origin.

However, despite this common ground it was also suggested that poststructuralism and critical theory in turn provided better accounts of communication and community than that provided by constitutive theory. Constitutive theory, as articulated by Frost, was handicapped by its claim that the highest form of recognition could only be achieved within the framework of the modern state. It was argued that limiting the form of community in this way prematurely discounted the possibility that concrete individuals may achieve recognition in a diverse range of communities at both substate and suprastate levels. Constitutive theory remains too prescriptive in its account of community and, therefore, unable fully to realise the goal of recognition of difference. For this reason, the contributions of constitutive theory remain of limited use for the project of developing a communicatively based cosmopolitanism.

Poststructuralist and critical theoretical accounts, in contrast to constitutive theory, are concerned to emphasise the possibilities for conversation and communication between concrete individuals, that are not tied explicitly to the state. Poststructuralists see the state and the state domain of discourse as unnecessarily exclusive and restrictive in its understanding of the possibilities for human agency and communication, and are concerned to deterritorialise community. Linklater, on the other hand, argues that an alternative reading of Hegel, this time informed by Marx, suggests that full recognition of human agency can only come about with the realisation of a cosmopolitan community. Linklater also shares with Ashley, Walker and Campbell the argument that recognition of the variety of concrete agents requires the detachment of ethical community from the modern state. They argue that such a detachment is necessary to securing an adequate and inclusive relation to diverse concrete 'others'. In this way, these theories move beyond the limitation of the cosmopolitan/communitarian divide.

Having made this move, however, the question that is raised again is 'of what does communication consist?' In this regard, this chapter suggested that Linklater's application of discourse ethics to the cosmopolitan project provided an account of communication that was more fully developed than the poststructuralist alternative. Discourse ethics consists of a rigorous attempt to provide the answer to the question 'of what does communication consist?' The principal achievement of Linklater's critical theory has been to introduce a model of conversation between participants inhabiting potentially radically different contexts but who are nonetheless conceived of as equals. In so doing, Linklater has provided the most detailed and systematic account of what a discursively based community concerned to do justice to difference might consist of.

Despite these advantages significant problems remain. The succeeding chapters argue that the openings for communication provided by poststructuralism and critical theory do not exhaust the meaning of 'good' conversation. Furthermore, it is argued that the resolutions of the tension between community and difference offered in them can still be improved upon. Specifically significant assimilatory potential remains in both poststructuralism and in Linklater's account of discourse ethics, which require further examination. A preliminary assessment suggests that both perspectives contain tensions between a practice of enlightenment (or emancipation) and a practice of communication. While this tension may be both productive and restrictive in the long run, it nonetheless raises the following questions: 'Does the project of universal emancipation and the creation of a community of self-determining autonomous beings require the universalisation of a particular "postconventional" agency?' and; 'To what extent does the creation of a universal principle of conversation require more substantive transformation of individuals and communities that is itself a process of assimilation rather than communication?'

Finally, by introducing a model of conversation Linklater gives the discussion a different focus. Linklater's introduction of discourse ethics directs attention beyond the issue of boundaries and towards examination of the meaning of communication itself. The next two chapters take up this task and introduce a model of conversation which provides both an alternative and a complement to discourse ethics.

3   Emancipation and legislation: the boundaries of conversation in poststructuralism and the critical theory of IR

In the previous chapter it was argued that both critical theorists and poststructuralist writers in IR shared the goal of a non-exclusionary and communicative relationship to difference. A reading of the works of Linklater, Ashley and Walker, and Connolly suggested that communication, as an act of recognition which did justice to difference, was a common element of both. In addition, it was also suggested that poststructuralism (in at least one variant) and critical theory came to focus on the issue of communication as a consequence of a commitment to the possibilities for human freedom. However, it was also suggested that Linklater's appropriation of Habermasian discourse ethics provided the most sophisticated treatment of the nature of communication and conversation in IR. Because it is premised on the principle of universal consent, discourse ethics provides a more just relation to difference through the formula of an unconstrained dialogue. This allows a more just orientation towards difference because no agent, no matter what their particular cultural starting point might be, is to be excluded from dialogue in advance: conversation is exemplified in the principle of equality in dialogue without requiring (uniform) identity. Stemming from this principle, Linklater argued that discourse ethics recognises the need for a universal and unconstrained dialogue in order to pursue consensus and agreement on questions of justice and inclusion. The task left to discourse ethics was the setting out of the nature of procedures necessary to ensure such communication. Discourse ethics, Linklater argued, provided the basis for a 'thin' conception of cosmopolitan community in which the demands of universalism and particularism could be reconciled.

The purpose of this chapter is further to advance the case for a 'thin' cosmopolitanism by examining the nature of good conversation in more depth. Chapter 2 concluded that Linklater's cosmopolitanism most closely approximated an ethics of communication balancing the standpoints of the concrete and generalised others. However, it was also concluded that Linklater's project might not be able to escape the tensions associated with the reconciliation of community and difference and this was evident in the form of a tension between a practice of assimilation and a practice of communication. This chapter argues that, while both discourse ethics and poststructuralist approaches help us to think more clearly about the meaning of a thin cosmopolitan community and help to provide a basis for conceiving of cosmopolitanism in communicative terms, their attempted resolutions of the tensions between the aspiration for community and the goal of recognising difference can still be improved upon. The argument which follows identifies the potentially assimilatory dimensions of their approaches to conversation and suggests that these dimensions stem from the identification of conversation with a Kantian concern with a politics of freedom. Discourse ethics in particular, suffers from an overdetermination as a result of this identification, and its model of conversation, therefore, is in need of further refinement. The argument begins by examining the limitations of the Kantian paradigm as embodied in poststructuralism and the discourse ethics model of conversation. The next chapter advances an alternative understanding of conversation based on the philosophical hermeneutics of Hans-Georg Gadamer. The focus of these two chapters, therefore, is on the specifics of the model of conversation and the meaning and nature of an inclusive and non-assimilatory dialogue.

Emancipation and legislation: reason, agency and practice in critical theory and poststructuralist IR

This section re-examines critical theory and poststructuralist accounts of community and communication in IR with the intention of highlighting their most problematic aspects. The substantial argument of this section is that, in so far as both critical theory and poststructuralism constitute their relationship to otherness purely in terms of expanding the realm of human freedom, they stand at risk of retaining both a restricted notion of equality and a potentially assimilative account of communication. More particularly because they equate morality with freedom, and freedom with critique, critical theory and poststructuralist IR necessarily engage in a practice in which equality is understood in terms of a capacity to practise reasoned self-critique. As a result, inclusion into the realm of communicative equals requires the exclusion of those facets which are deemed illegitimate, unreasonable or inconsistent with this capacity.

This point can best be understood in terms of what Kimberley Hutchings calls the legislative function of the Kantian critical project. Hutchings argues that the Kantian project is bedevilled by an inescapable paradox of 'limitation and legislation'.[1] Kant, and those who have followed him, have been faced with a paradox whereby critique refuses and questions all limitations on thought, and all claims to authoritative knowledge, while at the same time claiming a legislative, judicial role (which involves the placing of limitations) for itself. Kantian critique as a result, she argues, '... is characterised both as free debate and as the passing of "judicial sentences" ... '[2] The legislative or judicial role of critique is to define and exclude those modes of speech which are illegitimate, in particular, dogmatism and radical scepticism (relativism). According to Kant, these positions are illegitimate because they claim knowledge of things which are unknowable, in contrast to the claim of critique which accepts and recognises the limitations of human cognition.

In terms of providing a model of conversation the Kantian appeal to reason, along with the defence of freedom of thought and expression, encourages a plurality of voices while simultaneously excluding some voices from the realm of legitimate speech, it '... legitimates and encourages freedom of speech, while arguing that only certain speech is legitimate'.[3] According to Hutchings, this paradox is further troubled by the inability of reason to secure the grounds for its legislative, judgemental authority. In other words, how can critique claim authoritative knowledge of what is legitimate or illegitimate when it denies the possibility of authoritative knowledge?

The Kantian paradox of limitation and legislation provides for the possibility of assimilatory and exclusionary relations in the following ways. It is potentially exclusionary of modes of thought and speech which do not conform to the idea of critique, and deems them illegitimate for the purposes of negotiation or communication in the moral realm. It is potentially assimilatory because it suggests the possibility of

---

[1] K. Hutchings, *Kant, Critique and Politics* (London: Routledge, 1996). By referring to critical theory in this manner Hutchings is emphasising the Frankfurt school's position as a manifestation of the project first articulated by Kant. Accordingly many of the problems associated with critical theory have their roots in Kant's project.

[2] *Ibid.,* p. 32.   [3] *Ibid.,* p. 18.

a practice oriented towards the creation of a realm of discourse populated by those able to conform to the ideal of reason.

The Kantian paradox finds expression in both critical and poststructural approaches to IR.[4] In particular, what links these projects is the legislative function of the discourse and practices of freedom and enlightenment and it is this common ground which makes for the possibility of an unequal form of the self/other relationship in both. Both critical theory and Foucauldian poststructuralist IR hold that the purpose of freedom is best achieved through the exercise of critique. As such they find themselves in the same inescapable bind as Kant. They aspire to offer critique, the questioning of all limitations on human thought, as the path to and realisation of human freedom. However, in so doing, they also posit critique as the opposite to dogma, power and radical scepticism, or nihilism, which are deemed illegitimate and thus excluded. In both critical theory and poststructuralism this has direct ramifications on the possibilities for communication between radically different cultures and agents. In critical theory in particular, the exclusive and assimilatory potentials of the Kantian emphasis on critique and its opposition to tradition, provide contestable grounds for possible unjustifiable exclusion.

The argument below outlines the most important ways in which poststructuralism and critical theory provide evidence/examples of the legislative mode. The most important of these occurs where the voices of certain agents are excluded from the model of conversation provided by discourse ethics. Because poststructuralism does not provide a model of conversation as such it can not be compared on this issue in the same degree of detail, but it can, and is, addressed for what it does say about communication.

Agency and practice in poststructuralism

This section re-examines the poststructuralist position on communication and community. Concern about the legislative and exclusionary aspects of critical theory and discourse ethics is shared by

---

[4] What Hutchings' discussion of the legislative function of freedom raises is the difficulty of grounding the idea of reason outside of itself. If reason cannot be grounded in the way that its advocates would like, as Hutchings argues, then it must be a practice as vulnerable as any other. As a result, the legislative and judicial power of reason has its universality undermined. Reason, therefore, must appeal to its persuasive faculties rather than ontological or metaphysical grounds. According to Hutchings, Ashley and Walker, in adopting a register of freedom, likewise claim some sort of grounding for it and, therefore, are appealing to its legislative faculty.

poststructuralists. However, poststructuralists also argue that critical theory retains a high degree of logocentrism and they question
Habermas' goal of grounding critique in the presuppositions of argumentation. Furthermore, they understand discourse ethics as an attempt
at closure, in so far as it appears oriented towards definite and ultimate
consensus.[5] Poststructuralists also resist the logocentrism involved in
critical theory's understanding of reasoned discourse between rational
beings by problematising more completely the guiding concepts of reason and rationality, as well as the unified identity of the beings engaged
in discourse. In addition, they dispute the teleological and developmen-
tal/evolutionary model employed by Linklater and Habermas. Finally,
poststructuralists would have cause to be critical of Linklater's conception of international community on the grounds that, despite its claims,
it represents yet another exercise to determine the particular good life for
all. Some of these concerns are shared with philosophical hermeneutics
and will be taken up below.

In addition to a commitment to communication between real, situated
agents requiring the critique of boundaries and unjustifiable forms of
exclusion, as argued in the previous chapter, poststructuralist perspectives share with critical theory a commitment to practice in a 'register
of freedom'. However, by virtue of this mutual commitment poststructuralists also run the risk of envisioning a community populated by
'enlightened' beings and a practice oriented towards the realisation of
that community.

It was demonstrated in chapter 2 that Ashley and Walker offered an
understanding of freedom as Foucauldian resistance. The task of poststructuralism, in addition to the 'patient labour' of listening and speaking with others, was to engage in unsettling and disturbing practices in
order to increase the range of freedom and the variety of spaces within

---

[5] As Ashley and Walker argue '... any understanding of disciplined ethical conduct that
would aspire to cast all activities in the clarifying light of sovereign centre of universal
judgement – in the light of some given consensus, for example, or some canon for the
production of consensus – ironically depends on the exemption of certain activities from
the critical, juridical light to which it would refer... A universalistic ethical system, so
understood, always depends upon a reach of activity that exceeds the system's ethical
grasp... we cannot represent, formalise, or maximise deterritorialized modalities of ethical conduct. We cannot evoke a juridical model, define the good life and lay down the code
crucial to its fulfilment, as if bespeaking some universal consensus formed according to
rules of discourse already given, without at the same time covertly imposing a principle
of territoriality that these modalities refuse to entertain.' R. K. Ashley and R. B. J. Walker,
'Reading Dissidence / Writing the Discipline: Crisis and the Question of Sovereignty in
International Studies', *International Studies Quarterly*, 34 (1990), 367–426, pp. 390–1.

which individuals could carry out their 'labours of self-making'. This stream suggested that freedom was premised on the never-ending critique of sovereign identities and boundaries. Poststructuralist theorists in IR take an unequivocal stand against sovereign identities, discourses and presences and argue that totalisation could be resisted by revealing the contested, arbitrary, fluid and historical nature of identity and subjectivity. The recognition of subjectivity, of agency as 'socially constructed', contingent, arbitrary and malleable, is a necessary component in a poststructuralist ethics of freedom. Through recognition of the contingent nature of subjectivity and resistance to totalising and sovereign claims, the individual was more able to engage in 'their labours of self-making'. Ashley and Walker, therefore, suggest that freedom requires the exercise of non-sovereign identities.

The poststructuralist account of subjectivity and agency shares a great deal with the notion of autonomy in critical theory. Seen to be historical and contingent, subjects are capable, within flexible limits, of asserting and exercising agency and thereby transforming themselves and their social world.[6] In particular, critical theory and poststructuralism share an understanding of enlightenment as the realisation that it is 'man' and not nature who is the source of the social world, and all its inequalities and power structures.

As a result of this observation, poststructuralism and critical theory also share the goal of achieving freedom from indefensible, traditional, given beliefs about society, self and other through the use of reason. It will be recalled that Linklater endorsed the Habermasian understanding of reason's emancipatory power as simultaneously a means to, and the realisation of, an individual's freedom. Poststructuralism lends support to the use of reason in rendering visible and placing in question prejudices and, more particularly, totalising truth claims. At the same time, poststructuralism refuses to recognise the possibility of a consciousness free from distortion or the influences of 'irrational' considerations. For this reason, Devetak argues, critical theory and poststructuralism in IR can be understood to be engaged in rethinking the enlightenment project of 'modernity'. This project, he argues, 'is exactly this concern with the idea, meaning, and scope of emancipation. It is the breaking away from

---

[6] As noted in chapter 2 poststructuralists also problematise the meaning of autonomy and subjectivity to a degree not matched by critical theory. For poststructuralists the possibility of autonomy in the classical enlightenment sense is a much more difficult and impossible project because they appear to dispute while also aspiring to the possibility of individual subjectivity divorced from relations of power and domination.

the past, and past forms of injustice, and the need to shape a universal normative trajectory for the future.'[7] In particular, poststructuralists participate in this project in so far as they offer a politics of radical autonomy in which the destabilisation of sovereign identities and subjectivity is linked to an ethics of critical freedom. Furthermore, poststructuralists follow Foucault in depicting enlightenment as the questioning of limits. Freedom is found in the questioning and removal of limits previously seen to be final and absolute. In particular, they share the aspiration to subject all 'given' limits and truth claims to critical scrutiny and aim, as a consequence, according to Foucault, to 'separate out, from the contingency that has made us what we are, the possibility of no longer being, doing, or thinking what we are, do, or think'.[8] According to Devetak, this orientation towards limits requires '. . . the "permanent reactivation" of the critical attitude'.[9] While critical theory and poststructuralist international relations may offer differing interpretations of the meaning of enlightenment and autonomy, they nonetheless partake in a similar project by adopting a legislative practice oriented towards increasing the realm of freedom, however, so defined, or problematic, its meaning may be. Both endorse freedom understood as critique and offer it as the grounds for the exclusion of other modes of thought and speech.

While Ashley and Walker resist a developmental or teleological account of freedom and enlightenment they nonetheless find themselves engaged in a similar practice with similar problems to those facing critical theory. By theorising in 'a register of freedom' Ashley and Walker's account of freedom also '. . . take[s] on the explicit status of a Kantian regulative idea as a standard of judgement'.[10] For Ashley and Walker, freedom, therefore, inevitably functions simultaneously as both an emancipatory and a legislative ideal. In this sense and to this degree (and only to this degree) Ashley and Walker's account of practice is complicit in a potentially unequal relationship between self and other. This is so because from this position the other remains to be enlightened or emancipated

---

[7] R. Devetak, 'The Project of Modernity in International Relations Theory', *Millennium*, 24. 1 (1995), p. 35. For Devetak, what poststructuralists bring to this project is the task of subjecting the enlightenment tradition itself to critique and problematising its basic assumptions about subjectivity, freedom and knowledge. This does not mean they abandon it, only that it '. . . remains an open question, but one that must continually be re-posed'. *Ibid.*, p. 46. In this regard Foucault's text is exemplary.

[8] M. Foucault, 'What is Enlightenment', in P. Rabinow, *The Foucault Reader* (London: Penguin, 1984), p. 46.

[9] Devetak, 'The Project of Modernity', p. 46.

[10] Hutchings, *Kant, Critique and Politics*, p. 164.

from something like their immaturity (in the Kantian sense) and it is this which governs the orientation of the poststructuralist self towards the other. The poststructuralist practice of disturbance also suggests the goal of the creation of a community (or communities) populated by beings who share a similar self-understanding, that of reflexive post-structuralist individuals. Poststructuralism suggests that those who do not share this assessment of themselves as unfree are in need of enlightenment and, therefore, should be the subject of further critique or more correctly, should engage in more reflective self-critique. The poststructuralist account of freedom, like critical theory, suggests the expansion of the realm of those agents who understand themselves in a certain manner, that is, as postsovereign, reflexive, critical individuals. For this reason, despite both the aim of inclusion, and the recognition of the multiple meanings of freedom and communication with 'concrete' others, poststructuralist accounts of IR retain the potential for assimilation and prescription in the domain agency.

This aspect of poststructuralist thought comes through most clearly in Ashley and Walker's account of communication. For them communication does not have the same requirements for entry or participation as discourse ethics, they have no intention of developing a uniform model of conversation between post-conventional beings and furthermore, are not concerned with the development of 'thick' universal norms. The poststructuralist account of developing a 'universal moral trajectory' suggested by Devetak (above) appears to go only so far as the thin principle of inclusion. Thus while Ashley and Walker engage in a project of enlightenment, communication itself does not appear to be limited exclusively to enlightened agents. The pursuit of universal freedom in terms of a recognition of the arbitrary and historical nature of subjectivity is not an essential component of the ability to converse. Rather, the poststructuralist account of conversation is directed only at questioning the practices and beliefs which serve to prevent different agents from conversing with each other.

Ashley and Walker explicitly raise the question of how to engage ethically with those who do not share their self understanding or who 'in their specific marginal sites' comprehend the meaning of freedom differently. They ask, 'how is it possible to pursue and expand the realm of freedom and at the same time be sensitive to others?':

> If, in the process of testing limitations, one assumes that one's local strategic situation is a paradigm for the struggle for freedom wherever

it unfolds, then one is all too likely to be impatient with other's labors in other strategic situations... one is all too likely to be insensitive to the ways in which one's own conduct, one's way of questioning limitations – might ramify beyond one's locality and threaten to deprive others of the cultural resources by which they reply to the problems of freedom in other equally difficult strategic settings.[11]

Their response to this problematic is illuminating. In this situation there is a risk that an inappropriate response is likely to generate 'unfortunate results' which reduce the scope of freedom for all. To be insensitive in such a context is likely to produce a hardening of institutional boundaries on behalf of the 'other' and in response to a perceived threat. There is a danger of provoking the other into 'consecrate[ing] some semblance of a sovereign territorial ground they might call their own, even at a cost of freedom'.[12] Therefore, the best practice in this situation it is to engage in conversation: in 'the patient labour of listening and questioning'. But another question arises at this point: 'what is the purpose of this patient labour of conversation?' For Ashley and Walker it is 'to explore possible connections between the *strategic* situation of others and one's own, always sensitive to the problem of *expanding* the space and resources by which the ongoing struggle for freedom may be undertaken there as well as here'.[13] However, there is an ambiguity about this response. Conversation in this circumstance seems to be, on the one hand, the ethical way of engaging with radically different others, and on the other hand, an ethical way of engaging in *strategic* relation to others. In this conversation one engages with other, not in order to understand them *per se*, but rather in order to prevent a further hardening of boundaries that limits their's and one's own freedom. In this regard poststructuralism introduces the danger of engaging in a quasi-instrumentalist practice whereby communication with the other is over-determined by the *strategic* purpose of expanding the realm of freedom. That is, it proceeds to engage with the other presupposing the purpose of communication is the achievement of freedom, understood as self-critique. The point here is not to suggest that the relationship between self and other accompanying Ashley and Walker's project is a purely strategic one. Instead the intention is to bring to light a possible danger which might accompany a conversation with the other in

[11] Ashley and Walker, 'Reading Dissidence / Writing the Discipline', p. 394.
[12] *Ibid.*   [13] *Ibid.*

which the achievement of freedom, understood this way, provides its purpose or *telos*. The nature of this danger and its alternatives will be made clearer below and in the next chapter.

Finally, before proceeding to examine critical theory it is necessary to revisit the other stream of poststructuralist thought in IR. In chapter 2 it was argued that David Campbell had advocated an alternative poststructuralist ethics based on the work of Levinas. Campbell suggested that in contrast to conducting ethics in a register of freedom, Levinas argues that 'ethics redefines subjectivity as ... heteronomous responsibility'[14] to otherness. For Campbell, the radical interdependence of human subjectivity requires an acknowledgement of a universal obligation and responsibility to others, wheresoever they may be situated. While this ethics stems from a particular conception of human subjectivity as radical intersubjectivity, it resists ascribing the contents of particular identities to particular others. The engagement with the other is not motivated by a practice oriented to creating or realising a particular form of agency or community, but by a responsibility to them. In Campbell's account the other is engaged in conversation in order to understand their particular positions and problems and as a means of recognising and fulfilling a responsibility to them. This requires the other, Campbell notes, to be 'placed at a height' whereby the other's call, needs and wants orient the conversation. In this sense, Campbell's account provides a useful contrast to Ashley and Walker because in it there is no risk that the other will be seen as the object of our ends of enlightenment (even if our ends involve the recognition by the other of their own status as an end). Rather the other, for Campbell, is someone who places a demand on us and to whose voice we must listen and respond, that is: an end which 'we' must serve. For this reason Campbell's account is arguably less instrumental than Ashley and Walker's because the purpose of conversation is to fulfil moral responsibility, to allow an ethical life, to answer another's call and not to aspire to a realm of similarly 'free' agents.

Campbell acknowledges there are many problems and difficulties with the account of ethics that stem from the plurality of others to whom one can be responsible. However, these problems are not of concern here. Nonetheless there remains a need for caution in relation to Levinas' ethics for the following reason. There is a danger that placing the other

[14] D. Campbell, 'The Deterritorialisation of Responsibility: Levinas, Derrida, and Ethics After the End of Philosophy', *Alternatives*, 19 (1994), 455–84, p. 463.

at a height is not a relationship of equality as such. In this scenario the other's needs come before those of the self and the other is somehow seen to be more important or to have a superior demand. The question that can only be raised here is what place is there in this encounter for the needs of the 'self' and for the other's responsibility to the self. For the ethics of radical interdependence to realise a fully equal relationship it would seem that this responsibility must necessarily be reciprocal. Campbell does not employ Levinas' work in order to pursue a theory of community or justice and, as such, equality is not the foundational value of his ethics. However, as this enquiry is concerned with the idea of formulating an account of community that does justice to difference, the notion of equality is essential.

Discourse ethics: universality, dialogue and difference

It was argued in the previous chapter that Linklater's use of discourse ethics to provide the basis of a 'thin' cosmopolitanism represents a major advance in the pursuit of a universal community in which justice to difference could be achieved. The goal of a thin cosmopolitanism in which dialogue is the means of engagement between actors situated in different concrete circumstances, such as different cultures, stands as a motivating ideal and defensible aim. However, discourse ethics, both as conceived by Habermas and appropriated by Linklater, is not without its problems. In particular, the model of conversation supplied by discourse ethics and endorsed by Linklater is not as 'thin' as it appears at first sight and retains significant assimilatory potential. The problems arising from discourse ethics have their origins in Habermas' conception of the purpose of conversation. This section argues, following Benhabib, that the Habermasian *telos* of consensus and agreement repeats the paradox of limitation and legislation and places unnecessary restrictions on conversation which are potentially exclusive of difference. It is also argued that the Habermasian understanding of the necessary conditions of universal moral dialogue are likewise unnecessarily restrictive at the level of agency.

Benhabib suggests that by hitching the model of conversation exclusively to the *telos* of a rational consensus on universal validity claims between postconventional agents the formulation of communication provided by Habermas (and endorsed by Linklater) is unnecessarily restrictive and, in turn, exclusive of difference. Benhabib's criticism suggests that by emphasising Universalisation[U] discourse ethics restricts conversation to questions concerning the right and, in so doing, necessarily invokes the dual Kantian task of legislation and limitation, which, in turn, has major implications for the inclusivity of its model of conversation. Benhabib argues that because Habermas restricts conversation only to the task of determining those principles which might be acceptable to all participants in a practical discourse he risks creating a tension between the goals of inclusion and communication. The *telos* of 'understanding oriented towards rational agreement', that is towards consensus on the validity of normative statements, necessarily restricts our understanding of both the topics and the agents involved in discourse. Because conversation is limited exclusively to questions of 'the right' discourse ethics generates two possible types of exclusion: exclusion in relation to the possible topics of conversation and exclusion in relation to the identity of the agents of conversation.

In terms of envisioning a community in which justice to the members of radically different cultures is achieved through dialogue the exclusions which accompany Habermas' understanding of discourse ethics are problematic. However, the shortcomings of the particulars of Habermas' model of discourse ethics should not and do not present insurmountable obstacles to the defence and articulation of a thin cosmopolitan model of dialogue. Instead they simply further clarify the ground and enable us to seek alternative understandings of conversation which might capture the best elements of discourse ethics while at the same time losing those which are more problematic. The next chapter introduces and examines the philosophical hermeneutics of H. G. Gadamer and argues that Gadamer's perspective allows us to preserve many of the gains made by discourse ethics while losing many of its disadvantages in the pursuit of thin cosmopolitanism. The remainder of this chapter focuses on the limitations of Habermasian discourse ethics and Linklater's appropriation of it for international relations.

Universalisation and the right versus the good

In discourse ethics the *telos* of conversation is the achievement of substantive agreement on universal principles. For Habermas the primary defining goal, the *telos*, of conversation is consensual redemption of claims to universal moral validity among postconventional agents. As such discourse ethics is a deontological approach which seeks to define justice or 'the moral point of view' without defining 'the good'.[15] The goal of universal conversation is predicated upon the assumption of the priority of defining the 'moral point of view'. In Habermas' theory this standard is encapsulated in the principle of Universalisation[U] (see below). Discourse ethics, therefore, provides the procedures and conditions under which divergent agents engage in conversation to establish the validity of their moral claims. Thus the purpose of conversation is both to achieve substantive agreement and to regulate, adjudicate and assess these competing moral claims. Discourse ethics itself does not claim to provide substantive resolutions of moral problems, only the means by which they may be resolved.

It will be recalled that in chapter 1 Iris Marion Young distinguished between two different senses of universalism, the thin, inclusive sense and the thicker sense associated with the claim to neutrality in which the necessary procedures and methods for adjudicating between claims are emphasised. As noted above discourse ethics contains both these dimensions of universalism. The first refers to the principle of inclusion and consent. It is this principle which stipulates that discourse should *include* all competent agents who stand to be affected by a norm. The second sense refers to the *telos* of validation, the principle that norms cannot be considered *valid* unless they have secured universal consent. These two dimensions form the heart of discourse ethics and are encapsulated in the two interrelated principles of U (universalisation) and D (discourse) which state:

> [U] every valid norm has to fulfil the following condition: *All* affected can accept the consequences and the side-effects its *general* observance can be anticipated to have for the satisfaction of everyone's interests (and these consequences are preferred to those of known alternative possibilities for regulation).[16]

and

> [D] Only those norms can claim to be valid that meet (or could meet) with the approval of all affected in their capacity *as participants in a practical discourse.*[17]

According to Habermas, of these two, U comes before D and is the presupposition upon which discourse ethics rests.[18] U states the *conditions*

---

[15] See D. C. Hoy and T. McCarthy, *Critical Theory* (Oxford: Blackwell, 1994), p. 54.
[16] J. Habermas, *Moral Consciousness and Communicative Action* (Cambridge: Polity, 1990), p. 65.
[17] *Ibid.*, p. 66.   [18] See *ibid.*

of normative validity, in the form of the goal of consensus between rational agents. It also generates a principle of universal *inclusion*. For a norm to be valid it must not only be acceptable to all but must be acceptable to all on the basis of its observance by all. All participants can reasonably be expected to abide by the norm because all interests are satisfied by it. In order to assure consent everybody affected by a norm must be consulted. In other words, norms can only be considered valid and binding if they have universal consent.

The principle of D on the other hand stipulates the necessity of conversation, it states that U can only be realised by a genuine practical discourse. D introduces the argument that norms can be valid only if their acceptance can be assured in real practical discourse. But D also provides a principle of inclusion because it states that *all* affected must be included in the conversation.

Benhabib argues that in Habermas' theory the principle of inclusion is undermined by the orientation of conversation towards consent on validity claims.[19] She argues that U is unnecessary for achieving the goal of a universally inclusive conversation and provides unnecessarily restrictive criteria for conversation. Benhabib is correct in this identification because in addition to generating a principle of inclusion U also provides discourse ethics with the grounds for possible exclusions. U contributes to the legislative tendency because it excludes from conversation all statements, or all topics of conversation which are not oriented towards achieving universal redemption. The incorporation of U as the *telos* of conversation serves to define the purpose of conversation exclusively as mutual seeking for consensus in regard to claims of normative rightness (which, according to Habermas, are analogous to claims to truthfulness). The principle of universalisation formalises the content of what counts as acceptable speech. It states that only those utterances and claims which seek universal approval, that is, which ought to apply to everybody, are to be the subject of dialogue. Of crucial importance here is the dimension of rationality. Conversation is oriented towards *rational* agreement, that is, the possibility of consensus based upon the 'unforced force of the better argument', and only those principles which are truly rational can be universalised. Universalisation is both the criterion and the test of rationality. As a result, conversational participants are restricted to discussing those claims which seek universal redemption by everybody.

---

[19] See S. Benhabib, *Situating the Self* (Oxford: Blackwell, 1992).

This dimension of discourse ethics can best be explained as a result of its privileging of questions of 'right' over questions of the 'good'. As already noted U establishes discourse ethics as a deontological theory. Habermas is in agreement with Rawls in so far as both their theories seek to define 'the standpoint from which moral questions can be judged impartially'.[20] Both present scenarios which claim to 'show the participants the procedure they must follow if they want to solve moral problems'.[21] According to Habermas, such a position is the only one possible under conditions of modernity. Because discourse ethics takes 'modern pluralism seriously (it therefore) ... renounce[s] the classical philosophical claim to defend one uniquely privileged mode of life'.[22] These approaches conceive of the moral standpoint 'purely as a guide to action, concerned exclusively with what it is "right" to do, rather than what it is "good" to be'.[23] Discourse ethics, therefore, aims 'to define some criterion or procedure which allows us to derive all and only the things we are obliged to do ... '[24] It provides the impartial means by which different substantive conceptions of the good life are able to co-exist and sort out their differences. However, as a result questions of the 'good' are excluded from discussion.

In the context of discourse ethics, as formulated by Habermas, the hard and fast distinction between these two domains excludes discussion of the 'good' by bracketing it in the private realm: '*moral questions* which can in principle be decided rationally in terms of criteria of *justice* or the universalisability of interests are now distinguished from *evaluative questions*, which fall into the general category of the *good life* and are accessible to rational discussion only within the horizon of a concrete historical form of life ... '[25] For Habermas the 'moral point of view' is restricted to matters which are rationally redeemable and formalisable, that is, subject to rational argumentation and formalisation according to the principle of U, and which can hypothetically be acceptable to all participants in a practical discourse. Only matters of justice and obligation, of what it is morally 'right' to do, strictly speaking, can fulfil this criterion. As Benhabib argues: 'Habermas assumes that only judgments of justice possess a clearly discernible formal structure and thus can be studied along an evolutionary (rational) model, whereas judgments

---

[20] Habermas, J. *Justification and Application* (Cambridge: Polity, 1993), p. 48.
[21] *Ibid.*, p. 128.   [22] *Ibid.*, p. 123.   [23] Taylor quoted in *ibid.*, p. 3.
[24] M. Neufeld, 'The Right and the Good in International Ethics'. Paper Presented for the ISA Annual Convention. San Diego, April. (1996), p. 20.
[25] Habermas, *Moral Consciousness and Communicative Action*, p. 178.

concerning the good life are amorphous and do not lend themselves to the same kind of formal study.'[26] Personal conceptions of the good life and of what it means to be a good person, Habermas suggests, can be equated with aesthetic preferences or tastes in that they are not susceptible to rational argument. It is not possible to argue rationally about personal tastes as they are merely a matter of preference and individual constitution. For Habermas, as Benhabib puts it, '[A]ll other moral matters as pertain to the virtues, to normal emotion, to life conduct are questions which belong to the domain of "ethical life". They are non universalisable and non formalisable.'[27] The resolution of conflicts between different conceptions of the good and their general validity as ought statements cannot be subjected to the unforced force of the better argument and discursively redeemed. Thus 'ethics' as distinct from 'morality', the 'good' as distinct from the 'right', are not susceptible to 'rational' argumentation in the same sense. Those matters which are not rationally redeemable in this way have no place in discourse ethics.

However, by excluding questions of the good and orienting conversation *exclusively* towards the *telos* of consensus Habermas is unnecessarily restricting and legislating the topics of possible conversation. In so doing, not only is the nature of conversation unnecessarily narrowed but the likelihood of excluding radical difference is heightened. This dimension is revealed if we return to the concerns of both communitarians and gender oriented thinkers.

The communitarian and feminist arguments describing the limits of impartialist theories were discussed in chapter 2 in terms of the issue of agency. Many of these arguments have also been made in slightly different form against discourse ethics. In particular, it has been claimed that discourse ethics like other 'neutral', 'impartial' accounts of the right actually presupposes fairly 'thick', but disguised, accounts of the good. Mark Neufeld argues, following Charles Taylor, that deontological theories, including discourse ethics, are caught in a self-contradiction in relation to the good; 'they postulate not just first order goods, understood as desires or wants (for example, the individual purposes of states) but also higher order goods that stand qualitatively above others'.[28] By this he means that deontological theories are not neutral mediators between different conceptions of the good but also embody and advocate

---

[26] Benhabib, *Situating the Self*, p. 72.   [27] *Ibid.*, p. 40.
[28] Neufeld, 'The Right and the Good in International Ethics'. *Ibid.*, p. 9.

particular conceptions of what is a 'good'. The most obvious way in which this is so is that by their very goal of seeking to mediate between interests they presuppose both the existence of a pluralist society and its value as a good in itself. In other words, a philosophy of the right conducted in this vocabulary actually constitutes a thicker and more partial conception of community than is claimed by its exponents.

Thus from a communitarian position the danger accompanying discourse ethics is that despite its explicit attempt to engage with and include difference, its self-definition as an unambiguous account of the right means that it is open to the same charge made against Liberal cosmopolitans outlined in chapter 1: 'conceptions of the good/ good life are unreflectively smuggled in and not subject to critical review (and thus) the danger of falsely universalising and unnecessarily excluding difference becomes that much the greater'.[29] One of the crucial indicators of this is the way in which discourse ethics is gendered.

According to Benhabib, Habermas' emphasis on the maintenance of the distinction between right and the good, between the realm of the truly moral and the merely ethical, has damaging side-effects. In particular, Habermas' emphasis on U unnecessarily dictates the topics of conversation by narrowing the realm of the moral to that which can be formalised and judged according to the standard of rationality (defined as universalisability). The price of this distinction is that it excludes from dialogue matters which can be understood as moral in the everyday sense but which do not fit into Habermas' definition. As a result, discourse ethics repeats the tendency of other deontological theories to privilege the generalised over the concrete other. The emphasis on achieving agreement guided by the unforced force of the better argument runs the risk of repeating an emphasis on an abstract, disembodied 'reason'. More specifically discourse ethics, in so far as it privileges the generalised other, runs the risk of unnecessarily smuggling in gender biases and blindnesses regarding the capacity of agents and the topics of conversation.

Benhabib's argument here extends from an engagement with Carol Gilligan's critique of Kohlberg (upon which Habermas draws, see the discussion below) and her elaboration of the contents of an ethic of 'care'.[30] The ethic of care is a response to the emphasis on the generalised other in deontological theories of justice which place issues such

[29] *Ibid.*, p. 21.
[30] See V. Held (ed.), *Justice and Care: Essential Readings in Feminist Ethics* (Boulder: Westview, 1995).

111

as virtue, altruism, benevolence, solidarity and compassion, questions associated with the good life, but also with 'maternal thinking', firmly within the domain of moral theory. According to Benhabib, 'obligations and relations of care are genuinely moral ones, belonging to the center and not at the margins of morality'.[31]

From the perspective of an ethics of care many matters which are relevant for members of a community living together and which can be understood as moral, in the sense of concerning 'what ought *I* to do', should also be the subject of conversation between participants. An example of such everyday moral issues for instance might include the obligations one has to a friend versus the obligations one may have to family or to other 'important' (in Bernard Williams' sense) dimensions of one's life, such as work or a political cause.[32] As Benhabib puts it

> the moral issues which preoccupy us most and which touch us most deeply derive not from problems of justice in the economy and the polity, but precisely from the quality of our relations with others in 'the spheres of kinship, love friendship and sex; . . . for democratic citizens and economic agents, the moral issues that touch her most deeply arise in the personal domain'.[33]

For agents facing these sorts of questions the issues 'what ought I to do' and 'what sort of person should I be' are inextricable from each other, as it would be difficult to answer one without having an idea of how one should answer the other. Furthermore, the solutions to these problems are not necessarily to be formulated in terms of universal maxims or subject to universal validity tests. The questions are concerned with what 'I' as a specific individual ought to do in 'this' specific situation and not with what it is universally right to do, that is, with what everybody ought to do. While these obligations and concerns are not necessarily subject to a Universalisation test they do help to constitute the moral realm in the everyday experience and reflect the most obvious sorts of moral problems faced in everyday life.

The problem with Habermas' theory, according to Benhabib, is that its focus on the generalised other is gendered and excludes the concerns and capacities associated with women's experiences of moral life. The qualities associated with 'femininity' are relegated to the private realm. Benhabib argues that '[T]he restriction of the moral domain to

---

[31] Benhabib, *Situating the Self*, p. 186.
[32] See B. Williams, *Ethics and the Limits of Philosophy* (London: Fontana, 1985).
[33] Benhabib, *Situating the Self*, p. 185.

questions of justice . . . results in the privatisation of women's experience and lead to epistemological blindness toward the concrete other'.[34] As a result, discourse ethics cannot claim to be neutral in the sense of being without bias or partiality. Instead, as constituted by Habermas, discourse ethics privileges certain styles of engagement and certain types of moral experiences, those usually associated with the 'masculine' and risks unjustifiably excluding morally significant differences.

Furthermore, Benhabib suggests, there is no reason for thinking that such moral dilemmas are not amenable to reasoned discussion. In everyday situations moral agents can and do help clarify issues for each other and help each other decide what is the right thing to do by engaging in reasoned discussion. However, inclusion of such conversations in the moral realm is possible only if the notion of what counts as reasoned discussion is relaxed to include a larger more flexible concept of reason than that provided by its equation with universal validity. In this sense reason should be seen as inhabiting the processes of argumentation, understanding, explanation and persuasion and not the outcome alone.[35]

In sum, the point being made is that to restrict morality to those issues which are rationally formalisable is to restrict and distort the nature of reason, moral action and dialogue. The overall consequence of the emphasis on questions of right is that it serves to exclude the concerns of private life from the realm of dialogue and to restrict the topics of conversation. This restriction is legislative and exclusive precisely because it rules out certain topics and concerns, which can justifiably be considered moral, from the conversation pre-discursively. It prescribes not only the procedure but also the content of dialogue, that is of what are acceptable statements and topics, according to an already given definition of the moral realm, one which is constituted prior to engagement with the other. In this way, discourse ethics enacts the Kantian paradox of legislation and limitation.

Habermas has responded to many of these criticisms and attempted to incorporate them into his overall position. There is not the space to detail his response but a few points can be made. He argues that the concerns of the concrete other have their place in discourse ethics but only at the point of application of universal principles to specific contexts. The exact meaning of universalised principles he argues is never firmly

[34] *Ibid.* p. 164.   [35] For further discussion of this point see chapter 4.

established in some Archimedean point but is only established in the moment of application in specific discourses, that is, cultural/political contexts. The task of application requires the type of hermeneutic insights appropriate to the understanding of the 'concrete other'. Without a knowledge of the particular contexts and meanings structures of concrete others in genuine situations the universal principles are empty and abstract. However, Benhabib has responded by arguing that the relevance of the concrete other, and the ethic of care, goes much further than something that can simply be added at the point of application. The perspective of the concrete other is essential to understanding the very framing of universal claims and the meaning of universality for particular agents. It is by no means clear that members of different cultures or even of different groups within cultures (including western cultures) understand universality in the same way nor frame moral questions the same way. Therefore, the knowledge of the concrete other and the 'hermeneutic' skills that go with it need to be applied much earlier in the process, indeed they need to be applied from the very beginning, from the construction of the model of conversation itself and the goal of universality. Such a position is apparently not available to discourse ethics as Habermas understands, and this is in part because the rules of argumentation stem from the universal pragmatic presuppositions of speech.

Habermas claims that the rules of discourse ethics are pre-given and universal regardless of the self-understanding of any agent.[36] To engage in conversation, he argues, one must logically assume that one's claims as to what everybody ought to do can be verified in a universal conversation guided by the unforced force of the better argument. All such claims regardless of intention presuppose universality, according to Habermas. There is not the space in this enquiry to go into Habermas' attempt to ground discourse ethics in this fashion. Suffice it to say that there is something in the manner of the attempt to provide philosophical grounding for his project which is a source of disquiet. This aspect of Habermas' project seems to contradict the very goal of discourse ethics itself which is the validation of such claims in a dialogue between concrete subjects and not by philosophical fiat.

Finally, and most importantly, Habermas has not surrendered the task of defining 'the moral point of view' nor the necessity of excluding the

---

[36] 'Every person who accepts the universal and necessary communicative presuppositions of argumentative speech and who knows what means to justify a norm of action implicitly presupposes as valid the principle of universalisation...' Habermas, *Moral Consciousness and Communicative Action*, p. 86.

good from that viewpoint.[37] As such he has not modified those elements of the model of conversation which are exclusionary as outlined here.

Turning the discussion from Habermas to Linklater's use of discourse ethics in the context of a critical theory of international relations several points should be made. In so far as Linklater's account of moral conversation is different from Habermas' it can be addressed separately.

Linklater's use of discourse ethics has not been uncritical and in *The Transformation of Political Community* he clearly states how he thinks discourse ethics can be modified in light of the comments of its critics. Linklater accepts the claims of both Benhabib and others such as Neo-Aristotelians that discourse ethics needs to take into account the hermeneutic skill of understanding and application at a much earlier stage than acknowledged initially by Habermas.[38] Indeed he goes further than Habermas to accept that a hermeneutic perspective is necessary not only in terms of applying universal principles to particular situations but it also aids in reflecting on different understandings of the universals themselves.[39] Benhabib's critique of Habermas, Linklater argues, indicates 'engagement with the particularity of others is essential whenever agents become involved in any dialogue about whether there are any universal principles which ought to regulate their social interaction'.[40]

According to Linklater, the development of an account of universal dialogic cosmopolitanism does not need to be harnessed exclusively to Habermas' understanding of discourse ethics. For this reason Linklater has had little to say regarding Habermas' 'grounding' of discourse ethics nor some of Habermas' other larger philosophical claims as they have little bearing on his own project. Linklater has turned to discourse ethics primarily because it relates moral universalism to the principle of discursive inclusion. Therefore, while many significant differences remain between discourse ethics and its critics, dialogic universalism as a larger project is not necessarily fundamentally undermined by these criticisms. Rather Linklater argues it can accommodate many of them

---

[37] He has, however, acknowledged that a relationship between these two does exist and that one does indeed presuppose the other. See J. Habermas, 'Justice and Solidarity', in M. Kelly (ed.), *Hermeneutics and Critical Theory in Ethics and Politics* (Cambridge: MIT Press, 1990), pp. 32–52.
[38] For a suggestion of the manner in which discourse ethics can be made inclusive of 'concrete others' see A. Linklater, *The Transformation of Political Community: Ethical Foundations of the Post-Westphalian Era* (Cambridge: Polity Press, 1997).
[39] *Ibid.*, esp. pp. 94–5.   [40] *Ibid.*, p. 95.

while remaining true to its fundamental premises of Universalisation and discourse.

However, that said, Linklater has not addressed Benhabib's concerns regarding U nor has he addressed the problems with Habermas' distinction between the right and the good. In so far as this is the case then we can assume that U plays a similar role in his theory. Indeed rather than modify U Linklater at times appears to endorse it as the central plank of discourse ethics. Universalisability provides the test by which the rationality of competing claims can be measured. In this he appears to share Habermas' vision of the *telos* of moral conversation. Therefore, in so far as these dimensions remain unaddressed his account remains vulnerable to the same problems as Habermas'. As a result, Linklater's pursuit of universal inclusion is hindered by certain aspects of the Habermasian model of conversation upon which he draws so heavily.

Having outlined the restrictions and exclusions which accompany the understanding of conversation in discourse ethics it is necessary to turn to the other means whereby Habermas' model exhibits a tension between the goals of inclusion and communication, which is at the level of agency. The next section argues that the exclusionary potential of discourse ethics is reinforced by the dimension of Habermas' theory which argues that moral conversation regarding universal principles can only be conducted between postconventional agents guided by the unforced force of the better argument.

Agency and inclusion in discourse ethics

It will be recalled that the previous chapter concluded by raising the following questions: 'Does the project of universal emancipation and the creation of a community of self-determining autonomous beings require the universalisation of a particular "postconventional" agency?' and: 'To what extent does the creation of a universal principle of conversation require more substantive transformation of individuals and communities that is itself a process of assimilation rather than communication?' It is argued here that as long as conversation is understood exclusively to mean consensual validation of moral claims, that is matters concerning the right, then indeed discourse ethics does raise the possibility of an assimilatory account of agency. This is so because the Habermasian account is reliant on an account of agency which is teleological and developmental. The goal of communicative universality in discourse ethics can not be distinguished from the pursuit of freedom and as such Discourse ethics exhibits the Kantian dilemma of legislation and limitation.

In particular, the Habermasian project of determining the moral point of view necessarily legislates the topics of conversation *and* limits the types of agents who can practically engage in conversation, even while aspiring to universal inclusion. In attempting to describe the condition of free and equal communication discourse ethics, as formulated by Habermas, not only restricts discussion to matters of the 'right' but also raises the possibility of excluding those forms of agency (and corresponding modes of thought and speech) which are deemed incompatible with this goal. Again these aspects stem from the *telos* of universalisation.

It will be recalled that, according to Linklater, the goal of human freedom can only be realised in a discursive cosmopolitan community, in other words, when universality is achieved. For Linklater the *telos* of freedom is inextricably linked with universality. It was also argued discourse ethics contained elements of both the dimensions of universalism identified by Iris Marion Young. It contains both a principle stipulating that the conversation should *include* all competent agents who stand to be affected by a norm and a principle stating that norms cannot be considered *valid* unless they have secured universal consent.

These two forms of universalism directly correspond to Linklater's understanding of the meaning of human freedom and of a truly free human agent. Freedom in Linklater's critical theory has (at least) two mutually supportive definitions. First is a 'thin' sense of inclusion in conversation. Freedom in this first sense can only be realised in a cosmopolitan community of humankind in which all humans have the opportunity to participate equally in conversation regarding the arrangements of social life.

Accompanying this 'thin' understanding of freedom as inclusion is the 'thicker' interpretation premised on what Linklater calls the species capacity for individual autonomy. It is this second meaning which generates the potentially exclusionary dynamics of discourse ethics because it involves a substantially thicker and more prescriptive account of human agency than the idea of mere inclusion. In particular, Linklater follows Hegel in arguing that central to achievement of freedom is recognition of the capacity for rational human self-determination. This recognition in turn rests on the realisation that the social world is not subject to impersonal nature-like or god-given laws beyond the control of humans. According to Linklater

> Hegel argues that the formation of species-powers required man's transcendence of those societies in which men think they are governed by

natural powers and forces and believe that social distinctions have their origins in nature or confront men as naturally sanctioned ... But this is an alienated form of consciousness for what men are unaware of at this level of social organisation ... is the fact that it is their cultural framework which endows nature with authority over them: it is they themselves who have conferred social power and meaning upon natural phenomena.[41]

As Linklater sees it freedom understood as self-determination can only be fully exercised in a universally inclusive community where all can participate as equals in the negotiation of the forms of collective life; '... the existence of a moral community more inclusive than the sovereign state can be defended only on the basis of man's unique capacity for self-determination'.[42] In this way for Linklater freedom and universality are run together. Hence, the appeal of discourse ethics is that it captures both the 'thick' and 'thin' senses of freedom, freedom as individual autonomy and freedom as discursive inclusion. It provides an account of community that embodies the principles of freedom, equality and diversity in the form of a conversation between differently situated self-determining actors. To be free, and to see others as free and equal, is to engage in rational discussion regarding the arrangements of social life. Inclusion in conversation is both the means by which this capacity for self-determination is fully exercised and, it seems, a prerequisite for successful engagement. The freedom to participate in dialogue both simultaneously requires and realises a degree of human autonomy and self-determination on the part of the participants.

However, it follows from this that discourse ethics exhibits a tension between the principle that all those who stand to be affected by a norm are included and the contention that conversation regarding U can take place only between agents possessing what Habermas

---

[41] A. Linklater, *Men and Citizens in the Theory of International Relations*, 2nd edn (London: Macmillan, 1990), p. 145.

[42] *Ibid.*, p. xii. Linklater expands on this point thus: 'At this level of self consciousness, it would be necessary to accept the Kantian proposition that not to allow others to promote their self development is not to recognise their humanity, the capacities which differentiate them from the natural world. To understand the relationship between history and self-knowledge ... is to require acceptance of the Marxian claim that man should eliminate from his environment those obstacles to the further development of his distinctively human powers. With these understandings it becomes essential for men to determine what each individual owes the other members of his species by virtue of their common humanity, their equal status as free beings. They must seek satisfaction as self determining beings, as progressive beings with fundamental obligations to all other members of their species.' *Ibid.*, p. 198.

refers to as 'postconventional' consciousness. This tension stems from Habermas' controversial use of the work of Lawrence Kohlberg. Following Kohlberg, Habermas described a conception of moral development that involves the progression through three stages: the preconventional, the conventional and the postconventional. In Linklater's words:

> Pre-conventional morality exists when actors obey norms because they fear that non-compliance will be sanctioned by a higher authority; conventional moral norms are observed because actors are loyal to a specific social group; post-conventional morality occurs when actors stand back from authority structures and group membership and ask whether they are complying with principles which have universal validity... Post-conventionalism demonstrates a capacity for ethical reflectiveness in which agents recognise that moral codes are malleable social products rather than immutable conventions to which they must submit.[43]

Linklater describes this as a process of moral development in which agents learn how '... to formulate and institutionalise reflective and universal ethical principles'.[44] The postconventional agent 'assumes guidance by universal ethical principles that all humanity should follow'.[45] It is this capacity for universality which marks the postconventional stage as the highest stage of moral development.[46] Thus in line with the principle of a conversation informed by a *telos* of securing universal validity Habermas (and Linklater) endorse an evolutionary and developmental account of human agency. This account of the sort of consciousness that is required to engage in conversation equates individual human development with the awareness of the possibility of universality and equates universality (U) with maturity.

This aspect of discourse ethics, which stems from an over-determination by the goal of assessing the validity (rationality) of

---

[43] A. Linklater, 'The Achievements of Critical Theory', in S. Smith, K. Booth and M. Zalewski (eds.), *International Theory: Positivism and Beyond* (Cambridge: Cambridge University Press, 1996). p. 286.
[44] A. Linklater, 'Rationalisation Processes and International History', in M. Hoffman and N. J. R. Rengger (eds.), *Beyond the Inter-Paradigm Debate: Critical Theory and International Relations* (forthcoming), p. 7.
[45] Habermas, *Moral Consciousness and Communicative Action*, p. 124.
[46] The developmental structure of the moral learning process, as leading to universality, has a high degree of resonance with Linklater's earlier argument in 'Men and Citizens'. There he set out the idea of a scale of forms by which societies could be assessed according to their level of freedom. Post conventional morality corresponds to that of the emancipated being: it is critical of traditional moralities, guided by rational thought and *universal*. Autonomy and self-determination, therefore, are properties that belong only to those higher, more mature, forms of social development.

normative claims, is in tension with the goal of universal inclusion. More particularly it gives rise to the possible grounds for legitimating either the exclusion of certain agents *or* their assimilation. Habermas' resort to Kohlberg's theory only serves to entrench the Kantian dilemma and heighten the problems of discourse ethics not solve them. In discourse ethics the validity of moral claims is assessed in terms of an uncoerced dialogue between agents who are likely to be affected *and* who are conscious of the fallibility of all moral claims *and* are willing to submit their own values to universal scrutiny *and* who are not 'alienated' (in Hegel's terms). Agents engaged in rational dialogue oriented towards consensus must be able to stand back from their specific contexts, discourses, tradition and conventions. As rational agents reason alone, not tradition, authority, group affiliation or doctrine determines the universal validity of principles. The achievement of freedom, in other words, involves a postconventional consciousness in which the individual recognises his or her ability to rationally determine the content of their own life in the context of a conversation with others. In other words, conversation oriented towards U can occur only between subjects who have achieved a 'postconventional' level of consciousness: that is, morally mature, reasonable beings able to be governed by the unforced force of the better argument. Put more directly the achievement of universal rational discourse requires '... the development of reflective moral codes which affirm the value of the individual subject, the principle of autonomy and the ideal of a universal dialogue as the mechanism for endeavouring to resolve moral disputes'.[47] Discourse ethics is the mode of conduct appropriate to postconventional beings.

As a result, it can be seen that the account of the postconventional agent is an account of the necessary prerequisites for unconstrained dialogue but as such it also sets out the criteria of judgement by which certain types of agents might be excluded. Thus it appears that the criterion for inclusion in conversation is not only that one be affected by a norm but also that one recognise oneself as a self-determining agent. The pursuit of freedom in the form of a morally inclusive universal conversation in discourse ethics is, therefore, simultaneously an advocacy of a particular conception of agency. As such it involves an assimilative moment at the level of agency because it envisages a community

---

[47] Linklater, 'Rationalisation Processes', p. 16. According to Habermas 'The reason for doing right is that, as a rational person, one has seen the validity of principles and has become committed to them.' Habermas, *Moral Consciousness and Communicative Action*, p. 125.

of equally self-determining rational agents.[48] More specifically the procedure and *telos* of discourse ethics require 'constraints on the range of plural selves that may be encountered in moral discourse'.[49] Discourse ethics contains the possibility that certain forms of difference might not be able to engage in conversation as equals because they may be judged to be incapable of acting as postconventional thinkers. As Hutchings notes:

> The idea of communicative rationality, which is intersubjectively based and oriented towards understanding, is both presupposed in all discourse and *provides a standard against which both individual rational capacities and the organisation of societies can be judged.*[50]

The 'discourse' of discourse ethics, therefore, risks being open only to those deemed mature enough to enter it. As a result, the achievement of equality in discourse appears to require a fairly substantive common capacity which is associated with a particular account of agency.[51]

Conversation requires certain thick prerequisites: it requires a population of individuals who share the same qualities, that is individuals capable of being guided by the unforced force of the better argument. Discourse ethics so understood, can be seen to require a much thicker,

---

[48] Thus, as it was in Beitz, cosmopolitanism in critical theory remains linked to principles of equality and autonomy and as such risks sacrificing difference for identity. What changes is the form and degree in which these principles are articulated.

[49] K. Hutchings, 'Feminism, Universalism and Ethics', in V. Jabri and E. O'Gorman, *Women, Culture and International Relations* (Boulder: Lynne Rienner, 1999), p. 28.

[50] Hutchings, *Kant, Critique and Politics*, p. 62, emphasis added. This tendency in discourse ethics is echoed in Linklater's (earlier) interest in developing an 'international scale of forms' of those cultures/states/societies that aspire to and achieve universality and those that don't. The purpose of such a scale of forms is to assess and judge the other according to the degree to which they conform to the aspiration of universality.

[51] Despite her reservations in regard to Habermas' project, this tendency is indeed embraced by Benhabib, who accepts the model of the postconventional agent and endorses the substantive contents of the discourse ethics model. Benhabib argues 'Communicative Ethics promotes a universalist and post-conventionalist perspective on all ethical relations: it has implications for familial life no less than for democratic legislatures.' Benhabib, *Situating the Self*, p. 39. She also acknowledges, discourse ethics involves a much thicker conception of community than that of mere inclusion, because it presupposes and privileges 'a secular, universalist reflexive culture in which debate, articulation, and contention about value questions as well as conceptions of justice and the good have become a way of life', *ibid.* p. 42. However, Benhabib also argues that what she refers to as communicative ethics does not mean 'the advocate of conventional morality is *excluded* from the conversation; but the kinds of grounds such a person will bring into the moral conversation will not be sufficiently universalisable from the standpoint of all involved'. *Ibid.* However, she can only make this claim having previously rejected the Habermas' emphasis on U.

and therefore, exclusive, conception of agency or subjectivity than suggested by the idea of universality as inclusion. In this sense discourse ethics raises obstacles to communication with the radically different even while seeking to achieve universal inclusion. While discourse ethics attempts to articulate a form of cosmopolitanism that balances universalism and particularism in a discursive community, it nonetheless presupposes that the community will be populated by rational, autonomous, postconventional beings. The self–other relation here is equal only in so far as identity is common or all have developed the same consciousness. In this way Habermasian discourse ethics remains trapped in a paradox of limitation and legislation (which in turn is another manifestation of the difficulties involved in reconciling the tension between community and difference).

In addition to running the risk of assimilating identity into equality a number of other problems are raised by pursuing the model of conversation as a strictly Kantian project. In particular, in so far as it relies upon postconventional agency discourse ethics seems to make the possibility of justice to those who are not postconventional, or those who in Habermas' terms are situated outside the discourse of modernity (which is to say the same thing), more problematic.[52] For Habermas, a postconventional consciousness is that which characterises the discourse of modernity. This suggests that only those situated within the discourse of modernity have the appropriate skills to participate in discourse ethics.[53] This account of agency denies the possibility that those on 'lower' levels of development, who might inhabit a pre-modern or

---

[52] Not only does this account exclude those not engaged in the philosophical discourse of modernity but it also attributes reason as a property *specific* to that discourse, non modern forms of reasoning are not understood to be fully rational.

[53] There is a sense in which in a strict logical form this three level analysis makes sense, in that only those capable of reflective discourse can engage in reflective discourse. However, because discourse ethics is tied to specific historical–philosophical cultural formation it makes claims beyond those of strict logic and instead becomes engaged in quasi-anthropological statements regarding human capacities. Put simply as Hoy notes 'Habermas believes that an evolutionary theory of the development of rationality structures allows the anthropologist to criticise the practices of a less developed culture.' Hoy and McCarthy, *Critical Theory*, p. 204. The nature of the relationship between postconventionality and modernity is complex and ambiguous. Habermas and Benhabib have both made it clear that postconventionality is not tied to an account of human development at the societal level. That is, it is quite possible that those inhabiting pre-modern epochs in human history might exhibit the capacity to reflect critically upon their own and their societies practices and to do so in light of an abstract universality. However, despite this dimension discourse ethics is still troubled by an equation of reflexive thought with universality which forms the basis of its potential for exclusion, and the tension between its goals of inclusion and universality.

conventional consciousness and hold to traditional social practices and conceptions of the good life, may be able to engage in reasoned discussion. This might be so, for example, because they may continue to hold that moral laws are divinely ordained or exist independently of human thought.

The question raised by linking the possibility of a rational consensus to the concept of postconventional agents is, how does a universal postconventional theory of justice include those who do not share the same self understanding, that is, who are not, in Habermas' terms, part of the discourse of modernity? A truly moral relationship between modern and pre-modern agents appears impossible because those outside of the discourse of modernity are seen, like children, as not mature enough for reasoned discussion.[54] Hutchings notes that for both Kant and Habermas 'the formulation of the principle of morality poses problems for its actualisation outside of a kingdom of ends, or a fully rationalised lifeworld'.[55] If this is so then it implies that understanding and agreement are apparently ruled out between those at different stages of moral development. Thomas McCarthy puts the point this way: '. . . the social evolutionary components of Habermas' interpretative frame ensure that the interpretation of some types of traditional views will represent them from the start as "pre-modern" and hence not up to discursive par'.[56] Traditional, or pre-conventional moralities (i.e. those that are 'unreasonable' and that are not the product of consent freely given) are, it appears, to be excluded from conversation.[57] If traditional and pre-modern groups are still too tradition-bound and, therefore, incapable of rational discourse, how do we conduct relations with them morally? One answer seems to lie in Linklater's commitment to the project of emancipation.[58] However, this avenue also seems to lead to an overly assimilatory engagement.

---

[54] Or are we to assume that there is no 'outside' the discourse of modernity? In which case the 'totalisation' project might be thought to have succeeded.

[55] Hutchings, *Kant, Critique and Politics*, p. 75.

[56] Hoy and McCarthy, *Critical Theory*, p. 243.

[57] Benhabib for one endorses this exclusion.

[58] Linklater does in fact consider the question of how to relate to others in the absence of a universal kingdom of ends and his answer is, through discourse ethics. The emphasis in *Transformation* is, he states, '. . . on the harm *we* do to *them*, and on what *we* should do so that *they* are able to defend their interests in their relations with us'. A. Linklater, 'Transforming Political Community: A Response to the Critics', *Review of International Studies*, 25. 1 (1999), 165–75, p. 174. The point here is not that Linklater's answer to this question is emancipation, rather discourse ethics it seems requires a process of emancipation in order to be realised.

Discourse ethics and emancipation

The assimilative moment of conversation in discourse ethics is aggravated and compounded by Linklater's stress on the emancipatory *telos* of critical theory. Critical theory is constituted by an interest in emancipation understood as 'freeing human subjects from unnecessary social constraints and distorted patterns of culture and communication'[59] The critical theoretical interest in human emancipation requires the realisation of universal community in the form of a Kantian 'universal kingdom of ends': '... the purpose of social enquiry is to promote emancipation by providing enlightenment about the constraints upon human autonomy'.[60] Discourse ethics is able to provide both further theoretical support for this project, and an articulation of the nature of that community.[61] However, as we have noted this aspect of the Kantian project raises the prospect of a community of homogenous agents.

Because conversation is limited to the search for universalisable statements then it requires discourse amongst postconventional agents and any deviation from such agency, or from such a *telos* of conversation, is by nature an obstacle to discourse.[62] In this way the goal of inclusion, removing the obstacles to discourse, comes to mean not only the removal of political and moral practices of exclusion but also the creation of a realm of agents who understand themselves to be autonomous, free and self-determining, that is postconventional agents. In other words, inclusion comes with emancipation and equality, therefore, only comes with achievement of a shared consciousness.[63] Therefore, a conversation, the

[59] A. Linklater, *Beyond Realism and Marxism: Critical Theory and International Relations* (London: Macmillan, 1990), p. 4.

[60] A. Linklater, 'The Question of the Next Stage in International Relations: a Critical Theoretical Point of view', *Millennium*, 21. 1. Spring (1992), p. 87.

[61] According to Linklater 'discourse ethics reconceptualises the emancipatory project and retrieves the universalistic position within a compelling account of the historical development of species-wide moral competences'. A. Linklater, 'Citizenship and Sovereignty in the Post-Westphalian State', *European Journal of International Relations*, 2. 1, March (1996), 77–103, p. 86.

[62] Thanks to Michael Janover for this formulation.

[63] Critical theory's emancipatory project is open to a presumption of superiority, and, therefore, inequality, on behalf of the 'emancipated' towards the 'unemancipated'. It should be emphasised here that it is the practice of emancipation, and not the idea of freedom *per se*, that creates the opening for the assimilative relations between self and other. The *telos* of emancipation presupposes a condition of unfreedom for both self and other: The task then, is to liberate or emancipate both from this condition. In itself, this formulation understands both as equal in their need and capacity for emancipation. However, potential inequality arises when 'one' *recognises* one's own unfreedom and capacity for freedom and simultaneously sees that the other does not recognise themselves in this manner. As a result, the enlightened agent might engage with the unenlightened agent

telos of which is the consensus between post conventional agents, might require a practice directed towards the creation of a realm of similar agents.

In Linklater's work emancipation also takes two forms corresponding to the two forms of freedom. The first of these is the removal of any obstacle to discourse between humans. The second is the goal of expanding the realm of agents who understand themselves to be autonomous, free and self-determining. If freedom lies in self-determination, then emancipation comes about when humans understand that their world is made by their own actions and beliefs and therefore, is susceptible to consciously willed transformation. Emancipation means subjecting the social world to rational scrutiny and lifting or removing barriers to the exercise and recognition of human self-determination. However, in Linklater's critical theory, the distinction between the two appears nonsensical: the removal of obstacles to discourse is simultaneously the expansion of agents who understand themselves as free.[64] Thus the purpose of critical theory is to create a universal communication community in which all can engage in 'reasonable' discourse. In practice this means that the praxis of emancipation involves the universalisation of a particular account of human agency, that of individuals who understand themselves to be free, that is, rational postconventional beings.

These two meanings of freedom are in tension. The practice of critical theory as emancipation would seem to imply that the appropriate orientation towards the other is one concerned with enlightening and emancipating them from their pre-conventional and conventional moralities so that they can partake in conversation. Emancipation appears to be, not the goal, but the prerequisite of dialogue. This meaning of emancipation stands in tension with the goal of universal inclusion to the extent that it presupposes that discourse is only possible between similarly reflexive agents. This compounds a form of self–other relation that is potentially

for the purpose of reducing their ignorance. The presupposition is that the other is less free and in need of enlightenment because they do not share the same self-understanding. The assimilationist resonances of this argument can be evoked if we remember Las Casas' argument that Indians were worthy of inclusion on the grounds that they were capable of becoming Christians.

[64] According to Linklater this vision is not excessively assimilative of otherness, indeed, he argues, only an interest in emancipation can provide an adequate account of universal moral community. Linklater argues that it is a commitment to freedom that prevents the unjustifiable exclusion of the radically different from the realm of moral obligation. However, as this discussion indicates the critical theoretical ability to deliver in relation to 'radical' difference is in doubt.

assimilative in both the dimensions of equality and identity. The other's equality is only realised when they are emancipated, when they become modern, reflexive unalienated individuals, when they are assimilated.[65]

Furthermore, the legislative aspects of the Kantian paradigm are highlighted in this instance by the coexistence of two opposing categories, hierarchy and equality. The problem with an uncritical acceptance of Habermas' postconventional agent is that it implies a hierarchical relation between those more, or less, progressive participants in the conversation. While the principle may hold that those on different stages of development are equal, discursive equality is achieved only when one reaches the pinnacle of the hierarchy. For this reason the emancipatory *telos* of critical theory does not provide sufficient insurance against the possibility of generating an unequal relation to otherness capable of undermining communication between radically different agents.

These aspects of discourse ethics are testimony to the difficulties accompanying the task of attempting to reconcile the goals of community and difference. The tension between these two goals is evidenced in the tension within its core principles: the goal of universality as inclusion and as validation of norms. Whether discourse ethics as conceived by Habermas and Linklater does in fact overcome this contradiction because of its commitment to open dialogue is an open question. The point is that, at the very least, the language of hierarchy should be replaced by a language of equality and the language of emancipation by one of understanding and communication.[66]

The major point that has been made here is that because, for discourse ethics, conversation comes to mean consensual validation of universal moral claims among postconventional agents then any deviation from such form of agency or from this *telos* of conversation is by nature an obstacle to discourse. The goal of inclusion, removing the obstacles to discourse, might also mean not only the removal of political and moral practices of exclusion but also the creation of a realm of agents who understand themselves to be autonomous, free and self-determining. The conclusion that can be drawn from these observations for Linklater's

---

[65] While the achievement of emancipation or enlightenment can only be the result of a process of self awareness it stands to reason that if the fulfilment of the categorical imperative is universal conversation between postconventional agents then this goal arguably requires the *creation* of such a realm.

[66] Indeed Habermas himself has explicitly moved away from this language. See J. Habermas, *The Past as Future* (Cambridge: Polity, 1994), p. 104.

account of the nature of a thin cosmopolitanism is that in so far as he subscribes to Habermas' understanding of the *telos* of conversation then his conception also provokes the same concerns. Despite his efforts to emphasise the openness of conversation Linklater does not appear to have succeeded in adopting the inclusive dimension of discourse ethics (D) without simultaneously endorsing the legislative aspects which accompany the *telos* of U. Most importantly Linklater's formulation, like Habermas' does not rest at defining universalism in relation to the issue of inclusion alone but extends it to the process of the validation of norms. As a result, it involves a commitment to both a thick and a thin project.

At this point it is rewarding to return to Benhabib's critique of U. Benhabib argued that U introduces consequentalist complications by emphasising the need to gain consensus in order to validate norms. However, consensus, she argues, does not in itself guarantee validity. In her view '[C]onsent alone can never be a criterion of anything, neither of truth nor of moral validity'.[67] The consensual implications of U introduce an unnecessarily teleological element into discourse ethics because conversation becomes oriented towards achieving rational consensus regarding the right. She argues rather that it is rationality of the procedure which is of importance. This can be provided by D alone. Discourse ethics does not need the principle of U in order to facilitate inclusive moral dialogue. The core idea of conversation as procedure is enough upon which to base a defence of normative universalism: '...consent is a misleading term for capturing the core idea behind communicative ethics; namely the processual generation of reasonable agreement about moral principles via an open-ended moral conversation...'[68] Therefore, Benhabib argues, it is possible to reject U but keep D. We should not reject the goal of inclusion nor the generation of universal norms but these can be achieved without the over-determining *telos* of U.[69]

---

[67] Benhabib, *Situating the Self*, p. 37.   [68] *Ibid.*
[69] In rejecting the principles of U Benhabib also appears to be rejecting Habermas' attempt to provide a weak transcendental defence of the discourse ethics. Benhabib rejects the argument that the normative goals of discourse ethics can be 'grounded' in pragmatic presupposition of argumentation. The principle of mutual respect and inclusion in dialogue are ought statements which cannot be deduced from the pragmatic presuppositions of what a good argument consists of. She argues instead that the principle of universal inclusion in dialogue stems rather from an interpretation or immanent critique of western philosophical tradition (something like Rawls's reflexive equilibrium). In so doing, she is arguing that the U principle is an ought position and not a scientific statement.

What is of most interest in Benhabib's argument is that the effect of relinquishing the dimension of U from discourse ethics opens the possibility that we might provide communicative ethics with a broader focus which is arguably more inclusive of difference. By de-emphasising U we open conversation up to questions not concerned exclusively with

> what all would or could agree to as result of practical discourses to be morally permissible or impermissible, but what would be allowed and perhaps even necessary from the standpoint of continuing and sustaining the practice of the moral conversation among us (the emphasis shifts from) rational agreement, (towards) . . . sustaining those normative practices and moral relationship within which reasoned agreement as a way of life can flourish and continue.[70]

In addition to Benhabib's reservations we can add another which supports hers but proceeds in a slightly different direction. Benhabib's criticisms point to the possibility that the problems identified with discourse ethics might stem from the fact that it envisions conversation purely as a means for resolving moral disputes. The problems then are not with discourse ethics as an account of the 'moral point of view'. Rather the problem lies as much with the consignment of conversation exclusively to the task of dispute resolution and mediation between competing moral claims. If this is the case there is less at stake in abandoning the more problematic principle of U while keeping the goal of D. In so doing, we open the possibilities for investigating how conversation be maintained, encouraged and built. Relaxing the requirement of necessary consensus orients the goal of conversation towards other tasks such as community building and solidarity, without denying its role in dispute resolution or in the pursuit of universally agreeable norms. Indeed valid universal norms are most likely to be achieved only after, or in the context of, other conversations and after the generation of mutual understanding through a process of dialogue. To achieve both solidarity and justice, to build and maintain a discursive community, conversation must become both the means and the end. For this purpose we need a fuller, more comprehensive and less restrictive understanding of conversation than that provided by discourse ethics. The meaning and outline of such an understanding is pursued in the next chapter.

---

[70] Benhabib, *Situating the Self*, p. 38.

Conclusion

This chapter has attempted to demonstrate the manner in which the approaches to communication supplied by critical theory and post-structuralism in IR are problematic. It has been suggested that the Foucauldian strain of poststructuralist IR and Linklater's critical theory share a commitment to 'theorising in a register of freedom'. Following Hutchings it was suggested that as a result both these approaches could be identified as being subjected to what she referred to as the Kantian paradox of limitation and legislation. This paradox manifests itself in a dynamic which both encourages free communication and yet simultaneously appears to provide restrictions on it. In drawing attention to these possible problems in this fashion the purpose has not been to reject either the value of freedom or the goal of a universal community in which all are free. Nor has the intention been to suggest that either the Kantian paradox or the tension between community and difference can be escaped completely. Rather the intention has been to indicate the ways in which a certain definition of the meaning of freedom, especially when equated with the enlightenment ethos of critique, can affect the possibility of communication between radically different actors. If this chapter has succeeded in drawing attention to this dimension of the project of a thin dialogic cosmopolitanism then the next challenge becomes how to conceive of a universally inclusive dialogue in which all are free to speak, which reduces the potential for assimilation and exclusion detailed here. The next chapter offers one suggestion as to how this might be achieved.

4 Philosophical hermeneutics: understanding, practical reasoning and human solidarity

Every conversation presupposes a common language, or better, creates a common language. Something is placed in the centre, as the Greeks say, which the partners in dialogue both share, and concerning which they can exchange ideas with one another. Hence reaching an understanding on the subject matter of a conversation necessarily means that a common language must first be worked out in the conversation . . . in a successful conversation they both come under the influence of the truth of the object and are thus bound to one another in a new community. To reach an understanding in dialogue is not merely a matter of putting oneself forward and successfully asserting one's own point of view, but being transformed into communion in which we do not remain what we were.[1]

Chapter 2 identified Mark Neufeld's claim that the goal of a critical theory of international relations was the recreation of the Aristotelian *polis* on the global scale. Linklater's use of Habermasian discourse ethics, it was argued, had been the most successful attempt to think about how to proceed with this aim. Discourse ethics, Linklater argued, provided one conceptualisation of what such a recreation might look like. In Linklater's project the global *polis*, in order to be both inclusive and just, must necessarily take the form of a 'thin' cosmopolitan community modelled on discourse ethics. Chapter 3 argued that certain limits applied to this model as a result of its commitment to a strictly proceduralist, deontological conversation. The discussion concluded by suggesting that while discourse ethics provides many important criteria for understanding conversation it nonetheless has retained a tension between the goal of universal inclusion and a limitation on the forms of legitimate speech.

[1] H. G. Gadamer, *Truth and Method*, 2nd edn (trans. J. Weinsheimer and D. Marshall), (London: Sheed and Ward, 1989), p. 379.

It was suggested that this model contains the potential for a 'thicker' cosmopolitanism than suggested by Linklater's reading. This chapter presents the case for advancing a model of dialogue informed by philosophical hermeneutics and which entails a 'thinner' and thereby more inclusive vision of cosmopolitan community. Philosophical hermeneutics provides an alternative basis for thinking about conversation and the nature of a *polis* in which matters are decided through words and persuasion. The argument below is that the theory of understanding provided by philosophical hermeneutics supplies an account in which the goal of justice to difference through recognition in conversation might be more closely actualised. Philosophical hermeneutics provides the resources for such an account because of its orientation towards understanding, practical reasoning and the achievement of solidarity through dialogue.

The case for philosophical hermeneutics consists of several parts. The first requires analysing the model of conversation central to the hermeneutic account of understanding. Philosophical hermeneutics is a *philosophy* of understanding rather than a *theory* because it asks the question: 'what does it mean to say we have understood something?' or, rather, 'what is the meaning of understanding?' From this question conclusions are drawn about the nature of human 'Being-in-the-world' (*Dasein*) and these conclusions have significance for understanding the possibility of developing a universal communication community. The discussion begins by briefly outlining the nature and context of the philosophical hermeneutic theory of understanding. It presents Gadamer's case for the 'ontologisation' of hermeneutics through the recognition of the linguisticality of all understanding, and then moves to discuss the depiction of understanding as a dialogical 'fusion of horizons'. This metaphor demonstrates that for philosophical hermeneutics, understanding is conceived not as a purely private, subjective, act but rather as a dialogical, communicative and intersubjective one. Philosophical hermeneutics conceives of understanding as a *communicative* act, between equal but differently situated agents, in which self and other achieve recognition through dialogue. It is this dimension which provides the basis for an alternative model of dialogical community which preserves the strengths and cancels some of the weaknesses of those discussed in previous chapters.

The philosophical hermeneutic conception of the nature and purpose of conversation has much in common with discourse ethics but nonetheless provides an alternative model that avoids some of the potentially assimilatory dimensions. In particular, it is argued that Gadamer is able to articulate a better form of self–other relation by emphasising the central place of the experience of truth. The participants in a conversation, if genuinely seeking understanding, enter the conversation with the expectation of learning through encountering a new experience of truth. A claim to have achieved understanding involves coming to experience a new or different truth. This involves a form of learning because the other's difference offers a new experience. This encounter permits the other to be seen as both different and equal because, like the self, they may possess truth but this is a new and different truth. Therefore because a 'genuine' conversation oriented towards understanding is guided by the expectation of truth a less assimilatory relationship between self and other is achieved.

The philosophical hermeneutic account of understanding as dialogue between equal partners is situated within a practical philosophy that is also oriented towards the achievement of understanding, agreement and solidarity. Philosophical hermeneutics, Gadamer argues, is a practical philosophy which seeks to facilitate the exercise of practical reasoning, the chief virtue of the Aristotelian *polis*. Practical reasoning in turn requires the cultivation of solidarity between its members. Because philosophical hermeneutics is universalistic in its scope its *telos* is the creation of universal solidarity as the necessary conditions for the exercise of practical reasoning. Putting these two aspects of philosophical hermeneutics together, the model of dialogue and the pursuit of solidarity points to the pivotal place of communication. Platonic dialogue as understood by Gadamer both requires and creates a level of solidarity between the conversational partners and can, therefore, be seen as both means and end of a thin cosmopolitan community.

While the first part of the chapter examines these themes, the second explores the differences between this model and the one provided by discourse ethics. It argues that Gadamer's model provides a mean for overcoming certain of the limitations accompanying discourse ethics while nonetheless contributing to the goal of a thin dialogical and universal community. In particular it is argued that the most significant difference between the account of a conversation oriented towards truth in philosophical hermeneutics and that provided by discourse ethics, is the *telos* of understanding which underpins philosophical hermeneutics.

The hermeneutic claim to universality:
understanding as mode of being-in the-world

Hermeneutics, of which philosophical hermeneutics is only one branch, refers to the study of the relationship between meaning, interpretation and understanding. Historically, those engaged in this project have been concerned with questions of how best to interpret and understand a text or texts, originating with the Bible.[2] In the nineteenth century Wilhelm Dilthey argued that hermeneutics could provide a general methodology for the human sciences [*Geisteswissenschaften*]. Such a methodology would be distinct from, but equal in status and objectivity to, that of the natural sciences. It is with Dilthey that the famous distinction between explanation and understanding first originates.[3] Explanation is the task of the natural or physical sciences and understanding, that of the human sciences. This is because the *Geisteswissenschaften* are concerned with the understanding of meaning rather than brute facts: 'The human studies do not deal with facts and phenomena which are silent about man but with facts and phenomena which are meaningful only as they shed light on man's inner processes, his "inner" experience.'[4]

Dilthey's other major contribution was to assert that the human sciences are intrinsically historical sciences. Whilst knowledge in this realm is historical it is not, for Dilthey, precluded from being objective. The task of nineteenth-century hermeneutics then was to achieve objective understandings of inner experience via the interpretation of the 'works of man'(sic).

Gadamer's philosophical hermeneutics involves the use of the ontological insights of Martin Heidegger to deepen and reconceptualise the hermeneutic project begun by Dilthey. Gadamer starts *Truth and Method* with the question '. . . what kind of knowledge and what kind of truth'[5] do we attain when we study texts and traditions, when we engage in the human sciences? Beyond that question he asks 'what is understanding?' and '. . . how is understanding possible?'[6] Gadamer's answer to these questions provides his distinctive contribution to the pursuit of a discursive relationship of recognition between equal but different subjects.

---

[2] For an excellent introduction to the history of continental hermeneutics see R. Palmer, *Hermeneutics: Interpretation Theory in Schleiermacher, Dilthey, Heidegger and Gadamer* (Evanston: Northwestern University Press, 1969).
[3] For a discussion of the place of this distinction in IR see M. Hollis and S. Smith, *Explaining and Understanding International Relations* (Oxford: Clarendon Press, 1990).
[4] Palmer, *Hermeneutics*, pp. 103–4.   [5] Gadamer, *Truth and Method*, p. xxi.
[6] *Ibid.*, p. xxx.

His answer indicates the *ontological*, rather than the epistemological or methodological, dimensions of understanding. Like Dilthey he challenges the attempts to apply the methodology of the natural sciences to the human sciences. The human sciences, Gadamer argues, are informed by a different experience to that of the natural sciences, they are:

> connected to modes of experience that lie outside science: with the experience of philosophy, of art, and of history itself. These are all modes of experience in which a truth is communicated that cannot be verified by the methodological means proper to science.[7]

The essential common ingredient of these modes of experience is that they are interpretative. Thus, Gadamer's answer to the question 'what is understanding?' is 'all understanding is interpretation'.[8] When we say we understand something, we have in fact interpreted it.[9] As a result, hermeneutics becomes not the act of 'discovering' and understanding some 'original', deep, hidden, or objective meaning (or Truth), nor the act of recapturing the 'inner' experiences of humans (as in Dilthey) but rather the explication of a fundamental dimension of human experience.[10] Gadamer argues that understanding is not so much something we *do* but more the manner of our *experience (Erfahrung)* of the world. If all understanding is interpretation then our knowledge of and action in the world, our Being-in-the-World (*Dasein*), is also fundamentally interpretative or hermeneutic:

> Understanding is not conceived as a subjective process of man over and against an object but the way of being of man himself; hermeneutics is not defined as a general help discipline for the humanities but as a philosophical effort to account for understanding as an ontological – the ontological – process in man.[11]

---

[7] *Ibid.*, p. xxii.   [8] *Ibid.*, p. 274.

[9] Madison identifies these as the three main theses of Truth and Method '(1) To understand is in fact to interpret . . . (2) All understanding is essentially bound up with language . . . (3) The understanding of the meaning of the text is inseparable from its application.' G. B. Madison, *The Hermeneutics of Post-Modernity: Figures and Themes* (Bloomington: Indiana University Press, 1988), p. 114.

[10] Gadamer, unlike Dilthey is not concerned with creating a new science, nor is he concerned with creating an objective historical methodology. Philosophical hermeneutics describes not ' . . . a methodology of the human sciences, but an attempt to understand what the human sciences truly are, beyond their methodological self-consciousness, and what connects them with the totality of our experience of world'. Gadamer, *Truth and Method*, p. xxiii.

[11] Palmer, *Hermeneutics*, p. 163.

The ontological dimension of hermeneutics provides the basis for what Gadamer refers to as the hermeneutic, the claim to universality. The significance of this claim for the project of community and the question of recognition lies in its necessarily linguistic dimension. Gadamer bases his claim for the ontological dimension of hermeneutics on the universality of language as the medium for understanding. Understanding for Gadamer 'is not understanding of language, but understanding through language'.[12] The major argument of *Truth and Method* is that all knowledge is interpretation because all knowledge is constituted linguistically. According to Gadamer, not only do we understand and experience the world through language but language in a real sense discloses and manifests the world for us. Linguisticality is '... the fundamental mode of our being-in-the-world and the all embracing form of the constitution of the world'.[13] For Gadamer therefore: '[B]eing that can be understood is language.'[14] The linguisticality of human ontology makes for the most fundamental aspect of human situatedness. Because we are embedded in language in this way we are conditioned in the scope of our knowledge and experience.[15]

Intimately related to the argument for linguisticality is Gadamer's argument for the simultaneous historicity of human Being. If linguisticality is both the constitution of our world and the manner of our experience of it, then what is contained within it, what it carries or bears, is history and tradition. When Gadamer refers to tradition he does not mean tradition in the everyday sense but rather he is arguing that we are

[12] *Ibid.*, p. 139. In order to make this claim Gadamer employs an expressive view of language. One of the main elements of expressivism is that language is not simply a tool for understanding to be manipulated at will. Instead, it is the expression of being-in-the-world [Dasein]: '... words and language are not wrappings in which things are packed for the commerce of those who write and speak. It is in words and language that things first come into being and are [for us]'. Heidegger quoted in Palmer, *Hermeneutics*, p. 135. If language is the location of understanding and is thus constitutive of our experience it can never be transcended in the sense of achieving an extra linguistic or objective understanding. The attempt to reproduce the objectivity of the natural sciences in the social sciences through the manipulation of an objective language is thus limited by this embeddedness. To use or manipulate language can only be done through language because language is always present in any attempt to understand Language. For another account of expressivist views of language, see C. Taylor, 'Language and Human Nature', in M. Gibbons (ed.), *Interpreting Politics* (New York University Press, 1987).
[13] H. G. Gadamer, *Philosophical Hermeneutics* (Berkeley: University of California Press, 1977), p. 4.
[14] Gadamer, *Truth and Method*, p. 474.
[15] In this sense we are always in a position of less than complete knowledge or understanding. Gadamer argues 'It is the medium of language alone that, related to the totality of beings, mediates the finite historical nature of man to himself and to world.' *Ibid.*, p. 457.

'prejudiced' beings '... always already affected by history. It determines in advance both what seems to us worth inquiring about and what will appear as an object of investigation.'[16] Gadamer refers to this as effective history (*Wirkungsgeschichtliches*). As we understand through language we also understand through our situatedness in an historical tradition:

> [T]o Be historically means that knowledge of oneself can never be complete. All self-knowledge arises from what is historically pre-given... because it underlies all subjective intentions and actions and hence both prescribes and limits every possibility for understanding any tradition whatsoever in its historical alterity.[17]

According to Gadamer, all interpretation and understanding occur within the 'tradition' or horizon of consciousness constituted by the linguistic and historical tradition of the interpreter: the webs of meaning in which and through which we experience the world and which are the conditions of possibility of understanding. Tradition constitutes and is constituted by '... the prejudices that we bring with us ... [they] constitute ... the horizon of a particular present, for they represent that beyond which it is impossible to see'.[18]

The horizon of our tradition is, therefore, that which is formed by our embeddedness in language and history. It is 'the range of vision that

---

[16] *Ibid.*, p. 300. Gadamer's concept of effective history derives from his critique of the nineteenth-century historicist school. Historicists argued that the past could be understood 'in its own terms' and, therefore, it was not possible to judge one period by the standards of another. Gadamer argues that such a project requires an objectification of the past which is both impossible and which prevents actual understanding. Historicism does not recognise the manner in which the Historian unknowingly projects the understanding of the present onto the past. In so doing, it presupposes a clear distinction between past and present. This Gadamer denies: 'there is no pure seeing and understanding of history without reference to the present. On the contrary, history is seen and understood only and always through a consciousness standing in the present'. Palmer, *Hermeneutics*, p. 176. The present at the same time '... is seen and understood only through the intentions, ways of seeing and preconceptions bequeathed from the past.' *Ibid.*, p. 176. The past, Gadamer argues, can never be fully objectified as it is always operative within us and in ways in which we are not aware: we can never make our own position in history fully transparent to ourselves. Gadamer calls this the principle of effective history (*Wirkungsgeschichtliches*). Effective historical consciousness (*Wirkungsgeschichtliches Bewusstein*) is the consciousness of '... being exposed to history and to its action, in such a way that this action upon us cannot be objectified because it is part of the historical phenomenon itself'. P. Ricoeur, *Hermeneutics and the Human Sciences: Essays on Language, Action and Interpretation* (ed. Thompson, J. B.), (Cambridge: Cambridge University Press, 1981), p. 61. Thus we can never have complete knowledge of the efficacy of history: '... effective history still determines modern historical and scientific consciousness; and it does so beyond any possible knowledge of this domination'. Gadamer, *Truth and Method*, p. xxxiv.
[17] *Ibid.*, p. 302.   [18] *Ibid.*, p. 272.

includes everything that can be seen from a particular vantage point'.[19] For any given agent the universal characteristic of linguisticality takes the form of a particular linguistic and historical tradition. As a result, understanding does not occur in a vacuum, or from a 'neutral' or impartial position, and is not simply a subjective grasping of an objective truth but always an interpretation from within an historical tradition. The effect of historicity and language is that they form the horizon of our consciousness and the conditions for understanding. Because of our situatedness in tradition any understanding of our past, a text or another person, must be an understanding for us, in our particular situation. History and language make for our situatedness in 'tradition' and provide the productive 'prejudices' with which we understand the world and engage with it. In this sense philosophical hermeneutics begins from something like a communitarian premise regarding the particularity of norms and situatedness of agents in particular communities. For philosophical hermeneutics however, this situatedness does not restrict understanding to the particular community nor does it restrict practice to coexistence. On the contrary it is this situatedness of humans in linguistic and historical horizons that makes for our finitude and finitude provides limits, possibilities and motivation for both conversation and understanding.[20]

If the historicity and linguisticality of human experience provide the conditions in which we understand, experience and gain knowledge of the world, in other words, if they constitute our belongingness to the world, then these same determinants simultaneously make for our limits, our finitude. Finitude however, is simultaneously that which motivates and allows our search for understanding and which provides our openness to new knowledge and experiences. The search for meaning and understanding is, Gadamer argues, an implicit recognition of this finitude. Furthermore, the recognition of finitude, of not-knowing, is what makes us humble in the pursuit of knowledge. Finitude motivates and modifies the search for knowledge because it suggests, *not* that we should be content to remain ignorant, but that the search for truth and knowledge is never complete. Hermeneutic knowledge is also a

---

[19] *Ibid.*, p. 302.
[20] The philosophical hermeneutic emphasis on situatedness and tradition is compatible with Richard Rorty's philosophy which emphasises the inescapability of thinking from 'where we are now', i.e. from where we are situated historically, culturally and linguistically, as distinct from thinking from outside history in some Archimedean vantage point.

knowledge of the flexibility and mutability of limits, and, therefore, of the possibility of learning.

It is the relationship of openness and limitation which generates the hermeneutic conception of the self–other (what Gadamer refers to as the I–Thou) relationship because the recognition of finitude requires the search for knowledge to be necessarily dialogical. Being finite and situated beings we must engage in conversation in order to learn. It is in this context that Gadamer generates a model of understanding in conversation which achieves recognition of the other.

By including the dimension of historicity and linguisticality Gadamer radicalises and deepens the hermeneutic project. By expanding its realm from the interpretation of texts to the interpretation of human Being he is able to encompass the nature of what it means to have knowledge of the world. However, Gadamer's deepening of the hermeneutic project and his reflections on the possibility of understanding between agents situated within historical traditions, or contexts, also provides the basis for the dialogical dimension of his philosophy of understanding and a model of conversation which comes closer to achieving justice to difference.

The advantages of the dialogical account of understanding, and in particular the manner in which it generates a relationship of equality and recognition, can be initially illustrated by a comparison to two other forms of understanding. Gadamer distinguishes between three different types of understanding, involving three types of self–other relations.[21]

The first involves what he calls a knowledge of human nature. This form of understanding is informed by a means–end rationality which perceives the other merely as a means to 'our' end. It '... seeks to calculate how the other person will behave ... (and it sees) the other person as a tool that can be absolutely known and used'.[22] For Gadamer this type of knowledge reflects a 'naive faith in method and ... objectivity' as practised in scientistic models of social science.[23] According to Gadamer '... this orientation towards the Thou is purely self regarding and

---

[21] These types of understanding also bear strong resemblance to Todorov's categories of annihilation, assimilation, coexistence and communication.

[22] *Ibid.*, p. 359.

[23] This type of understanding also corresponds to Habermas' technical instrumental rationality. See J. Habermas, *Knowledge and Human Interests* (trans. Jeremy Shapiro), (London: Heineman, 1972).

contradicts the moral definition of man'[24] (as an end in himself [sic]). It can be seen as corresponding in some measure to the category of annihilation, in that the other's distinctive identity and equality are denied.

The second type of understanding reflects the historical consciousness which Gadamer identifies as characterising historicist approaches to history, and to what might be called a hermeneutics of recovery. This relationship corresponds in some degree to the category of assimilation but also interestingly to that of coexistence. This form of understanding is restricted to the goal of recovering an accurate representation of the self-understanding of the other. In this relationship the other, the Thou, is seen as a person who can be understood, like the self. However, the goal of this type of understanding is not only to know the other as well as they do but also to understand them better than they do themselves.

For Gadamer this is an improvement on the first form but is still not sufficient because in it

> the Thou loses the immediacy with which it makes its claim. It is understood but this means it is co-opted . . . by understanding the other, by claiming to know him, one robs his claims of their legitimacy . . . the claim to understand the other person in advance functions to keep the other person's claim at a distance.[25]

In this relationship the self is removed from the understanding of the other who is still objectified to the degree that they are unable to make any claim to truth upon the self. This approach '. . . makes him the object of objective knowledge, [and] involves the fundamental suspension of his claim to truth'.[26] In this sense the other is assimilated through the claim to know them while at the same time we have '. . . given up the claim to find . . . any truth valid and intelligible [applicable] for ourselves'.[27] The other in this way is denied their full equality because they are objectified.

The third type of understanding is dialogical understanding. It resembles and gives substantive content to Todorov's category of Communication. In this type of relationship what is being understood (be it a text, a work of art or another person) is capable of speaking

---

[24] Gadamer, *Truth and Method*, p. 358.   [25] *Ibid.*, pp. 359–60.
[26] *Ibid.*, p. 270. In historical consciousness 'we have as it were, withdrawn from the situation . . . He (the other) himself cannot be reached . . . The text that is understood historically is forced to abandon its claim that it is uttering something true.' *Ibid.*
[27] *Ibid.*

to the interpreter as a partner in conversation.[28] The relationship to the other here is not one of control but engagement, it allows the interpreter to see the other (the Thou) '... truly as a Thou – i.e. not to overlook his [sic] claim but to let him really say something to us'.[29]

The distinction between philosophical hermeneutics and historicism (the second type of understanding) rests on the notion that understanding refers to the subject matter (*Die Sache* or *Sache selbst*) of conversation, to what is said, not the sayer, the text not the writer. For Gadamer, 'to conduct a conversation means to allow oneself to be conducted by the subject matter to which the partners in the dialogue are oriented'.[30] The concept of the subject or the 'thing at hand' is what guides or motivates the conversation and to which one's interpretations always refer. The *Sache* is what the conversation is about and it is the other's interpretation of the *Sache* that we are attempting to see the truth of. It is also in relation to the *Sache* that we assess the accuracy or persuasiveness, to us, of the other's interpretation. Thus as Hoy states, although Gadamer

> believes that interpretations are always bound to a particular context, he does not think that we can interpret things any way we want. Interpretations are always guided by the *Sache*, and thus by a sense that there are right and wrong ways to say things that ought to be said.[31]

The concern with the *Sache* liberates us from the attempt to psychologise and relativise understanding. According to Gadamer, to be open to the other's truth claims is to be open towards what it is the other communicates. To understand '... means, primarily, to understand the content of what is said, and only secondarily to isolate and understand another's meaning as such'.[32] Furthermore, it does so by enabling us to

---

[28] '... a person trying to understand a text is prepared for it to tell him something ...' *Ibid.* Although Gadamer uses conversation as a metaphor for what happens in understanding a text there is, for him, no major difference between studying a text, understanding a work of art or engaging with another person in dialogue. Gadamer argues that all such encounters are dialogical in one form or another. For this reason Gadamer refers to the relationship between an interpreter and a text as an I–Thou relationship. Hence also the many references to texts in the quotations provided here.

[29] *Ibid.*, p. 361.   [30] *Ibid.*, p. 367.

[31] D. C. Hoy and T. McCarthy, *Critical Theory* (Oxford: Blackwell, 1994), p. 189.

[32] For Gadamer this is the essential similarity between understanding a text and reaching understanding in a conversation '... the chief thing that these apparently so different situations ... have in common is that both are concerned with a subject matter that is placed before them ... this understanding of the subject matter must take the form of language ... the way understanding occurs ... is the coming-into-language of the thing itself'. Gadamer, *Truth and Method*, p. 378. Gadamer here shares with Paul Ricoeur and

offer a critical position on ourselves by referring our understanding to something outside of ourselves.

A conversation, therefore, is not merely an exchange of information nor the acquisition of knowledge for strategic, or instrumental purposes (as in the case of say medical diagnosis which is a conversation but not necessarily a hermeneutic conversation). Nor is it about gaining knowledge of the other's mind or psychology. Instead it is for Gadamer 'a process of coming to an understanding'[33] in regards to the subject-matter [*Sache*] of conversation. The significance of emphasising the *Sache* is that it is the means by which the hermeneutic model of conversation avoids the objectification of the other and achieves recognition through being open to the possibility of truth. However, it is worth noting that for Gadamer the *Sache* is always a particular thing, text, interpretation, topic. Thus truth is always particular, situated and in reference to some subject. This particularist and situated notion of truth sits in contrast to the principle of discourse ethics which necessarily directs conversation *exclusively* to universalisable statements.

It is important to note that emphasising the subject orienting conversation does not involve denying the subjectivity or presence of the conversational partners themselves. Likewise, to emphasise learning from the other is not to deny the self nor to deny the truth that one has to offer.[34] The hermeneutic conversation is also not an example of Levinasian 'placing the other at a height'. On the contrary, for Gadamer acknowledging the orientation of a conversation towards the thing at hand is the only way of doing justice to, of acknowledging the full subjectivity, situatedness and *equality*, of self and other. Understanding in

---

Jacques Derrida the emphasis on separation of a text from its author's intention: '...the understanding of tradition does not take the traditionary text as an expression of another person's life, but as a meaning that is detached from the person who means it, from an I or a Thou'. *Ibid.*, p. 358. Gadamer's appeal to truth and the *Sache* suggests, on first reading, that he is referring to some sort of correspondence notion of truth and understanding. However, such an interpretation would be inaccurate. The purpose of Gadamer's account of historicity and linguisticality of all understanding is to move away from such endeavours while simultaneously resisting the obvious relativist implications of such a move.

[33] *Ibid.*, p. 385.

[34] 'The acceptance of the other certainly does not mean that one would not be completely conscious of one's own inalienable Being. It is rather one's own strength, especially the strength of one's own existential certainty, which permits one to be tolerant .... it (hermeneutic understanding) does not concern abandoning and extinguishing the self for the sake of universal acceptance, but rather the risking of one's own for the understanding and recognition of the other.' H. G. Gadamer, 'The Future of the European Humanities', pp. 193–208, in D. Misgeld and G. Nicholson, *Hans-Georg Gadamer on Education, Poetry and History* (Albany: SUNY, 1992), pp. 206–7.

the Gadamerian sense involves an orientation in which the other is not objectified but is engaged with in a mutual project in which both self and other achieve recognition.

If philosophical hermeneutics describes and seeks to achieve the third type of understanding the question then, to return to Gadamer's original task, is what does such an understanding between equals consist of? Gadamer argues that understanding is a result of a dialogical process of questioning and occurs in and when the participants achieve what he calls a fusion of horizons.

The dialogic model of understanding: the fusion of horizons

Gadamer's assertion of the linguisticality of human experience points to the possibility of understanding and conversation between radically different agents. Understanding, Gadamer argues, would not be conceivable without the prejudices provided by tradition. Therefore in contrast to the everyday meaning of tradition Gadamer emphasises the extent to which linguistic/historical traditions are not 'grids' or cages that are inflexible and closed. On the contrary, traditions are open, changing, and contain in Taylor's words 'doors to otherness'.[35] The everyday notion of tradition as something which is fixed and unchanging is misplaced when used as Gadamer intends because, he argues, '. . . the horizon of the past . . . tradition, is always in motion'.[36] Human existence is itself a process of movement and '. . . consists in the fact that it is never utterly bound to any one stand-point, and hence can never have a truly closed horizon'.[37] The horizon 'is . . . something into which we move and that moves with us. Horizons change for a person who is moving.'[38] The fact of human linguisticality in the form of tradition does not mean

[35] C. Taylor, 'Connolly, Foucault, and Truth', *Political Theory*, 13. 3, August (1985), 377–85, p. 382.
[36] Gadamer, *Truth and Method*, p. 271. Understanding is, therefore, not a matter of our correctly grasping an unchanging tradition. Instead it is as much a creative transformative act in which the historical tradition is transformed once again: 'understanding is to be thought of less as a subjective act than as participating in an event of tradition, a process of transmission in which past and present are constantly mediated'. *Ibid.*, p. 290. The experience of change allows or forces us to see things differently, it means our interpretations and understandings of the world transform over time with exposure to new circumstances and it is this which creates the possibility of understanding.
[37] *Ibid.*, p. 271. 'Just as the individual is never simply an individual, because he [sic] is always involved with others, so too the closed horizon that is supposed to enclose a culture is an abstraction.' *Ibid.* What Gadamer means here is not that cultures have not historically been isolated, temporally and spatially, from others, for example the Aztecs from the Spanish prior to 1492, but their isolation does not necessarily constitute a wall.
[38] *Ibid.*, p. 271.

that we are trapped within a pre-given order from which we cannot escape and which we are destined to repeat, instead: '[T]o be situated within a tradition does not limit the freedom of knowledge but makes it possible.'[39]

The common quality of linguisticality allows for what Gadamer calls the fusion of horizons of tradition. The act of understanding Gadamer argues occurs when the different linguistic/historical horizons of the participants, be it individuals, or a reader and a text, meet in a fusion: 'In the process of understanding there takes place a real fusing of horizons, which means that as the...horizon is projected, it is simultaneously removed.'[40] Therefore despite the plurality of human language, humans nonetheless all inhabit the same house of linguisticality. What we have in common is not this or that particular language, but linguisticality itself which both limits and enables communication. According to Gadamer, understanding is possible because linguisticality provides the bridge over the barriers formed by particular languages.

Understanding is referred to as a fusion because this word captures the idea that the individual horizons come to occupy the same place, while not necessarily losing their particular perspective. Understanding involves a fusion in the sense that it does not involve either the annihilation or assimilation of existing positions but rather their coming to inhabit a shared perspective. This shared meaning is, in an important sense, something new that exceeds and transforms the previous horizons without destroying them. It is in this sense that understanding '...always involves the attainment of a higher universality that overcomes, not only our particularity, but also that of the other'.[41] The fusion, therefore, occurs when both horizons remain and yet simultaneously come to share a new meaning, or simultaneously come to occupy the same territory or vantage point.

Understanding, therefore, engenders change in the traditions and the participants as they come to see things from a new perspective through their encounter with the other. By creating something new the hermeneutic conversation, in so far as it achieves understanding, brings

[39] *Ibid.*, p. 361 '...in whatever tradition we consider it, it is always a human – i.e. a verbally constituted – world that presents itself to us. As verbally constituted, every such world is of itself always open to every possible insight and hence to every expansion of its own world picture, and is accordingly available to others.' Gadamer, *Truth and Method*, p. 447.
[40] *Ibid.*, p. 273. [41] *Ibid.*, p. 271.

about a transformation of our own horizon, that is to say we are changed by the conversation. As Gadamer argues:

> We are continually shaping a common perspective when we speak a common language and so are active participants in the communicality of our experience of the world . . . Discussion bears fruit when a common language is found. Then the participants part from one another as changed beings. The individual perspectives with which they entered upon the discussion have been transformed, and so they are transformed themselves.[42]

For this reason, a fusion of horizons is not merely a matter of assimilating the other to 'our' horizon but a process in which both horizons undergo change and transformation.

The achievement of a fusion of horizons is the task of dialogue. Hermeneutic understanding, according to Gadamer, involves a dialogical movement between the participants. Understanding requires that we 'transpose' or 'place' ourselves into the horizon of the other. It requires that:

> into this other situation we must bring precisely, ourselves . . . If we put ourselves in someone else's shoes for example, then we will understand him[sic] – i.e. become aware of the otherness, indissoluble individuality of the other person – by putting ourselves in his position.[43]

However, Gadamer emphasises that the aim here is not totally to harmonise or *reconcile* the other to our existing knowledge. Transposing ourselves 'consists neither in the empathy of one individual for another, nor in subordinating another person to our own standards . . .'[44] but always in bringing ourselves into the other's position, seeing things as they see them and simultaneously acknowledging that we can only understand the other's horizon from the starting point of our own horizon. Gadamer argues that we can only understand the other, hear their particular voice and resist assimilation by acknowledging our prejudices and by realising that our situatedness always informs our understandings. Gadamer argues that only when we are aware of the fact that we always bring prejudices with us can we prevent them from over-determining the content of encounter. Only then is it possible to begin to hear the voice of the other. For this reason, 'it is constantly

---

[42] Gadamer, *Reason in the Age of Science*, p. 110.
[43] Gadamer, *Truth and Method*, p. 305.   [44] *Ibid.*, p. 305.

necessary to guard against overhastily assimilating the past to our own expectations of meaning. Only then can we listen to tradition in a way that permits it to make its own meaning heard.'[45] In other words, understanding is only possible because of our situatedness and belonging *and* a willingness to risk its disturbance. It is through such transpositioning that a new horizon is formed.

The possibility of understanding in a hermeneutic conversation has significant implications for the move beyond the cosmopolitan/communitarian divide and the pursuit of a communicatively based cosmopolitanism. The fusion of horizons in a hermeneutic conversation implies the possibility of the creation of something like a shared or even universal meaning. Such a conversation and agreement is possible, despite the different identities of the parties, and *because* of their situatedness: '[b]ecause of our belongingness to language and because of the belongingness of the text to language, a common horizon becomes possible'.[46] But primarily it suggests the possibility that rather than being restricted to those who already share a language conversation itself is actually a creative process wherein 'reaching an understanding on the subject matter . . . necessarily means that a common language must first be worked out in the conversation'.[47] The means for achieving a transposition, for placing ourselves in the other's shoes, and creating new shared meanings in a fusion of horizons is conversation or dialogue.

According to Gadamer, the process of reaching an understanding involves something like a process of question and answer between the interpreter and the text, the tradition or another person. In particular to place one's self in the other's horizon requires a process of question and answer in which both partners articulate the questions which concern them regarding a subject. According to Gadamer, to understand any historical text, statement or belief is to understand it as an answer to a question posed in relation to the *Sache*. In a process of understanding an historical text, for example, the interpreter asks certain questions of the text in order to ascertain its meaning. If the interpreter did not ask a

[45] *Ibid.*, '. . . a hermeneutically trained consciousness must be, from the start, sensitive to the text's alterity. But this kind of sensitivity involves neither "neutrality" with respect to content nor the extinction of one's self, but the foregrounding and appropriation of one's own fore-meanings and prejudices'. *Ibid.*, p. 269. Of course none of this is to say that having prejudices exposed is a guarantee that they will be 'overcome'.

[46] Palmer, *Hermeneutics*, p. 208.

[47] Gadamer, *Truth and Method*, p. 379. 'this understanding of the subject matter must take the form of language . . . the way understanding occurs . . . is the coming-into-language of the thing itself.' *Ibid.*, p. 378.

question, that would imply that they were already in possession of that which is to be understood, that is, the meaning of what is being said. Following this, the interpreter also comes to see the historical text as an *answer* to a certain question, and in order to appreciate how something is an answer one must also understand the question which it answers.[48] This dimension of conversation is integral to the process of coming to see the truth in what the other has to say. Understanding something as an answer also means understanding it as a valid answer, that is coming to see *that* it answers a question.[49] It is in the sense of understanding *how* a statement, text or law is an answer to a question, that we see its truth and learn from it.

The process of question and answer goes further than this, however, for the interpreter must also acknowledge the question that they themselves are attempting to ask and answer. It is the question which, in the case of history or a text for example, has prompted one's own enquiry. This dimension of understanding refers again to the questioner's own situatedness; the question that is asked is one that is formed in the context of the tradition and prejudices that the questioner brings.

Furthermore, in attempting to understand, one also acknowledges the question that one is being asked by the text:

> the voice that speaks to us from the past – whether text, work, trace – itself poses a question and places our meaning in openness. Reconstructing the question to which the text is presumed to be the answer itself takes place within a process of questioning through which we try to answer the question that the text asks us.[50]

Thus interpretation and understanding of a text actively involve the interpreter, who in turn is interrogated by the text. If we have a question which guides our interpretation then to some degree that question itself comes from the text but also from our own tradition. The text confronts us with something new and alien which we do not understand and in

---

[48] Kögler puts this clearly 'according to Gadamer understanding a question can mean nothing other than posing the question oneself. If a text is understood as an answer to a question, it is related back in a productive way to one's own questioning; that is to one's own problem situation. Only when a text is conceived in terms of a question can a dialogue be set into motion in such a way that the other's as well as one's own views can be treated as substantive and potentially true views.' H. H. Kögler, *The Power of Dialogue: Critical Hermeneutics After Gadamer and Foucault* (Cambridge, Mass.: MIT Press, 1996), p. 122.

[49] This does not mean that understanding requires us to see all answers as correct answers. On the contrary understanding involves endeavouring to discover if and how what is being understood answers the question.

[50] Gadamer, *Truth and Method*, p. 374.

so doing, prompts us to enquire into its meaning; 'recognising that an object is different, and not as we first thought, obviously presupposes the question whether it was this or that'.[51] If anything this dimension of recognition is the 'original' hermeneutic moment, in which the other, the different, the new and the incomprehensible are confronted and provoke the challenge of making sense of them.

Some commentators, such as Fred Dallmayr, have suggested that the metaphor of the fusion of horizons over-emphasises the possibility of consensus and agreement and, therefore, suggests an end to discussion and understanding. More particularly, he also suggests that it implies an eradication of difference in something like a final Hegelian synthesis.[52] To counter this perceived tendency, Dallmayr himself has highlighted Gadamer's later writings which emphasise the ongoing and never-completed task of understanding. Rather than engage with the particulars of Dallmayr's reading of *Truth and Method*, it is important to emphasise the ongoing nature of the hermeneutic conversation and Gadamer's rejection of any final Hegelian style synthesis.

For Gadamer, the purpose and the achievement of hermeneutic understanding is not the assimilation of the other into the self, instead it is the recognition that in understanding one comes to know the other as other, and the self as other. Complete or final understanding is never achieved but neither is total alterity maintained. Instead, what occurs resembles a conversation involving a continual too-ing and fro-ing of meanings. Conversation is the realm in which understanding is achieved and identity *and* difference articulated and negotiated. The purpose of conversation is not the eradication of difference in agreement, but instead the understanding of identity and difference through what is common: language.

That said, it is also important to note that conversation does not rule out the possibility of agreement or consensus. To do so would also be to over-prescribe the content and outcome of conversation. It may well be the case that in conversation different cultures can come to share agreements on 'thick' dimensions of community including the value of certain legislative norms and principles. But such convergence is not a requirement or the *telos* of a hermeneutic conversation. Rather, the *telos* of a hermeneutic conversation is understanding, and it is this which generates the fully equal relation between self and other. This *telos* both

---

[51] *Ibid.*, p. 362.
[52] F. R. Dallmayr, *Beyond Orientalism: Essays on Cross Cultural Encounter* (Albany: SUNY, 1996).

allows for difference and leaves open the possibility of convergence or consensus, in other words, agreement is neither legislated nor assumed. The different participants are able 'freely' to enter into discussion without any preconceptions as to what will be achieved working to prevent them from pursuing understanding.

If conversation is a process of question and answer between agents concerned to understand a subject matter, then, according to Gadamer, it is also, and fundamentally concerned with truth. It is the common orientation and expectation of encountering truth in conversation with an 'other' that provides the access to an opportunity for a more equal relationship between self and other.

The moment of equality in conversation occurs, not because understanding of the other is achieved, but rather because in conversation both self and other are seen equally as potential revealers or communicators of an experience of truth. At the same time the other is seen as different, because unknown, and what they have to say has not been revealed. To recognise their equality and their difference, one must be ready to learn from what they may have to say. Thus, in a genuine conversation the identity, of the other, or the content of what the Thou says, cannot be known beforehand. In other words, one must remain open to what one might learn in communication.

The concept of truth, therefore, is the crux of Gadamer's theory of understanding. Ironically truth itself however, is not treated systematically by Gadamer, in *Truth and Method* or elsewhere. Where he comes closest to doing so is the discussion of aesthetic experience in the first section of *Truth and Method*. It will be recalled that Gadamer's philosophical hermeneutics is based on the assumption that scientific method does not exhaust the possibilities for knowledge. Hermeneutic knowledge is knowledge of a different kind from that gained through scientific method. For Gadamer, the most convincing means of demonstrating this comes through the experience of art which is '... the most insistent admonition to scientific consciousness to acknowledge its own limits'.[53] The importance of art lies not merely in its aesthetic appeal, we don't appreciate it merely for its beauty, but for the meaning it has beyond its beauty. Art has meaning and significance because it presents a world to us:

> [T]he experience of encountering a work of art opens up a world; it is not mere gaping in sensuous pleasure at the outsides of forms. As soon

[53] Gadamer, *Truth and Method*, p. xxiii.

as we stop viewing a work as an object and see it as a world, when we see a world through it, then we realise that art is not sense perception but knowledge.[54]

We *communicate* with a work of art as a world-disclosing experience. In understanding a work of art we recognise, or rather we experience, something, a truth, of the world. As Palmer puts it 'when we see a great work of art and enter its world, we do not leave home so much as "come home". We say at once: truly it is so.'[55] A successful work of art says something to us and makes a claim about the world, a claim to truth, that is not scientific.

The meaning of encountering truth should not be understood as the encounter with a transcendental truth applicable to all. Rather to encounter truth is to have an experience (*Erlebnis*). An experience in this sense is a life-changing encounter, it involves both a dislocation from previous thoughts and an integration of new insights. Gadamer states that the experience of art '...suddenly tears the person experiencing it out of the context of his life and yet relates him back to the whole of his existence'.[56] To have understood is to have had such an experience. It is in this manner that the concept of experiencing truth should be understood in philosophical hermeneutics: understanding occurs as a moment of an experience of a truth of Being and the manner of such understanding is always dialogical. This characteristic provides the contrast between hermeneutical understanding and its alternatives.

This moment of experiencing a truth, or a world, has something of the quality of an application. Understanding, Gadamer argues 'always involves something like the application of the text... to the present situation of the interpreter'.[57] It is the moment of application which underlies the metaphor of the fusion of horizons. We can only understand the past (or a text) in so far as it says something to us, in so far as it has meaning and applicability to ourselves in our own situation. 'Genuine' understanding occurs when we have transposed ourselves into the other's situation, heard the other's voice and understood its applicability to ourselves.

The final dimension to Gadamer's definition of truth relates to the idea of the fusion of horizons as agreement. Coming to an understanding, hearing the voice of the other, coming to see a truth through a process

---

[54] Palmer, *Hermeneutics*, p. 167.   [55] *Ibid.*, p. 168.
[56] Gadamer, *Truth and Method*, p. 70.   [57] *Ibid.*, p. 274.

of question and answer is akin to coming to an agreement:

> it belongs to every true conversation that each person opens himself to the other, truly accepts his point of view as valid and transposes himself into the other to such an extent that he understands not the particular individual but what he says. What is to be grasped is the substantive rightness of his opinion, so that we can be at one with each other on the subject.[58]

The importance of agreement lies not so much in its content nor its achievement itself but, rather, that in being open to encountering truth one sees the other as an equal. According to Gadamer: '[T]he experience of the Thou also manifests the paradox that something standing over me asserts its rights and requires absolute recognition; and in that process is "understood". But... what is so understood is not the Thou but the truth of what the Thou says to us.'[59] Understanding, therefore, is oriented by the possibility of reaching an agreement concerning the meaning (not necessarily its moral rightness or universal validity) of a subject matter of conversation between fully equal participants.[60]

Socratic conversation

For Gadamer the ultimate model of conversation embodying this approach is the Socratic dialogue which presents a model of hermeneutic conversation/understanding in at least three senses: first: it is a conversation the purpose of which is to seek truth. It is not an argument in which the aim is to win through demonstrating the other's weakness: '[T]o test the assertions of the other person, one does not try to weaken them but rather to strengthen them, that is, to find their true strength in the subject itself.'[61] In a Socratic dialogue the manner of proceeding

---

[58] *Ibid.*, p. 385.   [59] *Ibid.*, p. xxxv.

[60] Richard Bernstein and D. C. Hoy have both argued that for this reason Gadamer's notion of truth is 'contingent upon an intersubjective consensus rather than upon a transcendental subject...' D. C. Hoy, *The Critical Circle* (Berkeley: University of California Press, 1978), p. 110. However, Risser has demonstrated that this is an oversimplification because it underplays the importance of Being, i.e. of that which is external to individual subjectivity. The consensus notion removes the reference to that which is being discussed, the *Sache*. See R. Bernstein,*Beyond Objectivism and Relativism* (Philadelphia: University of Pennsylvania Press, 1983), p. 155; J. Risser, *Hermeneutics and the Voice of the Other* (Albany: SUNY, 1997).

[61] Gadamer, *Truth and Method*, p. 199. According to Gadamer, 'The unique and continuing relevance of the Platonic dialogues is due to this art of strengthening, for in this process what is said is continually transformed into the uttermost possibilities of its rightness and truth, and overcomes all opposition that tries to limit its validity.' *Ibid.*, p. 368.

attempts to get at the 'truth' through mounting the strongest possible case for that which is being understood, the text, the other etc. In the moment of application one sees the truth or applicability of a statement or a text for oneself. This requires that one endeavours first to see if what one wishes to understand is truthful or applicable and then if that fails, and only then, to see why it doesn't, that is in what way the argument/text is weak or doesn't answer the question.

Second: Gadamer argues that the dialogic structure of question and answer requires genuine questions and a genuine openness and a desire to learn: 'The sense of every question is realised in passing through this state of indeterminacy, in which it becomes an open question. Every true question requires this openness.'[62] The Socratic dialogue is not a contest between opinions (or *doxa*) which, Gadamer argues, are removed from the search for truth and are self-contained. The structure of the genuine question presupposes, in contrast to mere opinion, that the question is not 'rhetorical' or 'pedagogical', in which the answer is already known, but actually open to the possibility of a new answer.

Third: the hermeneutic/Socratic conversation presupposes a certain degree of good will on the part of the participants. It presupposes that genuine understanding is the goal of the conversation and it is only under these conditions that conversation generates understanding and a new horizon.[63] Thus a Socratic conversation is a genuinely productive, transformative and creative encounter between partners and not merely an exchange or act of recovery.

Fourth: the attitude of openness to the truth stems from admission of one's own fallibility and ignorance, what Gadamer calls 'Socratic not-knowing'.[64] Gadamer argues that the Socratic questioning of experts was a means of articulating the limits of human understanding, of fini-tude. Central to the entire hermeneutic conception of understanding and dialogue (and especially in their ontological significance) is, Gadamer argues, a recognition of human finitude. Furthermore, the recognition of finitude underlying philosophical hermeneutics provides it with its account of self–other relations in so far as it provides the motivation

---

[62] *Ibid.*, p. 363.

[63] 'Reaching an understanding in conversation presupposes that both partners are ready for it and are trying to recognise the full value of what is alien and opposed to them. If this happens mutually, and each of the partners, while simultaneously holding onto his own arguments weighs the counter arguments, it is finally possible to achieve – a common diction and a common dictum.' *Ibid.*, p. 387.

[64] See chapter 2, 'Socratic Knowing and Not-Knowing', in H. G. Gadamer, *The Knowledge of the Good in Platonic–Aristotelian Philosophy* (Yale University Press, 1986).

for learning. It is only through not-knowing, acknowledging one's limits and ignorance, that dialogue becomes necessary and one can ask a question and be open to the answers that may be heard in response: 'In order to be able to ask, one must want to know, and that means knowing that one does not know.'[65]

In conclusion then the philosophical hermeneutic answer to the question 'what is understanding?' starts with the recognition that understanding involves communication between self and other. Coming to an understanding requires an orientation towards otherness which is open to the possibility of experiencing 'truth' and to what the other may have to teach the self regarding the subject at hand. Understanding depicted as a fusion of horizons involves a conversational metaphor illustrating this condition. The hermeneutic model of understanding in conversation has the following consequences: first, humans as linguistically situated agents cannot attain perfect knowledge of ourselves or others. Whatever knowledge we possess is always informed by our prejudices; second, recognition of finitude, acknowledgement of one's own limits, allows for the possibility of learning, that others can communicate some truth to us; third, the act of understanding creates a realm of common meaning in so far as we have come to *share* an understanding. This is what happens when we have really understood something.

Phronesis

Philosophical hermeneutics is, Gadamer emphasises, a practical philosophy. Gadamer sees Aristotle's discussion of *phronesis*, or practical wisdom, as illustrative of a process of reasoning that is essentially hermeneutic. If Philosophical hermeneutics as a practical philosophy begins with an understanding of knowledge as interpretative, situated and intersubjective, then the concept of *phronesis* illustrates the understanding of reason as a contextualised practice. The virtues associated with Socratic conversation and a dialogic engagement with others in a spirit of openness are characteristic of the exercise of *phronesis*, according to Gadamer. Therefore in order to understand the nature of Philosophical hermeneutics it is necessary to understand Gadamer's interpretation of the meaning of *phronesis*. Furthermore, *phronesis* represents an alternative to a practice of emancipation dedicated towards the creation of a realm of suitable agents and has direct relevance to the task of developing a thin cosmopolitan community.

---

[65] Gadamer, *Truth and Method*, p. 363.

This section briefly outlines Gadamer's interpretation of the meaning of *phronesis* as a model of hermeneutic reasoning by way of a comparison with the practice of *techne*. The adoption of *phronesis* by Gadamer points to the fact that Philosophical hermeneutics shares with Habermasian critical theory the aim of combating the dominance of the technical instrumental (*techne*) model of reason. Technical instrumental rationality shares with the first model of understanding a relationship of inequality and objectification towards other agents. If dialogical understanding is the appropriate mode of understanding between linguistically constituted agents then *phronesis* or practical reasoning is the form of practice appropriate to philosophical hermeneutics. For this reason practical wisdom or *phronesis* can be best understood in the first instance in relation to *techne*.[66]

Phronesis can be distinguished from *techne* in several important ways: first, *phronesis* involves an understanding of the relationship between means and ends and between the right and the good which distinguishes it from technical or instrumental understandings of reason and practice. *Techne* involves a simple relation between means and ends: ends are set in advance and reason is used in determining how to apply established means to achieve them. In the social realm this corresponds to the idea that 'the good' can be determined in advance and in abstraction outside of the particular circumstance or community to whom it refers. In *phronesis* both means and ends are subjects of deliberation and specifically: '... what separates it fundamentally from technical expertise is that it expressly asks the question of the good too'.[67] The relationship between means and ends is also, therefore, more complex and bi-directional. For Gadamer *phronesis* represents '[M]oral knowledge ... of a special kind'[68] whereby knowledge of the good is not permanent or unchanging but always in process, in question and a matter of negotiation. A practice of *phronesis* suggests a conception of community in which the question of the good, 'How ought we to live?' is never finally answered and in which the common negotiation of this question itself helps to constitute the community.

---

[66] In Gadamer's engagement with Habermas it also became necessary to distinguish *phronesis* from Habermas' version of emancipation.

[67] Gadamer, *Reason in The Age of Science*, p. 93.

[68] *Truth and Method*, p. 322. 'Moral knowledge can never be knowable in advance like knowledge that can be taught. The relation between means and ends here is not such that one can know the right means in advance, and this is because the right end is not a mere object of knowledge either. There can be no anterior certainty concerning what the good life is directed towards as a whole.' *Ibid.*, p. 321.

Second: *phronesis* involves a less abstract conception of application than *techne*. Gadamer argues that in *techne* knowledge is applied to an object by an actor who is situated outside and who remains unaffected by this application. For Gadamer, *phronesis* involves applicability in the sense that to understand a particular situation, text, or law, for example one must have some idea of its applicability to oneself. The common element is that the interpreter of the law or the text is situated and must acknowledge their situatedness. Without such acknowledgement neither the text nor the law is properly understood. The understanding of the issue at hand, the text or the law, takes place within a context in which it is applied.

Third: where *techne* involves the gaining and application of abstract, universal knowledge outside of and not determined by its situation *phronesis* involves knowledge of particular situations and circumstances. Practical reasoning involves a different relationship between universal and particular. Where *techne* suggests that application is simply a moment of applying universal to particular *phronesis* suggests that application determines the meaning of both universal and particular. Practical wisdom cannot be defined in the abstract because there are no universal rules to guide it. According to Gadamer, Aristotle's discussion of *phronesis* in the *Nicomachean Ethics* illustrates the manner in which general or universal principles or commonly held values are mediated and applied in particular circumstances. In *phronesis* '. . . the meaning of any universal, or any norm, is only justified and determined in and through its concretization'.[69] In this sense practical wisdom is knowledge of what to do or how to act in a particular situation and involves understanding what is at stake in that situation 'of what it is right to do here and now'. If a text's meaning is only realised in its application, moral principles likewise are only realised in concrete situations. Therefore to act justly one needs to know the specifics of the situation. Gadamer argues that for those employing practical reasoning the question of justice '. . . is totally relative to the ethical situation in which we find ourselves. We cannot say in a general and abstract way which actions are just and which are not: there are no just actions "in themselves", independent of what the situation requires'.[70] The decision regarding how to interpret the universal in particular circumstances, the decision as to what a certain

[69] Gadamer, *Reason in the Age of Science*, p. 82.
[70] H. G. Gadamer, 'The Problem of Historical Consciousness', in P. Rabinow and W. M. Sullivan, *Interpretive Social Science: A Reader* (University of California Press, 1979), p. 140.

value might mean or be translated into in certain circumstances, is always open and is always defined, in part, by its application.

The best example that Gadamer gives of the type of reasoning involved in *phronesis* relates to jurisprudence and the application of the law. The role of the jurist according to Gadamer, does not require the mere technical application of pre-existing laws to a particular situation. The jurist instead must interpret a law in a particular case. This means that the meaning of the law must be decided in that case, which conversely means that the meaning of the law cannot be understood in advance or *in abstracto*, without its particular moment of application. Thus not only is the particular justice determined in the moment of application but so is the universal (law), or as Gadamer states, in practical reason 'the "universal" derives its determinacy by means of the singular'.[71] This is made most obvious in those instances where the law is seen to be outdated or rigidified, for example the case of rape in marriage. In such a situation the justice of the law is in doubt and is revealed to be so in a particular circumstance and the law (hopefully) is revised or rejected in order to make it more 'just'. Such a move requires reflection and practical wisdom and not merely technical, instrumental application of an existing knowledge. The jurist must reflect upon the justice of the law in light of the justice of a particular situation, such reflection is outside the ambit of a technical knowledge in which no reflection as to the good, or the just, or the universal, is conceded. However, the jurist must also have a knowledge of the ethos surrounding the law and the values of those affected by it. They must be 'placed' in the situation. It is in this sense that practical reasoning involves 'a question of perceiving what is at stake in a given situation'.[72]

Fourth: *techne* involves knowledge which can be taught and transferred simply from one actor to another. *Phronesis* on the other hand, requires wisdom and insight which can only be gained by experience. The practice of *phronesis* requires a degree of wisdom and perception, to know specifics or to be familiar with the letter of the law is not enough: 'it requires experience as well as knowledge'.[73] In particular, *phronesis* requires the exercise of judgement drawing upon a knowledge and understanding of a situation that excels what may simply be taught. Thus *phronesis* is also unlike *techne* in that it is not a knowledge that is readily

---

[71] Gadamer, *Reason in the Age of Science*, p. 81.
[72] Hoy, *The Critical Circle*, p. 58.   [73] *Ibid.*

transmittable or transferable. Rather than a skill to be taught, it is an awareness, or consciousness, that needs to be cultivated: 'It refers to a non-objectified and largely non-objectifiable accumulation of "understanding" which we often call wisdom.'[74]

However, it is important to emphasise that while *phronesis* is a form of knowledge it also places emphasis on 'not-knowing'. Knowledge, as Gadamer seems to understand it here, suggests both certainty and a lack of choice or deliberation. In contrast the actor informed by *phronesis* does not 'know' how to act in a certain situation, instead they use their experience, knowledge and judgement to come to *understand* a situation, to perceive what is at stake or at issue and to make a decision as to how to act or what is right to do. The actor does not 'know' how to act in advance but instead *gains* understanding of a situation.

Gadamer describes such not-knowing as the product of 'experience' (*Erfahrung*).[75] Experience is what enables and what comes from genuine understanding. Experience, for Gadamer, is knowledge of the limits of human capacities and powers in the face of finitude. Experience teaches us that we are not ultimately in control of our destiny: '[I]n experience man's powers to do and his planning reason come up against their limits.'[76] In the face of this we require not dogmatism and rigidity but openness to future experience. The experience of finitude results in an openness to new possibilities:

> Experience, in the true sense of its meaning, teaches one inwardly to know that he is not lord over time. It is the experienced man who knows the limits of all anticipation, the insecurity of all human plans. *Yet this does not render him rigid and dogmatic but rather open for new experience.*[77]

This openness generates a willingness to understand, to risk one's self, to acknowledge ignorance and to learn one's limits and expand them at the same time. The concept of experience suggests that in many ways the most important aspect of Gadamer's use of *phronesis* is its description of a process of understanding as a mediation between finitude and openness. This process of mediation is capable of delivering a more just and equal relationship to difference because of the crucial place of finitude.

---

[74] Palmer, *Hermeneutics*, p. 195.
[75] *Erfahrung* refers to the sense of being experienced rather than of having an experience (*Erlbenis*) mentioned above.
[76] *Ibid.*, p. 197.   [77] *Ibid.*, p. 195.

The practical and political manifestation of a hermeneutic inter-est in understanding and the endorsement of the Socratic model of conversation is the cultivation of a realm in which practical reasoning can occur. The account of understanding as dialogue between equal part-ners is situated within a practical philosophy that is oriented towards the achievement of understanding and solidarity. Practical reasoning requires the cultivation of solidarity between its members. However, de-spite the usual association of such appeals with a communitarian project Gadamer's account of practical reasoning buttresses and is consistent with the model of conversation but is, furthermore, the basis for the ex-pansion of that model to the globe. Because philosophical hermeneutics is universalistic in its scope its *telos* then is the creation of universal soli-darity as the necessary conditions for the exercise of practical reasoning. This dimension of philosophical hermeneutics will be returned to at the conclusion of this chapter.

Philosophical hermeneutics as practical philosophy: understanding and solidarity

The argument thus far has focused on the possibilities for understanding and conversation presented by the philosophical hermeneutic theory of understanding and how the model of conversation arising from this theory compares with discourse ethics. What has not been emphasised is that aspect of philosophical hermeneutics which is a more active en-dorsement of the expansion of community. This section suggests that in contrast to a primary concern with the communitarian goals of the transmission of tradition from one generation to the next, which in turn suggests a practice of coexistence, philosophical hermeneutics is equally concerned with the expansion of community.

The hermeneutic appeal to the horizon of tradition as the founda-tion of reason suggests an essentially communitarian project that is concerned chiefly with the practice of reasoning within an established tradition. The adoption of a practice oriented towards understanding encapsulated in the Aristotelian conception of *phronesis*, or practical wisdom as an alternative to a practice of emancipation is normally associated with communitarian thinkers such as Alasdair Macintyre.[78] Gadamer acknowledges that the Aristotelian term *phronesis* can be understood as a form of reasoning appropriate to a particular situation, that is, it is a contextual use of reason usually situated in a particular

---

[78] See A. Macintyre, *After Virtue* (University of Notre Dame Press, 1984, 2nd edn).

community or *nomoi*. Aristotle refers to this as the *Ethos* in which 'normative notions always stand under the presupposition of their normative validity'.[79] For Richard Bernstein, the appeal to *phronesis* buttresses the interpretation of philosophical hermeneutics as communitarian in so far as its exercise is restricted to a particular community in which norms are shared. He suggests that this announces the limits of the philosophical hermeneutic enterprise especially in the normatively fractured societies of the modern west.[80] However, his reading of philosophical hermeneutics unnecessarily restricts hermeneutic ambition and underestimates the significance of its claim to universality.

Philosophical hermeneutics it has already been noted is a practical philosophy. In later works, principally *Reason in the Age of Science,* Gadamer makes a distinction between *phronesis* as practical reason and hermeneutics, or understanding, as a practical philosophy. The key to this distinction lies in Gadamer's acknowledgement that for Aristotle *phronesis* occurs within the context of a 'thick' community or ethos. The thrust of Gadamer's work, however, is that hermeneutics and the practice that it entails should not be restricted in their ambition. The hermeneutic situation, that of interpretation and understanding in the context of linguistically carried tradition, is universal. Therefore the type of practice appropriate to it should not be restricted to or contained within traditions or a particular community but rather equally directed *across* them and to the creation of solidarity between them.[81]

---

[79] Gadamer, *Reason in the Age of Science*, p. 133.

[80] 'Given a community in which there is a living shared acceptance of ethical principles and norms, then *phronesis* as the mediation of such universals in particular situations makes sense. The problem for us today . . . is that we are in a state of great confusion and uncertainty . . . about what norms or "universals" ought to govern our practical lives . . . we are living in a time when the very conditions required for the exercise of *phronesis* . . . are themselves threatened or do not exist.' Bernstein, *Beyond Objectivism and Relativism,* p. 157. For Bernstein it seems that Habermas' critical theory provides the necessary next step and in that sense goes beyond philosophical hermeneutics.

[81] The term *phronesis*, therefore, does not capture the full range of Gadamer's approach to practice or to hermeneutics as a practical philosophy because of its association with the idea of established community. A more appropriate term to describe the broader concept of practice at work in philosophical hermeneutics is that of practical reasoning. Practical reasoning refers to a dimension of the 'hermeneutic claim to universality', to a form of practice that is not restricted to a particular 'ethos' but which nonetheless shares the general characteristics of *phronesis*. The distinction between *phronesis* and practical reasoning here serves to highlight the difference between a local instance of hermeneutic practice, *phronesis*, and a general one; practical reasoning.

The practical and political manifestation of a hermeneutic interest in understanding is the cultivation of a realm in which practical reasoning can occur. As Bernstein notes 'If we follow out the logic of Gadamer's own line of thinking, if we are really concerned with the "sense of what is feasible, what is possible, what is correct, here and now", then this demands that we turn our attention to the question of how we can nurture the type of communities required for the flourishing of *phronesis*'.[82] The pursuit of a realm in which practical reasoning can occur requires recognition and creation of a degree of solidarity between its members. Solidarity Gadamer argues '. . . is the decisive condition and basis of all social reason'.[83] This being the case the first task of philosophical hermeneutics is the pursuit of solidarity. Solidarity does not mean belonging to a fully-fledged, common historical tradition or 'thick' community. Rather, it is an expansion of the area of identification and of 'we' feeling, premised perhaps merely on acknowledgement of a shared historical predicament, situation or of a common future.[84] Gadamer argues that it resembles friendship, or the Greek notion of *synesis*: '. . . the person who is understanding does not know and judge as one who stands apart and is unaffected, but rather he thinks along with the other from the perspective of a specific bond of belonging, as if he too were affected'.[85] Philosophical hermeneutics sees understanding as both creating and requiring solidarity. The exercise of practical reasoning both relies on pre-existing solidarities or horizons and enables the creation of new ones. In other words, if we are to engage in universal conversation we require solidarity in order to allow communal reasoning to occur.

Because philosophical hermeneutics is universalistic in its claims this means that it is concerned ultimately with the creation of universal solidarity as the necessary conditions for the exercise of practical reasoning on a global scale. Indeed Gadamer is explicit in seeking to enable a universal realm of solidarity amongst different cultures of the world and he sees philosophical hermeneutics as precisely the philosophy appropriate to such a project.

---

[82] Bernstein, *Beyond Objectivism and Relativism*, p. 158.
[83] Gadamer, *Reason in the Age of Science*, p. 87.
[84] In his later writings Gadamer highlights the recognition of the environmental crisis as a possible source of new solidarities. For a discussion of this sense of 'we'-ness from a different perspective see M. Cochran, *Normative Theory in International Relations* (Cambridge, 1999).
[85] Gadamer, *Truth and Method*, p. 323.

Insofar as hermeneutics is more than a theory of the human sciences, it also has the human situation in the world in its entirety in view. Thus it must be possible to include different cultures, religions, etc. and their relations... And if we then have to become part of a new world civilisation, if this is our task, then we shall need a philosophy which is similar to my hermeneutics: a philosophy which teaches us to see the justification for the other's point of view and which thus makes us doubt our own.[86]

In other words, philosophical hermeneutics is consistent with the goal of seeking to re-create the achievements of the Aristotelian *polis* on the global scale. The necessity of solidarity, therefore, suggests that if there is a single *telos* to philosophical hermeneutics then it is the creation of universal solidarity through the expansion of the realm of understanding to include those inhabiting other traditions. Philosophical hermeneutics attempts to direct attention to existing solidarities and to awaken the possibility of new solidarities in which understanding and practical reasoning can operate: the task of hermeneutic practice is the pursuit of 'new normative and common solidarities that let practical reason speak again'.[87] It is oriented towards the creation and expansion of community in the 'thin' sense of solidarity or 'we' feeling and identification. The creation of new solidarities requires an effort to understand and, above all, engage in conversation. This, if anything, is the meaning of the metaphor of the fusion of horizons and forms the major ethical thrust of Gadamer's overall project.[88] Hermeneutic philosophy, therefore, gives rise to a practice of understanding defined in its most broad ambit.[89] The universality of the hermeneutic situation suggests the possibility of a 'reawakening consciousness of solidarity of a humanity that slowly begins to know itself as humanity, for this means knowing that it belongs

---

[86] H. G. Gadamer, 'Interview: The 1920s, 1930s and the Present: National Socialism, German History and German Culture', pp. 135–53 in Misgeld and Nicholson, *Hans-Georg Gadamer*, p. 152.

[87] Gadamer, *Reason in the Age of Science*, p. 87.

[88] For Gadamer this task is directed primarily against what he sees as the replacement of practical reason with *techne* in the political and social decision making of modern technological societies.

[89] In its ultimate form then Gadamer sees the task of hermeneutics as contributing to '... the rediscovery of solidarities that could enter into the future society of humanity'. *Ibid.*, p. 87. '... I ask whether in foreign civilisations that are now being drawn technologically over into the ambit of European–American civilization – China, Japan, and especially India – Much of the religious and social traditions of their Ancient cultures does not still live on under the cover of European furnishings and American jobs, and whether whatever lives on may not perhaps bring about an awareness out of necessity once again of new normative and common solidarities that let practical reason speak again.' *Ibid.*

together for better or worse and that it has to solve the problems of its life on this planet'.[90] In other words, one of the goals of philosophical hermeneutics is to increase human understanding and solidarity across the globe and across cultural divides as a contribution to the development of a thin cosmopolitan community.

The vision of cosmopolitanism that might be informed by philosophical hermeneutics is, therefore, obviously different from the thick vision presented by liberals, such as Beitz, where universality is privileged over particularity, homogeneity is endorsed and otherness denied. It also does not fall prey to the criticisms which often confront discourse ethics, including that conversation is necessarily oriented towards a final consensus and agreement. Instead philosophical hermeneutics suggests a multicultural cosmopolitanism in which, through conversation, various cultures and individuals learn to 'experience the other and the others, as the other of ourself, in order to participate with one another'.[91] A part of this of course is also to learn to 'live with the other, as the other of the other'.[92] It is this 'learning to live and participate' with others which is, for Gadamer, the meaning of solidarity.

The model of conversation in discourse ethics and philosophical hermeneutics

The account of conversation and understanding in philosophical hermeneutics outlined above bears many resemblances to a communitarian concern for the situatedness of concrete agents. Furthermore, it has been demonstrated that philosophical hermeneutics develops a philosophy of communication and a model of conversation from these premises that allows for an equal relationship through dialogue between concrete others. While the situatedness of agents in a philosophical hermeneutic conversation has been emphasised, it is necessary at this point to detail further the account of agency in philosophical hermeneutics in order to emphasise the radically *inclusive* dimension of hermeneutic understanding. In particular, having outlined the philosophical hermeneutic account of understanding as a dialogical process it is necessary to demonstrate to what extent and in which ways this model is less assimilatory and more inclusive than the Habermasian discourse

---

[90] *Ibid.*, p. 86.
[91] 'The Diversity of Europe: Inheritance and Future', pp. 221–36 in Misgeld and Nicholson, *Hans-Georg Gadamer*, p. 236.
[92] *Ibid.*, p. 234.

ethics model discussed in chapter 3. It was argued there that because discourse was directed exclusively towards questions of 'the right' and was informed by a *telos* of agreement on those principles which might be universalisable, it generated two possible types of exclusion: exclusion in relation to possible topics of conversation and exclusion in relation to the identity of the agents of conversation. The model of conversation and understanding provided by philosophical hermeneutics is less exclusionary and less assimilatory along both these axes.

It was also argued in chapter 3 that discourse ethics provided a potentially exclusionary account of conversation in so far as it emphasised that conversation concerning universalisable principles was possible only between postconventional agents. The account of understanding provided by philosophical hermeneutics and outlined above avoids this problem by emphasising the universality of understanding and simultaneously removing the opposition between reason and tradition. The issue of agency and inclusion is, therefore, predominantly a question about the possibility and nature of reasoning. Thus in order to understand more fully how philosophical hermeneutics provides a more inclusive account of conversation it is necessary to examine the concept of reason and its relation to agency.

Reason, understanding and agency in philosophical hermeneutics

The radically inclusive dimension of philosophical hermeneutics stems from, and is directly related to, its conception of reason as a capacity of language.[93] The model of conversation outlined above rests upon the hermeneutic claim to universality: all understanding is interpretation. The metaphor of the fusion of horizons depicted a universal property of *all* understanding through language. Therefore, the model of conversation presented by Gadamer is universal in that it is a property of all humans, or all who possess language. This model is also premised on an account of understanding in which 'reason' is a universal phenomenon by virtue of being a property of language. Understanding, or the fusion of horizons, is the achievement not only of tradition but of reason also. In philosophical hermeneutics reason is akin to understanding and understanding is essentially linguistic and universal. The philosophical

---

[93] It is important to stress here that the possession of reason itself is not the criterion for moral inclusion. Rather, reason allows conversation and the engagement with others, and conversation provides merely the means for this engagement and not the moral justification.

hermeneutic account of conversation can be seen to involve a radically inclusive account of conversation because in it reasoned conversation is a capacity of all linguistically constituted agents. In other words, in the Habermasian view rationality is equated with universal validity whereas Gadamer's equates reason with the universal capacity for understanding.

The key to Gadamer's account of reason can be found in the section of *Truth and Method* examining 'the prejudice of the enlightenment'. Many commentators imply that the strength of Gadamer's 'rehabilitation of prejudice' lies solely in its demonstration of the difficulty of rendering tradition completely transparent through reason. That is, the principle of effective history indicates the *difficulties* of pursuing enlightenment. For similar reasons, Gadamer's insights have also been used to buttress the argument that enlightenment is an ongoing and never-ending project.[94] However, there is another reading which demonstrates that the enlightenment's opposition between tradition and reason was ill-founded and misleading from the beginning. This critique also demonstrates the manner in which 'reason' is not exclusively a property of enlightened or, in Habermas' terms, postconventional agents.

Gadamer argues that the task of the enlightenment is to effect the replacement of tradition and authority with the sovereignty of reason. In doing so the enlightenment project became set in a dogmatic opposition to tradition and as a consequence established a false dichotomy between tradition and reason.[95] Gadamer's particular concern is to demonstrate that the enlightenment project maintained a prejudice against authority, or a prejudice against prejudice.[96] He aims to demonstrate the manner

[94] Gadamer asserts that reason 'would become vacuous and undialectical... if it tried to think the idea of a completed reflection, in which society would lift itself out of the continuing process of emancipation – the process of loosening itself from traditional ties and binding itself to newly constructed validities – so as to achieve an ultimate, free and rational self-possession.' *Truth and Method*, p. 571. See for instance Bernstein, *Beyond Objectivism and Relativism*, and also R. Devetak, 'The Project of Modernity in International Relations Theory', *Millennium*, 24. 1 (1995).

[95] Gadamer's account here shares something with Foucault's observation that the enlightenment generated a form of '... intellectual blackmail of "being for or against the enlightenment"'. M. Foucault, 'What is Enlightenment', in P. Rabinow, *The Foucault Reader* (London: Penguin, 1984), p. 45. Foucault's argument is that enlightenment, as a process, needs to be separated from the development of the specific ideology of eighteenth-century humanism. Separating them allows the articulation of a more general and less particular account in which it is no longer necessary to choose to be for or against enlightenment. In such an account it would be possible to partake in the enlightenment project without endorsing the particular conception of human subjectivity associated with humanism.

[96] It is this issue which formed the core of the so-called Habermas–Gadamer debate which is discussed in the next chapter.

in which tradition and prejudice provide the conditions of reasoning and could, therefore, generate knowledge and be the bearers of truth. Tradition and prejudice, he argues, are not in themselves illegitimate. Indeed reason is a property of tradition, it does not occur within a vacuum or have properties that can be divorced from the tradition from whence it came. As a result, reason and enlightenment do not stand in heroic opposition to tradition, but should be understood as the continuation of a tradition itself. Furthermore, the enlightenment conception of reason relies on unacknowledged authority. What makes something reasonable is not merely its ability to be persuasive, to make sense 'in itself', but what counts as persuasive always depends on the tradition. Tradition, therefore, is viewed as authoritative.[97]

Because Gadamer disputes the idea that reason can be persuasive in and of itself, divorced from its context, philosophical hermeneutics is sceptical towards the possibility of being moved by the unforced force of the better argument alone. The force of an argument will always be related to the horizons of meaning of those to whom it is addressed. Contra the enlightenment, or rather the critique of tradition, Gadamer argues that if all understanding occurs in the horizon of linguistic tradition then the knowledge gained by reason is also similarly situated. Reason and critique are, therefore, not objective but conditional, and as such, limited in their insights. The rehabilitation of prejudice and authority is not a rejection of critique but rather an acknowledgement of the historical and temporal conditions in which critique, as a form of understanding, takes place. Gadamer does not deny the necessity of reflection, only that reflection 'dissolves' tradition or equals emancipation. Philosophical hermeneutics, therefore, informs reason with a recognition of finitude.

Gadamer's aim is not to undermine the pursuit of freedom, enlightenment or the criticism of authority, merely to resist the opposition between them.[98] The point is, rather, that tradition is not merely a limitation of which we must be aware, but is also a positive, productive

---

[97] 'even in a state of perfect enlightenment we cannot ground everything we hold to be true through strict proof or conclusive deduction. Rather we must permanently rely on something and ultimately on someone, in whom we have trust. Our entire communicative life rests on this.' H. G. Gadamer, *The Enigma of Health* (Cambridge: Polity, 1996), p. 121. In this sense Gadamer seeks to address the impossibility of reason's grounding itself which was identified by Hutchings.

[98] Indeed Gadamer has been explicit in his defence of freedom. See for instance his comments on Hegel in Gadamer, *Reason in the Age of Science*, esp. p. 37 where he states 'The principle of freedom is unimpugnable and irrevocable. It is no longer possible for anyone still to affirm the unfreedom of humanity. The principle that all are free never

and creative element in the reasoning process. Thus it is possible to concur with Dallmayr's assessment that: '[U]nder these auspices, tradition and modernity are no longer binary opposites or poles of a historical trajectory, but rather ways of life intimately entwined with each other . . .'[99]

As a result, however, a philosophical hermeneutic position rejects the developmental account of reason, and the idea that the postconventional agent can be sharply differentiated from the conventional agent, provided by Habermas. According to Gadamer, change, reflection, critique (all exclusive properties of postconventional agents, according to Habermas) are themselves all part of the 'process' of tradition as a vehicle of understanding: '[T]radition is not the vindication of what has come down from the past but the further creation of moral and social life; it depends on being made conscious and freely carried on.'[100] In short in so far as philosophical hermeneutics rejects the opposition of enlightenment and tradition then it also rejects the opposition between the conventional and the postconventional agent. Thus, the qualities of reason and enlightenment, the ability to reflect, change and understand the self and others in a new light, which Habermas, Linklater and Benhabib ascribe to postconventional agents alone, are, in philosophical hermeneutics, qualities that characterise the process of understanding and the possession of linguisticality itself and which, therefore, are not restricted to enlightened individuals.[101] Where this account of agency differs from the description of the postconventional agent is that it drops the *telos* of universalisation. Because Gadamer does not insist on relating understanding to universalisation he does associate reflection, critique and change exclusively with the capacity to ask 'are these interpretations, norms, meanings, capable of being adopted by all?'

There is a crucial implication which follows from this argument: if understanding and reasoning are properties of all linguistically situated agents then conversation between concrete others does not require the creation of a community of similarly 'thickly' constituted agents, and

---

again can be shaken.' But Gadamer's understanding of freedom is not the same as Kant's and his philosophy can be understood as an attempt to avoid or at least relax the tension identified by Hutchings.

[99] Dallmayr, *Beyond Orientalism*, p. 168.   [100] Gadamer, *Truth and Method*, p. 571.

[101] If there is a moment of assimilation in philosophical hermeneutics then it occurs in the argument that all humans possess reason as a consequence of being linguistically and historically situated. Thus philosophical hermeneutics does not escape the assimilationist moment altogether. However, it can be argued that it reduces that moment significantly.

opens the conversation to more universal participation. The philosophical hermeneutic account of understanding suggests that if one collapses the distinction between reason and tradition then it is no longer possible to maintain a praxis dedicated solely to the removal of tradition and its replacement by reason. Philosophical hermeneutics provides a conception of reason as a value that cannot necessarily be associated with particular stages of human development nor with the capacity to think in terms of how the species as a whole might react to one's propositions. Reasoned conversation is a property of all humans who possess language. For this reason, Gadamer's account of conversation potentially encompasses the entire range of human subjects without necessarily implying that they all share the same identity or that conversation must be withheld until they have achieved the right level of competence.

This extension of the nature of the reasoned agent is only possible by rejecting the sharp distinction between reason and tradition and its correlate distinctions between public/private, right/good, moral/ethical realms. In so far as philosophical hermeneutics rejects the dichotomy between reason and tradition then it also rejects these dichotomies as well. These dichotomies all rest, in Habermas' work, on the possibility of securing a distinction between that which is rational, by which he means consistent with the unforced force of the better argument, and that which is not. If we remove this distinction then we create the possibility of more inclusive conversation by 'thinning out' or making the meaning of reason less determinate or fixed in its goals.

Philosophical hermeneutics seeks a universally inclusive conversation. It understands conversation as a universal capacity and because it relaxes the equation of reason with the possibility of universal acceptance it does not repeat the paradox of limitation and legislation in the same way. Philosophical hermeneutics does not stipulate the formal requirements of conversation, beyond a certain willingness or good faith, and so does not exhibit the same tension as discourse ethics between universal inclusion and the need to set criteria for communicative competence.

In sum then, it can be argued that Gadamer's entire thesis on the universality and nature of understanding, on the linguisticality of understanding, is an argument for the universality of 'reason' and reflection. Understanding, or the fusion of horizons through conversation, can and does occur in any human society or individual. The prerequisites for conversation are in a sense already in place by virtue of linguisticality.

This means that the philosophical hermeneutic conversation is less exclusive at the level of agency and that it is radically inclusive of all linguistically constituted beings capable of understanding. In a sense the philosophical hermeneutic account lowers or broadens the conditions of possibility for a universal communication community by extending and simultaneously 'thinning out' the conception of a reasoned agent. Philosophical hermeneutics rejects the implication that a reasoning agent is one solely oriented to universalism. Instead what is meant by a reasoned agent is extended to include, in principle, any linguistically constituted agent. In the philosophical hermeneutic account the other is understood as a linguistically constituted agent from the start and, therefore, inherently capable of understanding and conversation. It does not assume ignorance or 'immaturity' on the part of the other: '. . . the knowledge of practical wisdom is not a knowledge that is conscious of its ascendancy over the ignorant'.[102] Philosophical hermeneutics informed with a recognition of finitude on the part of the self, therefore, contains no presumption of superiority. This means that the orientation to the other is concerned from the beginning with the 'thinner' goal of understanding in conversation rather than emancipation. It is for this reason that philosophical hermeneutics is able to embody the relation of equality to otherness through a category of communication in a way that is unavailable to critical theory.

Having outlined the advantages of the philosophical hermeneutic conception of agency and how this makes for a radical inclusivity the task now is to compare the specifics of this model with discourse ethics in order to highlight the advantages of the former. It was argued in chapter 3 that discourse ethics relied too heavily on a model of conversation which emphasised questions of the right and the achievement of universalisation. The danger of this emphasis lay in the exclusion of certain topics from conversation, and, therefore, of the interests and concerns of particular concrete others. It was suggested, therefore, that a model of conversation was necessary which could be more inclusive of a wider range of concerns and agents. It was also suggested, following Benhabib, that attention should be directed towards the means and conditions whereby conversation itself, could continue. This section examines and demonstrates the manner in which the philosophical hermeneutic model of conversation preserves the strength and cancels

[102] *Ibid.*, p. 293.

the weaknesses of Habermasian discourse ethics and helps to provide a 'thinner', less assimilatory, more inclusive conception of cosmopolitan conversation.

In order to understand fully the differences between these two models it is useful to examine the common elements and points of convergence between the two approaches. The two models of conversation converge and share the following strengths. Conversation in both is directed towards something like Habermas' formulation of 'understanding oriented towards agreement'. Both philosophical hermeneutics and discourse ethics understand that in some ways a conversation has a goal of agreement at its end. The orientation towards agreement serves to motivate the conversation and to help provide momentum. More importantly both models suggest that understanding has been achieved when agreement is reached. However, significant differences over the meaning of agreement are also present and will be discussed below.

For both discourse ethics and philosophical hermeneutics the question of agreement is linked to the possibility of a certain type of truth.[103] Both models of conversation share the understanding that dialogue is oriented towards truth to the degree that it is about something more than access to the other's self-understanding. In both accounts the notion of truth functions as a means of escaping from the psychologistic functions of understanding and as a means of enabling reflection on oneself and the other. This concept of truth also has a critical function and works as a kind of regulator orienting the conversation to the possibility of learning and away from merely the transmission of existing knowledge and taken for granted understandings. It also serves a regulative function preventing a conversation from slipping into a pure relativistic contest.[104] In discourse ethics this takes the form of a search for universalisable principles determined by a willingness to be guided by the unforced force of the better argument whereas in philosophical hermeneutics truth comes into play in relation to the concept of the *Sache* and in the possibility of learning from the other. In discourse ethics the

---

[103] For Habermas moral rightness is analogous though not identical with truth. See J. Habermas, *Moral Consciousness and Communicative Action* (Cambridge: Polity, 1990), pp. 58–60.

[104] This is an important qualification which Linklater has emphasised in his latest writings, where he is at pains to point out the open-ended and possibly inconclusive nature of genuine dialogue and which serves to bring the approaches of critical theory and philosophical hermeneutics closer to each other. See Linklater, *The Transformation of Political Community*.

participants are guided in their search for universalisable principles by the unforced force of the better argument. In philosophical hermeneutics it is the possibility that the other may be capable of revealing a truth to us in relation to a subject matter of conversation which enables us to treat them as equal.

In addition, and as a result of a commitment to truth, both require a recognition of finitude in so far as they require an openness towards the other participants in dialogue and towards the possibility of learning from them. The possibility of learning from the other involves recognition that the other, like the self, could articulate a certain but different truth and, therefore, could be seen as both equal and different. Linklater for instance emphasises that crucial to discourse ethics is an openness amongst the participants in a rational discourse to the possibility that they can learn from the other. For those engaged in discourse ethics: 'there is no a priori certainty as to who shall learn from whom'.[105] This openness implies a willingness to reflect upon the self and to change one's self understandings or beliefs in the light of new or different interpretations and knowledge. The possibility of understanding as depicted in the metaphor of the fusion of horizons is also contingent upon the possibility of change and transposition from one's own horizon. Change is a necessary part, or risk, of understanding. Both philosophical hermeneutics and discourse ethics, therefore, hold in common the argument that dialogue can only occur when the participants are willing to risk themselves and learn from others: '... dialogue requires that agents are prepared to question their own truth claims, respect the claims of others and anticipate that all points of departure will be modified in the course of dialogue'.[106]

Furthermore, discourse ethics and philosophical hermeneutics agree that this type of conversation is to be distinguished from a strategic conversation in which the aim is to achieve knowledge of the other in order to control them (as for instance in the example of Cortês). Likewise both models distinguish a conversation oriented towards mutual comprehension and agreement from an argument in which the purpose is to prove 'oneself' right and win over the other. It is not the purpose of conversation to 'convert' the other to one's cause or position. Instead it is a process of mutual engagement and exchange oriented towards mutual

[105] A. Linklater, 'Citizenship and Sovereignty in the Post-Westphalian State', *European Journal of International Relations*, 2. 1, March (1996), 77–103, p. 86.
[106] *Ibid.*, p. 87. Linklater also adds the rather thick rider that this requires participants to be guided by the unforced force of the better argument.

enlightenment in which all can learn. In this respect the other is seen as a dialogic equal in discourse ethics and philosophical hermeneutics and both, therefore, involve a high degree of communication.

However, despite these commonalities, substantial differences remain over the exact meaning and emphases placed on all these common elements, in particular, the concepts of agreement, truth and learning.[107] These differences in turn can be traced to the more significant point of departure regarding the ultimate purpose or *telos* of conversation. As a result of being motivated by the goal of understanding philosophical hermeneutics is able to preserve some of the strengths and cancel some of the weaknesses of the discourse ethics model. Philosophical hermeneutics preserves the strengths of the discourse ethics model in those areas outlined above where there is a commonly held position. Philosophical hermeneutics preserves the strengths of conversation oriented towards truth, of openness towards others, of the possibility of agreement, and on the goal of universal inclusion. However, it cancels out some of the weaknesses of discourse ethics on these issues as well. In particular, three areas can be identified in which the goal of understanding provides a more inclusive and less exclusionary approach to conversation: the goal of inclusion, the right versus good, openness to others and the possibility of learning.

Superficially at least philosophical hermeneutics and discourse ethics share the belief that conversation requires 'understanding directed towards agreement'. However, further examination reveals more profound differences on the significance of agreement and its relation to conversation. In particular, the Habermasian model involves a thicker and

---

[107] Both approaches share a view that open dialogue and the 'reversibility' of perspectives are essential to being open to the other's point of view. In discourse ethics this was classified as being open to the possibility of learning and was the achievement of the post-conventional agent. However, such learning, for Habermas and apparently for Linklater, is really only of one type: learning regarding that which can be universalised. Linklater gives further support to this when he argues that discourse should proceed in the attempt to assess which principles, both in the west and in other societies, have transcultural validity or appeal. This search would involve a conversation which sought to discover only those beliefs in other cultures which are capable of universalisation. These appear to constitute a predisposition towards what counts as learning in this situation. In this fashion, and because it asserts that all normative claims seek universal redemption, discourse ethics appears to discount the very possibility of 'particular' learning. Discourse ethics, therefore, delimits *in advance* the possible scope for understanding and, therefore, for hearing the voice of the other. The self is closed off to the particularity of the other and their truth because the other becomes merely a source of verification (or not) of universalisable norms. Learning for philosophical hermeneutics is not associated with a developmental process as it is for Habermas and Linklater. Instead it merely involves acquiring an awareness of different possibilities of being and a gaining of experience (*Erfahrung*).

more specific conception of agreement than does philosophical hermeneutics which in turn stems from a significantly different under-standing of the purpose of conversation. For Habermas 'understanding oriented towards agreement' is understood to mean that conversation is oriented towards rational agreement on universal principles of moral life. Discourse ethics argued that norms were only valid if they were consented to by all those affected. The purpose of conversation then is to secure the consent and agreement of genuine agents to universal principles.

In contrast to this, philosophical hermeneutics presents a model of conversation oriented towards the much thinner goal of 'understand-ing'. To engage in 'understanding oriented towards agreement' does not necessarily mean to be engaged in a discursive test of universal va-lidity claims, rather, it can also mean something like coming to share a particular understanding of the *Sache*. Agreement means simply that the self can 'understand' the other's point of view and has success-fully 'stood in the other's shoes'. As was argued above Gadamer states that when understanding occurs it is always something like agreement. What he means here is that one agrees with another in so far as one can comprehend their position and is able to say, 'yes I see what you mean and why you mean it and how you have come to see things this way'. As Georgia Warnke notes '[W]e need not ultimately agree with the text or text analogue we are studying. It may not be an option for us to adopt Zande beliefs in witchcraft . . . But Gadamer's contention is that whatever the outcome of conversation – the result is an achieve-ment of understanding . . .'[108] This is the sense in which philosophical hermeneutics perceives understanding oriented towards agreement. To be able to recognise that the other is comprehensible is not the same as being able to come to share their opinion, in the sense of saying, 'yes I see what you mean and I believe that you are right and I shall adjust my opinions/beliefs/practices accordingly'. Philosophical hermeneutics depicts understanding oriented toward agreement in the first of these two senses, discourse ethics depicts the second type of agreement. How-ever, in both there are other possible outcomes, or rather neither pre-clude the possibility of either agreement or disagreement. Nonetheless

---

[108] G. Warnke, 'Walzer, Rawls and Gadamer: Hermeneutics and Political Theory', in K. Wright (ed.), *Festivals of Interpretation: Essays on Hans-Georg Gadamer's Work* (Albany: SUNY, 1990), p. 156. It is important to emphasise that to have agreed or understood in this sense is to have 'experienced' (*erlebnis*) the other's position or horizon and not merely to have recovered their self-understanding.

it is the *possibility* of agreement in philosophical hermeneutics which constitutes an acknowledgement of the other's equality. The other can be understood and agreed with, in so far as they can be comprehended, without necessarily being understood as revealing knowledge which is *universally* valid or of significance. As Warnke argues, understanding is a matter of 'expanding our ideas, altering our practices and, in general, educating ourselves. There is no need to think that there is only one way to realise these interpretive aims.'[109] Therefore there is no guarantee that having understood another's position in a fusion of horizons one will necessarily agree that their propositions can be universalised. Rather it simply means that having engaged with another in conversation one has recognised them as equal by seeking to understand their position and understand them and allowing their experience of truth to speak to us.

As a result, if for discourse ethics the *telos* of conversation is a consensus between postconventional agents regarding universalisable principles, then for philosophical hermeneutics the purpose or *telos* of conversation is simply that of hermeneutic *understanding* in its broadest sense. Philosophical hermeneutics eschews the task of determining universal principles which should govern conversation and in this sense it is not a purely procedural account of conversation as the means of determining the right. Philosophical hermeneutics does not understand the task of philosophy as defining procedures prior to dialogical engagement.[110] Rather the task of philosophical hermeneutics has been to reflect on what understanding means and what is involved in coming to an understanding. Conversation is oriented towards achieving a fusion of horizons between the different participants in relation to the subject matter of conversation. In philosophical hermeneutics conversation is the means of reaching an understanding on a matter of common interest or concern, in the process the other is seen as a dialogical equal through having their truth claims recognised. Unlike discourse ethics

---

[109] Quoted in Hoy and McCarthy, *Critical Theory*, p. 261.

[110] It may well be argued that it is precisely this refusal to address procedural, institutional and societal conditional questions that represents the principal weakness of philosophical hermeneutics. It is not the aim here to develop an account of the conditions under which this type of communication may flourish. And it may well be that were it to do so then philosophical hermeneutics would suffer from the same problems that accrue to critical theory. If a philosophical hermeneutic account were to address these particular questions then it would invariably be drawn into describing a thicker form of community and a thicker form of praxis. This is a very important question but not the concern of this book. The goal here is to provide a philosophical account of what conversation and communication should involve in terms of a model of conversation.

the philosophical hermeneutic conversation is not overdetermined by the goal of universalisation as understood by Habermas and does not contain the *telos* of developing universally justified, valid, regulative and legislative norms. The philosophical hermeneutic conversation is not a model of justice understood in the strict Kantian sense but it is a model of conversation which is nonetheless capable of delivering justice understood as recognition. While it does not rule out the possibility of universal agreement, such agreement is not the measure by which conversation is assessed. It is this difference which makes the most difference and which leads to the less assimilatory elements of philosophical hermeneutics. By eschewing the Habermasian goal of justice defined deontologically, as the definition of what everybody ought to do, philosophical hermeneutics avoids those assimilative tendencies of the discourse ethics model outlined in the previous chapter while at the same time remaining committed to the values of freedom and equality.

As a result of its *telos* of understanding philosophical hermeneutics does not restrict either the tasks or the topics of conversation. This thin version of cosmopolitanism informed by philosophical hermeneutics differs from Habermasian discourse ethics in that a conversation modelled on its insights is one in which deliberation about the meaning of the good life can occur. A conversation informed by philosophical hermeneutics does not rule out questions of the right and the achievement of universalisation but neither does it restrict agents in their enquiries or the subject matters of conversation. Conversation involves discussing whatever it takes to come to an understanding with each other. As a result the philosophical hermeneutic model does not restrict conversation exclusively to matters of right. Questions of the good life are up for discussion as well as questions of the right because both are required to have a complete engagement with the other. Because motivated by the goal of understanding a conversation informed by philosophical hermeneutics does not need to enforce a separation between those matters which are public and those which are merely private.

In this sense the philosophical hermeneutic model preserves the emphasis on the abstract other while being more inclusive of concrete otherness. It is abstract in that it is oriented towards the possibility of understanding *any* and all linguistically constituted agents and yet concrete because understanding requires an engagement with all the particularity of agents and their concerns, their horizon of meaning. Or rather philosophical hermeneutics acknowledges that conversation cannot be restricted to questions of the right, that it is not possible to maintain that distinction when it comes to understanding and, therefore, understanding involves discussion of the good. By dropping the requirement that conversation can only concern 'questions of right' philosophical hermeneutics opens up the possible topics and purposes of conversation allowing a more complete and overall more inclusive and less assimilatory engagement between participants.

An interesting observation can be made against the theories of the right at this juncture. By conceiving itself as a discourse concerned with mediating between conflicts of interests the impartialist position demonstrates characteristics of both assimilationist and coexistence categories. The assimilatory characteristics of the goal of impartiality were demonstrated in chapter 2. Where impartialist accounts display elements of a coexistence approach it is to the extent that the goal of mediation of *interests* effectively excludes the identity of participants and more importantly the *content* or *truth* of their conception of the good from the realm of discussion. In other words, the other is engaged with only in so far as their actions, beliefs and so on have an effect upon the self.

The philosophical hermeneutic account of conversation avoids both these problems because it is not restricted to a purely procedural role. Because it eschews the supposedly neutral position of theories of the right it paradoxically allows for more just relationships between 'others' in a *thinner* conception of community. If one understands conversation as concerned not just with the mediation of interests and the resolution of conflicts but with addressing the question of what is the good life, or better still, how shall we live, then the other is seen as a partner who participates with oneself in a common project. Under these circumstances the purpose of conversation also includes the building of solidarity rather than the mediation of interests alone. From this perspective the other is seen as participating with oneself in a mutual task of comprehension and understanding and, consequently, one is more truly open to the other and what they have to say.

The discussion of the good life in this form of thin cosmopolitanism is not a 'requirement': it does not demand that 'internal' conceptions of the good life must be held up for universal approval. Rather a conception of community informed by philosophical hermeneutics sees the cosmopolitan conversation itself, whether it be limited to principles of coexistence or thicker principles of the right, as discussion regarding the good life (understood as 'how shall we live'). An approach informed by philosophical hermeneutics does not restrict discussion of the good life to domestic politics. Furthermore, it is not concerned to provide one thick universal account of the good life, rather, like poststructuralism, it refuses a hard and fast distinction between internal and external accounts.

In addition, because philosophical hermeneutics is expressly committed to conversation about the good it is consequently less likely to 'smuggle in' such conceptions unreflectively or to present itself as an account of 'the moral position'. Emphasising questions of the good also suggests that the degree to which any individual or society wishes to enter into thicker relations or converge upon more substantive conceptions of the good life and the right are themselves a part of the discussion.

The conception of community at work in philosophical hermeneutics is thicker than some and amounts to a substantive preference for one form of life over another. It is not possible to deny that what Gadamer offers us is something like a different conception of the good, as a discursive community. Philosophical hermeneutics is as affected by its prejudices as any perspective. Philosophical hermeneutics does privilege a particular form of life by suggesting that some modes of reasoning and action are inappropriate. Thus dialogical understanding is privileged over its alternatives such as *techne*. However, the model of conversation presented by Gadamer allows for a more thorough contestation and reflection on its prejudices by not over-determining the content and purpose of conversation. In addition, the project of being inclusive of difference rests itself upon a thick and universalistic claim that diversity is good and difference demands respect and ethical treatment. Furthermore, the model of conversation being developed here is based on the values of equality and freedom and seeks to encourage the exercise of both. It can however, be argued that the emphasis on finitude is intended to work as a brake and a corrective to the assimilative moment in Gadamer's conception of the good, thereby rendering it more open, inclusive and 'thinner'.

Finally, in so far as it is impossible to reconcile completely the goals of community and difference, that it is impossible to conceive of a community defined in any way, without it being, in some sense, thick or substantive, then philosophical hermeneutics does not escape this tension as the brief discussion in the preceding paragraphs demonstrates. However, the point then is not to deny the situatedness and particularity of the hermeneutic account of community and conversation but rather to make that account as thin as possible in order to be as inclusive as possible.

However, if the philosophical hermeneutic conversation can be distinguished from the model of conversation developed by critical theory as argued above it nonetheless shares the goal of inclusion of 'the other' in conversation. If conversation and understanding are human capacities then, from a philosophical hermeneutic perspective, there is no reason, at this level, to exclude any such being from the realm of dialogue. However, while Aristotle's discussion of *phronesis* is, Gadamer suggests, the type of reasoning and practice that is appropriate to a hermeneutic consciousness, practical reasoning is not restricted to those who have cultivated a hermeneutic consciousness and does not require the existence of a community of similar individuals in order to be exercised. Philosophical hermeneutics, therefore, does not *necessarily* involve a praxis oriented towards the expansion of the realm of individuals who share the consciousness of finitude or effective historical consciousness. Practical reasoning does not require a community of hermeneuts in order to function. It is this dimension which contributes to its radical inclusiveness.

Furthermore, the philosophical hermeneutic emphasis on understanding directs attention to the role of conversation in *building* community and solidarity which is largely absent from critical theory and poststructuralist thought. This emphasis sits in contrast to the deontological emphasis of discourse ethics with its stress on the regulative, legislative mode of conversation. As Habermas himself notes the deontological model itself assumes a certain level of solidarity and trust between participants.[111] Philosophical hermeneutics in contrast is consistent with the possibility and pursuit of consensus but is motivated by the goal of understanding and creation of shared horizons rather than exclusively the goal of determining the 'right'. Therefore the philosophical hermeneutic model preserves the goal of inclusion, the essential moral insight of discourse ethics, based on the recognition of others as ends in themselves, while cancelling the pure *telos* of establishing universal validity. Philosophical hermeneutics remains consistent with the principles of inclusion central to discourse ethics, because no agent is *a priori* ruled out of conversation, but this goal is not subordinated to the goal of universal validity. Philosophical hermeneutics is consistent with a vision of conversation which does not require the principles of universalisation (U) in order to guarantee discursive inclusion (D).

[111] See discussion of this in the next chapter.

In addition, the dimension of Gadamer's conceptions of practical reasoning which focuses on the relationship between means and ends provides this form of praxis with a more flexible approach to questions of community and in particular, the nature of cosmopolitanism than is suggested by the deontological Kantianism of discourse ethics. Because practical reasoning involves a conception of practice in which means and ends are both reflected on it, therefore, suggests that both the means for pursuing cosmopolitanism and the form of cosmopolitanism itself must and can be subjected to reflection in any given situation. Thus cosmopolitanism can only be defined in its actualisation. Rather than defining in advance a form of cosmopolitanism in which rules are laid down in advance a practice informed by philosophical hermeneutics suggests a flexibility when it comes to the forms that cosmopolitanism will take in specific situations. This includes whether or not involvement in the cosmopolitan project itself will be desirable or attainable in any given situation. This is especially so in the case of a cosmopolitanism concerned with the idea of justice to the radically different. Thicker forms of moral agreement and solidarity may come about as a result of conversation but the decision to proceed on such conversation is itself to be decided not philosophically but discursively. Philosophical hermeneutics preserves the possibility of reaching further and creating a more substantive, 'thick', conception of community without legislating or requiring that eventuality.

Finally, from this position the likelihood of failure in achieving universal consent at any given time does not prevent those concerned with acting justly towards others from acting in a manner consistent with a thin cosmopolitanism (that is in a conversational mode oriented towards the possibility of understanding). The hermeneutic account of practical reasoning provides some guidance as to how to act morally when the 'thick' cosmopolitan community has not been achieved. For this reason the greatest advantage of practical reasoning lies in the fact that it has no pre-determined ends in relation to otherness, other than understanding. Thus it has no plans upon the other nor any prescription laid out in advance which dictates the encounter. If the ends of conversation or engagement are determined in advance then the voice of the other is unable to get itself heard and their equality denied. Thus, for example, confronted with individuals who resist or do not share the same consciousness, an approach informed by philosophical hermeneutics is capable of maintaining a just relationship. Instead it merely asks the question again: what does justice mean in this particular situation?

Faced with the 'other' who resists or does not share its consciousness or understanding, a position informed by philosophical hermeneutics is able to keep the question of justice open and in dialogue. Because of this it is possible to remain open to what the other has to say because the other's difference does not prevent them from being perceived as an equal in conversation. This account resists the traditional dynamic of IR in which the lack of a thick homogenous cosmopolitan community can only mean the perpetuation of exclusive and self-interested communities and, instead, contemplates the nature of moral action in the absence of a universal kingdom of ends. In the absence of a final universal consensus or completed community of emancipated beings there is instead the task of living together in difference, a task which requires a mediation of means and ends, universal and particular and the pragmatic development of wisdom and understanding in which differences and agreements are worked through.

Conclusion

This chapter has demonstrated the position of philosophical hermeneutics on knowledge and conversation. The argument made for philosophical hermeneutics can be summarised as follows. A hermeneutic conversation provides a relationship to otherness that is concerned with understanding. It argued that the concept of conversation as one oriented towards truth and understanding provides an orientation towards the other which neither denies difference nor assimilates it. In particular, it was argued that the hermeneutic model of a conversation provided an account of communication that recognised equality without it imposing identity and that recognised difference without it degenerating into inferiority. In this sense, it was argued that Gadamer's formulation of conversation as an engagement with otherness directed by an openness to 'truth', provided a model of a relationship to difference that was able to escape the categories of assimilation and coexistence. It depicted the relationship between self and other as a relationship between equals oriented towards mutual understanding and towards the truth of a subject over which they are engaged. The motivation for and condition of this conversation is provided by human finitude. Thus, the hermeneutic concept of the self–other relation is informed and fundamentally structured by the recognition of finitude. The search for understanding does not rule out the search for universal consensus or agreement and it is possible that conversation oriented towards understanding may identify universally acceptable positions. However, a philosophical hermeneutic approach suggests that it is dangerous and prescriptive to assume that this is the ultimate, or even the initial, purpose of conversation. Instead, conversation must begin *at least* with understanding, and only then move on to thicker goals, in light of the achievements of understanding. Because the goal of philosophical hermeneutics is understanding, this involves both the inclusion of other but also the creation of new shared meaning horizons. In this sense then the possibility of creating universal conceptions of both the right and the good is left open. The creation of a single universal horizon, while not necessarily likely, is possible. Its creation however, can not be considered as merely the creation of a universal community of right but also the creation of a universal realm of solidarity which preserves distinctions between 'us' and 'them' while simultaneously creating solidarity amongst 'us' all.

5 Philosophical hermeneutics and its critics

The principle that all are free can never again be shaken.[1]

The account presented in the previous chapters argued for the principal contributions of philosophical hermeneutics to the development of a thin cosmopolitanism. However, philosophical hermeneutics is not without its critics, nor its own limitations and exclusions. Therefore, in order to build the case for a philosophical hermeneutic approach it is necessary to engage with these critics. Out of this engagement a better sense of the requirements of a cosmopolitanism encompassing the principles of communication can be determined and the case for a thin cosmopolitanism made stronger. This chapter examines the principal criticisms of philosophical hermeneutics and uses them to help formulate a more complete account of conversation.

The most relevant criticisms made against philosophical hermeneutics generally fall into two types. Perhaps the most longstanding, and common, of these arguments is that philosophical hermeneutics is essentially conservative. This charge is usually, but not exclusively, made from a critical theoretical perspective. Critical theorists also often make the related assertion that philosophical hermeneutics suffers from a form of philosophical idealism and is dismissive of, or blind to, material conditions which contribute to the formation of horizons of meaning. Philosophical hermeneutics has also been subjected to criticism from poststructuralists such as Jacques Derrida who charge that its arguments are embedded in a metaphysics of the will and, more importantly, that it privileges continuity over discontinuity and closure over disruption.

[1] H. G. Gadamer, *Reason in the Age of Science* (Cambridge: MIT Press, 1981), p. 37.

180

This chapter engages with the relevant dimensions of these claims, beginning with critical theory, before proceeding to those problems identified by Derrida.[2] The chapter concludes by rearticulating a model of conversation and an understanding of community which is informed by philosophical hermeneutics, critical theory and poststructuralism and identifying those elements which might form the basis of a common perspective.

Philosophical hermeneutics and critical theory

Perhaps the most persistent and detailed criticisms of philosophical hermeneutics have come from critical theory. Of course, the most important and sustained of these were made by Habermas in the context of what has now become known as the Habermas/Gadamer debate which followed the publication of *Truth and Method*.[3] There followed an exchange in which the most important similarities and differences between philosophical hermeneutics and critical theory were clarified. At the same time the differences between them came to be seen as less stark than first suggested. There is no need or space to recount this debate in full. Instead it is useful to highlight the most important issues around which the debates revolved and to highlight those criticisms of Gadamer's position which seem to have survived the debate.

From the perspective of Habermasian critical theory philosophical hermeneutics opens itself to the charge of conservatism because of its emphasis on effective history, the authority of tradition and its appeal to *phronesis*. From this point of view Gadamer's rehabilitation of 'tradition and prejudice', and his argument that all understanding occurs within tradition, dismisses the possibility of critical reflection. If all

---

[2] The discussion in chapters 3, and 4, has focused on the 'Foucauldian' stream of poststructuralist thought which has been evident in international relations. The introduction of Derrida at this juncture serves to bring in another dimension of poststructuralist thought and one which provides for a deeper engagement with the concerns of philosophical hermeneutics. In addition, as the focus here is on the limitations of philosophical hermeneutics it is necessary to address the concerns arising at its 'origins' so to speak, i.e. that is in the philosophical realm. In this realm Habermas is the best representative of critical theory and Derrida of poststructuralism.

[3] For details of this debate see. J. Habermas, 'A Review of Gadamer's *Truth and Method*' (trans. T. McCarthy and F. Dallmayr), in B. R. Wachterhauser, *Hermeneutics and Modern Philosophy* (Albany: SUNY, 1986). J. Habermas, 'The Hermeneutic Claim to Universality', in M. Gibbons, *Interpreting Politics*, pp. 174–202, and H. G. Gadamer, 'Reply to My Critics', in H. Bleicher, *Contemporary Hermeneutics: Figures and Themes* (London: Routledge and Kegan Paul, 1980), also chapters 1 and 2 of H. G. Gadamer, *Philosophical Hermeneutics* (Berkeley: University of California Press, 1977).

understanding is interpretation in the sense that Gadamer means it then critical reflection which seeks to stand back from tradition and to offer rational criticism of that tradition is impossible. Critical reflection appears to be nothing other than the 'prejudice' of enlightenment, one prejudice among many. For Habermas, critical reflection achieves its power precisely because it is able to stand back from prejudices and subject them to rational critique, but such a practice is denied by a philosophical hermeneutic starting point. According to Habermas, 'Gadamer's prejudice for the rights of prejudices certified by tradition denies the power of reflection.'[4] For Habermas this collapse of reflection and tradition means that philosophical hermeneutics reduces reason to a context-specific faculty and denies its transcultural validity.[5] As a result of this dimension of the universality of hermeneutics, Habermas implies that it must necessarily privilege the status quo as it seeks to legitimise current prejudices only by reference to the authority of tradition.

According to Habermas, by restricting knowledge to 'everyday language' (by which he means nonscientific language) Gadamer denies reflexivity. Habermas argues that Gadamer is positing an opposition of truth to method. That is, he thinks Gadamer wants to deny the possibility that a vocabulary constituted outside everyday language, such as a technical or scientific one, can produce reflections [truth]. Truth for Gadamer can only occur within the tradition [of everyday communicative experience], which is inaccessible by this type of distantiation. This is a problem for Habermas because the linguistic tradition will be a product of power and evinces distorted understandings. In other words, tradition is also a source of untruth. So, for Habermas, the level of hermeneutic understanding, because it occurs in everyday language, is essentially pre-reflexive, pre-theoretical and, therefore, uncritical. In contrast, Habermas argues reason 'proves itself in being able to reject the claim of tradition . . . Authority and knowledge do not converge.'[6] In becoming reflective, hermeneutics steps out of tradition and becomes something else. In doing this, in objectifying or distancing itself, it becomes a social science, indeed it becomes critical theory. Critical theory, therefore, draws upon the reflective capacity of reason and rationality to

---

[4] Habermas, 'A Review ', p. 269.
[5] In this Habermas seems to associate philosophical hermeneutics with 'deep contextualists' such as MacIntyre and Rorty. See J. Habermas, *Justification and Application* (Cambridge: Polity, 1993), esp pp. 101–5.
[6] Habermas, 'A Review', p. 269.

define itself and defend its goal of enlightenment whereby it constitutes itself as an emancipatory theory.

Habermas later drew upon the reflective capacity of reason to establish the categories of agency drawn from Kohlberg. The distinction Habermas drew between a critical theory and philosophical hermeneutics parallels the distinction between the conventional and the postconventional consciousness. It is only the postconventional consciousness which is able to reflect fully upon and transcend their context and agree to be guided by universalisable principles. As was noted in the previous chapter, Gadamer's collapsing of the distinction between reason and tradition also meant a rejection of the distinction between the conventional and postconventional agent.

Furthermore, Habermas has also claimed that it is rationality alone which provides the necessary universality with which to understand and develop consensus between different traditions. The universal fusion of horizons, implied by Gadamer's metaphor, can only be achieved in reference to some regulative ideal, such as rationality or the idea of the unforced force of the better argument.[7] Therefore, philosophical hermeneutics is necessarily conservative and not up to the task of developing a universal communication community.

However, as the discussion in the previous chapter would suggest Habermas' reading of Gadamer is, at least in part, misguided because it misunderstands Gadamer's claims in relation to reason and understanding. In this debate, Habermas accused Gadamer of defending tradition over reason and of denying reason its emancipatory power. Gadamer defended the claim that what counted as reasonable rested on an authority other than its own which is handed down from the past in the form of tradition. What Gadamer did not claim was that reason necessarily sits in opposition to tradition. Nor did Gadamer deny the desirability of reflection, or presuppose the inherent legitimacy of any particular aspect of tradition. Tradition is exposed to scrutiny through the encounter with the other and this encounter in turn helps to reveal the limitations of tradition, or in Gadamer's words, to reveal which prejudices are legitimate and which are not. In other words, Gadamer's understanding of tradition does not imply that any given aspect of tradition is necessarily legitimate, but that any test of its legitimacy can also only come about in the context of the language which tradition itself has bequeathed. That language however, is not necessarily the same, as it is through the

---

[7] See Habermas, *Justification and Application*, p. 105.

encounter with differences that the language is changed. Thus, rather than underestimating the power of reflection, Gadamer seeks merely to counter what he sees as the enlightenment's over-estimation of reason's ability to see through its own prejudices.

If Gadamer is correct, then it is true that there is nothing in philosophical hermeneutics which rejects critique, or the use of reason to understand and engage with prejudices. As Bernstein has put it, 'every encounter with tradition is intrinsically critical'.[8] Gadamer simply offers a different description of what it is that occurs when we have claimed to understood something, and a different interpretation of what it is to 'reason'. In this sense, philosophical hermeneutics is not necessarily conservative. Indeed philosophical hermeneutics can only be understood as *necessarily* conservative if a strict division between modern and conservative, between enlightenment and tradition, or conventional and postconventional agency is enforced. However, it is precisely such a strict division that Gadamer is engaged in undermining.

Nonetheless, Habermas has succeeded in pointing out some other important omissions or apparent blindnesses in Gadamer's philosophy, which suggest some of its limitations. These limitations however, are neither fundamental nor fatal, but they do bring to light those elements of philosophical hermeneutics which are in need of supplementation.

In addition to the criticisms made above, Habermas, and others such as Bernstein, argue that philosophical hermeneutics suffers from a blindness towards certain aspects of language, and that this blindness is symptomatic of a general tendency. Habermas argued that in addition to being the vehicle of tradition and the manner of our 'being-in-the-world', language is also a vehicle, or a tool, for the expression of power relations. Language, he argues, 'is also a medium of domination and social power; it serves to legitimate relations of organized force'.[9] Our understandings or traditions are not just the passing down of a form of life, but they are also the expression of power relations and material interests, or rather the form of life they hand down is also constituted by certain power relations. Language, Habermas argues, is also used to mask deception or distort understanding in order to conceal:

> [I]nsofar as the legitimations do not articulate the power relations whose institutionalizations they make possible, insofar as these

[8] R. Bernstein, *Beyond Objectivism and Relativism* (Philadelphia: University of Pennsylvania Press, 1983), p. 149.
[9] Habermas, 'A Review', p. 272.

relations merely manifest themselves in the legitimations, language is also ideological. Here it is a question not of deceptions within a language but of deceptions with language as such. Hermeneutic experience that encounters this dependency of the symbolic framework on *actual conditions* changes into critique of ideology.[10]

According to Habermas, philosophical hermeneutics' focus on linguisticality and the deep nature of human-being-in-the-world means that it ignores the role of social forces and in doing so it is blind to the play of power in a tradition or society.[11] Furthermore, from Habermas' perspective philosophical hermeneutics ignores the argument that linguisticality is itself mediated by changes in the material circumstances of life. So, in other words, Habermas accuses Gadamer of a form of idealism, in which all social phenomena are reduced to language, while at the same time ignoring the limits of language as world disclosure. The ability to identify and criticise these dimensions of language is the role of critical theory and the critique of ideology.

While these points are important they do not, in themselves, in Gadamer's words, represent a 'philosophical going beyond'[12] nor do they undermine philosophical hermeneutics, or the position outlined in *Truth and Method*. Rather, and despite Habermas' claims to have secured the grounds for a critical theory from outside the specific horizon of western enlightenment, these criticisms can all be reinterpreted within the horizon of philosophical hermeneutics. The role of material or social forces in providing stimulus, and in forging particular human understandings, does not undermine Gadamer's claim that these understandings occur in, and because of, linguisticality. Social forces only have meaning, can only be understood, because they occur within language. As Gadamer put it in a letter to Bernstein 'Our experiences of things, indeed even of everyday life, of modes of production, and yes also of the sphere of our vital concerns, are one and all hermeneutic.'[13] Furthermore, the intrinsically critical nature of the encounter with tradition, and with the other, is also consistent with a recognition that

---

[10] *Ibid.*, p. 272, emphasis added.
[11] As Bernstein notes 'Habermas does not really disagree with what Gadamer means by dialogue, conversation, and questioning, but is rather . . . constantly drawing our attention to those systemic features of contemporary society that inhibit, distort or prevent such dialogue from being concretely embodied in our everyday practices.' Bernstein, *Beyond Objectivism and Relativism*, p. 224.
[12] 'A letter from Hans-Georg Gadamer, in R. Bernstein, *Beyond Objectivism and Relativism*, p. 264.
[13] *Ibid.*, p. 263.

language can function as a tool of power, and that certain prejudices may not be legitimate. Thus, it can be suggested that critical theory and philosophical hermeneutics are concerned with similar dynamics, and with describing and explaining the conditions of understanding and reflection. Where they differ is that they claim a different epistemological status for their descriptions.

In addition, while it is true that Gadamer says very little about the way in which power might distort the construction of horizons of meaning, this does not necessarily mean that Gadamer is blind to the ubiquity of power in political relations. In contrast to Habermas' claim that Gadamer is unaware of or blind to the role of domination and power, Dieter Misgeld has argued that Gadamer is only too aware of power. It is because power is a pervasive and ineradicable dimension of the human social world that philosophical hermeneutics cannot envision a world free from domination. Gadamer cannot conceive of a world in which social differences are eliminated and as a result, he rejects and is deeply suspicious of any solution which attempts to engineer such an outcome. This is one reason why Gadamer defends Aristotelian practical reasoning and the cultivation of *phronesis*, involving the prudent weighing of alternative possibilities, against emancipatory or utopian practices. It is, Misgeld argues, because Gadamer 'is so much aware of the presence of these factors (power-coercion) that he refuses to transform philosophical hermeneutics into a *critique* of domination'.[14] Unfortunately as a result, Gadamer's recognition of domination also means that he underestimates the importance of those movements which, since the enlightenment, have attempted to increase the realm of human freedom. Gadamer either fails to address them at all, or, where he does, he 'fails to perceive the difference between emancipatory and technocratic politics'.[15] Thus while Gadamer is legitimately sceptical of the epistemological claims to have eradicated the influence of tradition which accompanies the discourse of emancipation, he also nonetheless downplays the practical significance of emancipatory movements such as feminism, anti-colonialism and anti-racism, which have sought to increase the ability of previously excluded voices from taking their place in the 'conversation of humankind', and,

[14] D. Misgeld, 'Poetry, Dialogue and Negotiation: Liberal Culture and Conservative Politics in Hans-Georg Gadamer's Thought', in K. Wright, *Festivals of Interpretation: Essays on Hans–Georg Gadamer's Work* (Albany: SUNY, 1990), pp. 136–60, p. 171.
[15] *Ibid.*, p. 173.

more specifically, in the political processes of modern states. In so far as Misgeld is correct, then Gadamer's philosophy practises certain exclusions and blindnesses as a result of its emphasis on understanding, and is in need of supplementation.

What these reflections on the relation of philosophical hermeneutics to power suggest is that, with one exception, philosophical hermeneutics has not been directed towards an understanding of the obstacles to achieving dialogue and to the realisation of the type of solidarity in which practical reasoning can flourish. Richard Bernstein argues that philosophical hermeneutics must address the question of 'what it is that blocks and prevents such dialogue, and what is to be done, "what is feasible, what is possible, what is correct, here and now" to make such a genuine dialogue a concrete reality'.[16] In philosophical hermeneutics the investigation into how communication may be encouraged, and into what features of human social life might prevent the realisation of discursive communities, has been limited to the critique of the dominance of *techne* or instrumental rationality, in the modern world. Gadamer's primary aim has been to challenge the idea of 'planning reason' or technical instrumental rationality, first in the form of historicism and later in the form of 'social science' based on natural sciences. He has indicated how both these approaches stand in the way of 'genuine' understanding but has said little about other forms of communication, practice or belief which may prevent genuine understanding.

The investigation into these aspects of human communication has been the focus of critical theory, with its emphasis on understanding the practices of inclusion and exclusion over time. In directing our attention to what it is that blocks dialogue and prevents a genuine act of understanding, critical theory directs the attention of philosophical hermeneutics away from the meaning of understanding and towards the socio-cultural obstacles to understanding. As Bernstein puts it, critical theory reminds us that '[I]f the possibility (of dialogue) is to be more than an empty "ought", and if it is to be concretely embodied in social practices, this requires a transformation of the material conditions that block and distort communication'.[17] This is indeed a necessary step towards the creation of the conditions for practical reasoning and solidarity in the

---

[16] R. Bernstein, *Beyond Objectivism and Relativism*, p. 163.
[17] *Ibid.*, p. 190. Bernstein's point is that investigation into these material conditions requires going beyond, or outside, the philosophical hermeneutic concern with meaning alone.

modern international order, and in so far as philosophical hermeneutics ignores, or is uninterested in, these questions then it remains insufficient in itself. Philosophical hermeneutics, therefore, requires supplementing with the insights and interests of other approaches, such as critical theory, which do direct attention to the obstacles to dialogue.

One final comment can be made, and which should not be forgotten in this context, is that where philosophical hermeneutics and critical theory differ in this regard, is at the level of epistemological and cognitive obstacles to understanding. As we have seen, from Habermas' perspective, one of these obstacles to genuine communication is the persistence of conventional consciousness: that is, of consciousness tied to tradition. Philosophical hermeneutics, it has been argued, does not see tradition itself as an epistemological obstacle to communication. For Habermas, achieving a universal communication community requires the removal of the epistemological obstacles as well as the sociological ones. Gadamer does not agree that tradition forms an obstacle in the way Habermas argues, therefore, there is no need to reject tradition per se, only those prejudices which prevent the achievement of a fusion of horizons.

Philosophical hermeneutics and deconstruction

Critical theorists have not been alone in their criticisms of philosophical hermeneutics and its 'rehabilitation of tradition and prejudice'. From the position of the poststructuralism of Jacques Derrida, philosophical hermeneutics seems the heir to an outdated and anachronistic logocentrism.[18] In 1981 Derrida and Gadamer met in an arranged encounter in Paris which, in tone as much as substance, revealed a great deal about their respective philosophies and the absence or presence of common ground between them. The following discussion briefly outlines the substance of this 'encounter', in order to highlight what was revealed about the relevant similarities and differences between philosophical hermeneutics and Derrida's deconstruction.[19]

---

[18] See also for instance the oversimplified contribution by Caputo in D. P. Michelfelder and R. E. Palmer (eds.), *Dialogue and Deconstruction: The Gadamer–Derrida Encounter* (Albany: SUNY, 1989).
[19] See *ibid*. For an interesting and illuminating discussion of the relationship between Derrida and Gadamer see also F. R. Dallmayr, *Beyond Orientalism: Essays on Cross Cultural Encounter* (Albany: SUNY,1996); and D. C. Hoy, *The Critical Circle* (Berkeley: University of California Press, 1978).

The most important point made by Derrida against Gadamer is that we should question the philosophical hermeneutic emphasis on solidarity, agreement and continuity. This questioning of the very *telos* of philosophical hermeneutics, at face value, suggests an absolute limit to its ambitions. However, rather than suggesting a strict dichotomy between radically different projects, Derrida's position also serves to direct attention to otherwise backgrounded aspects of understanding and communication. Derrida's deconstructive approach provides a crucial difference of emphasis which serves both to supplement philosophical hermeneutics and remind it of the limits of understanding. In this sense deconstruction, by emphasising the obstacles to and limits of understanding, helps contribute to the goal of a dialogical community, in which a primary aim is the recognition and awareness of difference and 'otherness'.

In many ways philosophical hermeneutics has more in common with poststructuralism and deconstruction than it does with Habermasian critical theory. Philosophical hermeneutics and poststructuralism both reject Habermas' problematic and ambiguous references to objectivity and the ideal of a social science in favour of a more thoroughly interpretive discourse. In this sense they are more fully hermeneutic and anti-foundationalist than critical theory. And it is this which had resulted in Gadamer occasionally being referred to as postmodern or poststructuralist. However, despite these similarities, significant differences do remain.

In his response to Gadamer's Paris paper 'Text and Interpretation', Derrida posed three brief questions. The first concerned Gadamer's passing mention of 'good will towards the text'. Derrida suggested Gadamer's use of this term signified a deeper issue in hermeneutics. He asked: '[D]oes not this way of speaking, in its very necessity, belong to a particular epoch, namely that of a metaphysics of the will?'[20] His obvious intention here is to suggest that philosophical hermeneutics remains within what he sees as the problematic horizon of metaphysics. This question addresses Derrida's concern with logocentrism and metaphysics and the aporias involved in attempting somehow to think beyond these concepts and preoccupations. In this context Derrida attempted to demonstrate how, even in those who think they are escaping metaphysics [Gadamer/Heidegger], metaphysics persists. And, in

---

[20] J. Derrida 'Three Questions to Hans-Georg Gadamer', in Michelfelder and Palmer, *Dialogue and Deconstruction*, p. 53.

this particular case, the search for meaning and truth, even understanding, is a continuation of the metaphysics of presence.[21]

Derrida's particular problem with Gadamer, it would seem, is Gadamer's continuation of the project of the 'hermeneutics of Being' which, he argued, Heidegger later abandoned. Returning to his question to Gadamer, this particular charge relates to interpretation of Heidegger from different periods and in particular, to Heidegger's interpretation of Nietzsche. Derrida criticises Heidegger's reading of Nietzsche and argues instead that Nietzsche did more to disrupt metaphysics than Heidegger's search for Being. Derrida sees Nietzsche as going further in destroying metaphysics than Heidegger, precisely because Nietzsche reveals meaning as 'the will to meaning'. That is, he reveals meaning to be nothing other than the play of power without any hidden essence, or truth, to conceal or to be revealed. Nietzsche, like Gadamer, remains within a metaphysics of the will but does more to reach out of it because he emphasises the arbitrary and the disruptive. Derrida wants to argue that Heidegger, Nietzsche and others are still caught by metaphysics, but he also wants to argue that it is an aporia that can't be escaped; so he therefore acknowledges that he can't escape it either:

> [T]here is no sense in doing without the concepts of metaphysics in order to shake metaphysics. We have no language – no syntax and no lexicon – which is foreign to this history; we can pronounce no single destructive proposition which has not already had to slip into the form, the logic, and the implicit postulations of precisely what it seeks to contest.[22]

In his question to Gadamer, Derrida can be understood as reminding Gadamer that philosophical hermeneutics is also caught in this aporia.[23]

---

[21] Derrida's critique of Metaphysics is, according to Bernstein, a critique of 'the history of the search for a series of substitutions of center for center by which we seek a "reassuring certitude", a "metaphysical comfort", . . .', R. Bernstein, *The New Constellation* (Oxford: Polity, 1991), p. 175. Metaphysics is dangerous because '. . . it also (always) establishes ethical–ontological hierarchies in which there is subordination and violence . . . (Derrida's) critique, his protest against metaphysics is primarily ethical–political. It is the invidious and pernicious tendency toward hierarchy, subordination and repression that informs his rhetoric and tropes.' *Ibid.* p. 175.

[22] J. Derrida, *Limited Inc.* (Evanston: Northwestern University Press, 1988), p. 183.

[23] As David Hoy puts it 'Hermeneutics may not think of itself as a version of metaphysics, but the hermeneutic desire to decipher the univocal meaning of the text may mirror the desire of metaphysics for a complete and comprehensive account of the meaning of everything, for the truth of the whole and the unity of the world.' Hoy, *The Critical Circle*, p. 56. As Gadamer himself puts it, '. . . in taking up and continuing hermeneutics as philosophy, [I] would appear at best as the lost sheep in the dried up pastures of metaphysics', H. G. Gadamer, 'Letter to Dallmayr', in Michelfelder and Palmer, *Dialogue and Deconstruction*, p. 94.

But Derrida also wants to resist it and to challenge metaphysics, and perhaps develop a 'quite different way of thinking about texts'.[24] For Derrida, this quite different way of thinking in the face of such continuity, is to emphasise and disclose rupture. This different way of thinking informs his subsequent questions to Gadamer.

Derrida's second question concerned what he argued was Gadamer's intention to 'integrate psychoanalysis into general hermeneutics'. In such a situation he asks: '[W]hat to do about good will – the condition for consensus even in disagreement – ... what would good will mean in psychoanalysis ... ?'[25] This question directs our attention towards that aspect of the psychoanalytic process in which the aim is to understand, not what the other wants to be understood, but exactly that which the patient wishes to conceal and which they don't want to be understood. In this case it would seem that psychoanalysis requires a degree of bad will or suspicion. As he goes on to suggest, for Derrida, Nietzsche's approach is a better form of hermeneutics in this regard. Derrida argues that the Nietzschean approach to meaning and the possibility of understanding is better placed for asking the necessary type questions for understanding this situation. Does not good will, Derrida suggests, cover up what is *not* said, what is hidden and not acknowledged?

The third and most important question (for this enquiry) asked:

> [W]hether one speaks of consensus or of misunderstanding (as in Schleiermacher), one needs to ask whether the precondition for *Verstehen*, far from being the continuity of rapport ... is not rather the interruption of rapport, a certain rapport of interruption, the suspending of all mediation?[26]

This question is a more direct statement of this same proposition: 'Does real understanding [*Verstehen*] or knowledge come about through goodwill or through rupture, through consensus or through dispersion, and through discontinuity?' Understanding, it would seem, can only come about by shattering any instance of agreement and showing what it hides and excludes.

Derrida's position here can be better understood if related to his discussion of the undecidability of the text. Derridean deconstruction implies that any attempt to find meaning is/must be an attempt to establish the straightforward relationship between signified and signifier and, as

---

[24] Derrida, 'Three Questions', p. 54.   [25] *Ibid.*, p. 53.   [26] *Ibid.*

such, is rooted in metaphysics. It must be an attempt to decide on a final, true and definitive meaning in isolation from other meanings, a meaning in its essence. What deconstruction attempts to show is that such attempts both hide and reveal the very instability of meaning and of language:

> this is the possibility on which I want to insist: the possibility of every mark, spoken or written, and which constitutes every mark in writing before and outside of every Horizon of semio-linguistic communication in writing, which is to say in the possibility of its functioning being cut-off at a certain point, from its 'original' desire-to-say-what-one-means (*voulour dire*) and from its participation in a saturable and constraining context. *Every sign, linguistic or nonlinguistic, spoken or written (in the current sense of this opposition) on a small or large unit, can be cited, put between quotation marks; in so doing it can break with every given context, engendering an infinity of new contexts in a manner which is absolutely illimitable. This does not imply that the mark is valid outside of a context, but on the contrary that there are only contexts without any center or absolute anchoring (ancrage).*[27]

Because language only 'refers' to itself then meanings are arbitrary or undecidable, words can come to mean something completely different from what may have been their original usage or intention. What Derrida argues is that words only get their meaning in relation to each other in a play of differences, and not by reference to an external reality or some essential conceptual kernel:

> the signified concept is never present in and of itself, in a sufficient presence that would refer only to itself. Essentially and lawfully, every concept is inscribed in a chain or in a system within which it refers to the other, to other concepts, by means of the systematic play of differences.[28]

Thus meanings and words are not, in Rorty's phrase 'the mirror of nature' nor the representation in language of something else. But the relationship of words to each other is not overdetermined by tradition, or by one particular context. Instead, Derrida is suggesting an ability of meanings to become detached from certain contexts and attached to new ones. Thus Derrida emphasises the infinite flexibility of language and the limits of tradition to determine the context of meaning. Disrupture and undecidability emphasise, exacerbate and encourage this dimension of

[27] Derrida, *Limited Inc.*, p. 12.   [28] *Ibid.*, p. 11.

language and meaning. In this way, the issues of undecidability and of rupture and discontinuity are related, the outcome of the undecidability of texts is the end of the hermeneutic search for Meaning (*Verstehen*) as something transferred in its essence through tradition. Therefore, for Derrida, undecidability means that rupture is as, if not more, significant than continuity. This emphasis on undecidability and rupture suggests that the type of understanding and communication sought by philosophical hermeneutics is impossible. Indeed, because meaning cannot be fixed, it suggests that understanding is something to be mistrusted.

However, to portray philosophical hermeneutics as blind to rupture and discontinuity is misleading. The depiction of understanding in a fusion of horizons also involves an element of displacement. Gadamer affirms 'that understanding is always an understanding-differently (*andersverstehen*). What is pushed aside or dislocated when my word reaches another person, and especially when a text reaches its reader, can never be fixed in a rigid identity.'[29]

In a sense, philosophical hermeneutics and deconstruction focus on different sides of the same coin; the aporia which lies at the heart of linguisticality; the capacity of language to both enable and hinder communication. The question which they both explore, as Gadamer puts it, is:

> What, in the final analysis, is linguisticality? Is it a bridge or barrier? Is it a bridge built of things that are the same for each self over which one communicates with the other over the flowing stream of otherness? Or is it a barrier that limits our self abandonment and that cuts us off from the possibility of ever completely expressing ourselves and communicating with others?[30]

What is revealed in Derrida's questions to Gadamer is not necessarily any radical difference over the nature of language. Philosophical

---

[29] Gadamer, 'Letter to Dallmayr', p. 96.
[30] Gadamer, 'Text and Interpretation', in Michelfelder and Palmer, *Dialogue and Deconstruction*, p. 27. In so far as Gadamer has an answer to this and where he can be seen to differ from Derrida, concerns the *precondition* of interruption. As he says in his reply to Derrida: 'Now certainly I would not want to say that the solidarities that bind human beings together and make them partners in a dialogue always are sufficient to enable them to achieve understanding and total mutual agreement. Just the same would apply with regard to the inner dialogue the soul has with itself. Of course we encounter limits again and again; we speak past each other and are even at cross purposes with ourselves. *But in my opinion we could not do this at all if we had not travelled a long way together, perhaps without even acknowledging it to ourselves. All human solidarity, all social stability, presupposes this.'* Gadamer, 'Destruktion and Deconstruction', in Michelfelder and Palmer, *Dialogue and Deconstruction*, p. 57.

hermeneutics and deconstructionist poststructuralism share a view of the linguisticality of the human world and a conception that this means that knowledge is always interpretation and is in question. Instead, what comes to light in the discussion is the importance of both continuity/discontinuity, understanding/misunderstanding and goodwill/suspicion or rupture. Derrida's last question best signifies the difference that makes a difference in this regard. At the risk of oversimplifying the issues, it can be suggested that where Gadamer sees understanding as requiring continuity, Derrida looks for and brings out discontinuities and ruptures which also heighten understanding. However, while not denying significant differences, it can be suggested that the most productive way to read these two positions is not as mutually exclusive and radically opposed orientations, but rather, as different and complementary approaches to the possibility of understanding.[31]

James Risser has characterised the differences between Gadamer and Derrida as representative of the 'two faces of Socrates'. Socrates, Risser argues, 'appears on the scene not to answer but to question, to be vigilant against unquestioned authority that would confuse what appears to be with what really is . . . Socrates takes up this questioning of others in the humility of his own ignorance.'[32] This questioning stance has two functions, represented by the two faces: one is the posing of ceaseless questions and the shaking up of accepted beliefs, the questioning of prejudices and unmasking of power through reason; the other is the use of critical questioning to bring about a better understanding, a greater wisdom, a more compelling interpretation. Thus, the two faces are that of the gadfly, who seeks to disrupt all settled knowledge through a vigilant questioning and 'the midwife who seeks to bring wisdom to birth'.[33]

The approach of Derrida, Risser argues, is characteristic of the first face. In seeking disrupture, Derrida reminds us that there are no ultimate assurances of truth. He seeks to confront those who claim to know, or to be able absolutely to present something as truth, with a questioning attitude which disrupts this stance and reminds them of the tenuousness of their claim to truth and their finitude. Gadamer, on the other hand,

---

[31] Such is the interpretation offered by John D. Caputo which relies on an oversimplified account of philosophical hermeneutics to present a very dichotomous reading of the relationship between the two which seems rather to fly against the strategy of rejecting binaries.

[32] James Risser, *Hermeneutics and the Voice of the Other* (Albany: SUNY, 1997), p. 169.

[33] *Ibid.*, p. 171.

represents another face of Socrates, the one which uses questioning as means of coming to agreement, or at least a better understanding, on a subject, and thereby achieving a sort of wisdom. Questioning and conversation in Gadamer's Socratic stance not only subject dogmatism (*doxa*) to reason but also help create common ground, or solidarity, *in* conversation. Risser argues that both the faces of Socrates require a certain vigilance. The first face requires the vigilance of criticism of ultimate truths, while the second requires the 'vigilance in the conversation that we are . . .',[34] a vigilant attention which seeks that which is common and 'the continuing effort to find common ground'.[35]

Risser's characterisation captures much of what is important in both Gadamer and Derrida, as well as the intertwining and interdependence of their approaches in a common though multifaceted exploration of the meaning of reason and communication. This identification of the two faces of Socrates leads to a recognition of the mutually illuminating aspects of poststructuralism, philosophical hermeneutics and critical theory. If we understand the issues involved this way, then it becomes possible to see how a mutually illuminating relationship exists between these different philosophies which may help to contribute to the development of a thin dialogic cosmopolitanism capable of doing justice to difference.

The task of reciprocal illumination

The arguments presented here and in the previous chapters have been constructed with the intent of demonstrating not only the achievements of the various approaches but also the manner in which they can be seen to have incompletely met the goals, or realised certain of the values they pursue. The purpose of introducing philosophical hermeneutics has been to contribute to those achievements and to provide a means for remedying some of the lingering residues of assimilationist relations in the existing field of work. This chapter has begun to argue for the ways in which critical theory and poststructuralism are both capable of illuminating certain tendencies in each other and in philosophical hermeneutics. Such a process of reciprocal illumination is necessary if a more complete account of 'good' conversation, which aims to achieve justice to difference, is to be sought and achieved. The most important

---

[34] *Ibid.*   [35] *Ibid.*, p. 172.

matters in which such a reciprocal illumination can be achieved can be summarised as follows.

In regard to critical theory it has been argued, philosophical hermeneutics does not concern itself with examining the material or societal conditions in which dialogue can be undertaken. Critical theory, on the other hand, can invoke its Marxist heritage to suggest that there are material and social forms of inequality which actively serve to exclude others from conversation. What is required then, is the identification and removal of these obstacles in order to facilitate maximum inclusion in conversation. Such concerns have not been central to philosophical hermeneutics and serve to correct its emphasis on the ontological and philosophic obstacles to understanding.

In regard to poststructuralism, it is as a response to the Derridean reading of Gadamer that the aspect of Gadamer's thought most expressly concerned with the 'voice of the other' has been brought to the fore. The poststructuralist emphasis on rupture and discontinuity, and the suspicion of the search for consensus, also serve to illuminate and balance the reading of Gadamer which emphasises the synthetic aspect of understanding, as against the agonal and incomplete aspect of understanding, and the 'irretrievability' of the other's meaning. The readings of Risser, Dallmayr and others have emphasised the component of philosophical hermeneutics, in which understanding is always also 'understanding-differently'.[36]

Poststructuralism and critical theory, together, also illuminate the absence of an account of power in philosophical hermeneutics. They illuminate how agreement and consensus may reflect relations of power, inequality and 'distorted' communication, rather than genuine mutual understanding. Likewise, the poststructuralist emphasis on difference and exclusion serves to continually pose the questions of 'who' and 'what' are excluded, and why, to the participants of any philosophical hermeneutic conversation, as well as in relation to any 'fusion of horizons' which may emerge from it. In these ways, poststructuralism and critical theory illuminate the possibilities for assimilation in the hermeneutic account of conversation as a fusion of horizons.

However, in addition to illuminating certain limitations of the philosophical hermeneutic project, critical theory and poststructuralism have also served to illuminate each other. For example, it is clear that

---

[36] Gadamer, 'Letter to Dallmayr', in Michelfelder and Palmer, *Dialogue and Deconstruction*, p. 96.

Linklater's continuing development of the critical theoretical agenda has been deeply influenced by poststructuralist thought. Nowhere is this more evident than in *The Transformation of Political Community*, where he argues that the work of Rorty, Foucault, Derrida and Lyotard add crucial dimensions to the project of a cosmopolitan community. In particular, Foucault's enquiry into the construction of difference and marginalisation contributes to the goal of facilitating inclusion, by highlighting the processes in which different societies 'construct and exclude the moral other'. According to Linklater, Foucault raised the question and provided new ways of understanding how:

> societies construct self-constituting dichotomies between the normal and the abnormal . . . how as the dominant understanding of rationality comes to be established, societies construct the 'other' who does not belong and who becomes the object of strategies of marginalisation, normalisation and control.[37]

For Linklater, understanding these processes is crucial to moving beyond practices of unjustifiable exclusion and towards the realisation of cosmopolitan community that does justice to difference.

Another area in which poststructuralist concerns have made themselves felt in Linklater's project, stems from the critique of totalisation, which draws attention to the danger of convergence or assimilation in the cosmopolitan community. Linklater's defence of the manner in which discourse ethics is inclusive of a wide range of differences, and without requiring the annihilation of particular or parochial identities, in addition to his acknowledgement of the never completed dimensions of conversation, derives in part from a desire to counteract the totalising elements of cosmopolitanism. In this fashion, certain tendencies in the critical theoretical project have been illuminated by poststructuralism.[38]

From the perspective of critical theory, poststructuralism is also in need of illumination. According to Linklater, the poststructuralist celebration of diversity is situated within an unacknowledged universalism, whereby difference is hailed as a universal good. In so doing, poststructuralism rests on certain unacknowledged and undefended universal

[37] A. Linklater, *Men and Citizens in the Theory of International Relations*, 2nd edn (London: Macmillan, 1990).
[38] To appreciate the full extent of Linklater's engagement with poststructuralism see A. Linklater, *The Transformation of Political Community* (Cambridge: Polity, 1997).

claims. Linklater argues that, as a result, much of poststructuralism tends to avoid

> the issues of deciding what can and what cannot – what ought and what ought not to – be universalised. It has failed to raise the key question of how the defence of universality and the claim for difference might be woven into a single theoretical perspective.[39]

While the poststructuralist preoccupation with difference is needed to counteract the assimilative tendencies of cosmopolitanism, from Linklater's position, the particularist and relativist tendencies of post-structuralism need to be balanced by the Kantian preoccupation with universalism. From this perspective the task of a coherent account of community in IR requires the balancing of the needs of the universal and the particular. Likewise, philosophical hermeneutics illuminates those elements of poststructuralism which neglect or dismiss continuity, understanding, and the possibility of solidarity. Philosophical hermeneutics reflects and emphasises the manner in which language is a bridge, as well as a barrier, to understanding.

Finally, however, in addition to those insights which philosophical hermeneutics supplies and which have been outlined above, there is one other dimension, so far unstated, but perhaps of comprehensive importance. In *The New Constellations* Richard Bernstein argued that what perhaps best illuminates the meaning of poststructuralism and postmodernism can be characterised as their distinctive mood or *Stimmung*. He suggested that

> it is best to use the expression 'modern/postmodern' to signify what Heidegger calls a *Stimmung*, a mood – one which is amorphous, protean, and shifting but which nevertheless exerts a powerful influence on the ways in which we think, act and experience.[40]

The distinctive *Stimmung* of poststructuralism/postmodernism is one '... of deconstruction, destabilisation, rupture and fracture – of resistance to all forms of abstract totality, universalism, and rationalism'.[41] It is this mood which can be detected in the face of Socrates represented by Derrida.

In this vein, it can be suggested that it is the *Stimmung* of philosophical hermeneutics which most distinguishes it from critical theory and post-structuralism, but which also provides its greatest contribution to the

---

[39] Linklater, *Men and Citizens*, p. 216. [40] Bernstein, *The New Constellation*, p. 11.
[41] *Ibid.*, p. 57.

mutual task of seeking a just world order. The *Stimmung* of philosophical hermeneutics, which can be detected in the face of Socrates represented by Gadamer, is one of reconciliation, understanding, solidarity and community. This *Stimmung* contrasts with the mood displayed in Socrates' other face which expresses scepticism and is constitutive of both critical theory and poststructuralism. It was argued above that one aspect common to critical theory and poststructuralist approaches is the task of uncovering the lack of real agreement between differently situated agents.[42]

This dimension of critical theory and poststructuralism emphasises scepticism and the role of critique: they suggest an ever-vigilant and critical stance towards any assumed or given understandings and agreements. In particular, one of the tasks of critical theory is to identify agreements or understanding that rest on, for want of a better term, false consciousness.[43] Furthermore, some instances of poststructuralism also seem to argue that communication is impossible because any understanding is always already an act of violence or assimilation.

If this is the case then the most important contribution that philosophical hermeneutics can make is to emphasise the possibility of continuity and understanding. Where enlightenment or emancipatory approaches seek or address disrupture, change and discontinuity, philosophical hermeneutics also seeks meaning, understanding, continuity, stability and coherence. As Gadamer concludes

> [B]ut though the will of man is more than ever intensifying its criticism of what has gone before to the point of becoming utopian or eschatological consciousness, the hermeneutic consciousness seeks to confront that will with something of the truth of remembrance: with what is still and ever again real.[44]

[42] Critical theory approaches the object of understanding with the goal of revealing that which is taken to be true as untruth: 'It is for this reason that every consensus, as the outcome of an understanding of meaning, is, in principle, suspect of having been enforced through pseudo communication: in earlier days, people talked about delusion when misunderstanding and self mis-understanding continued unaffected under the appearance of factual agreement.' J. Habermas, 'The Hermeneutic Claim to Universality', in M. Gibbons, *Interpreting Politics* (New York University Press, 1987), p. 197.

[43] As Gadamer notes the idea of false consciousness retains a presence in the critique of ideology central to Habermas' earlier work and by which he attempted to distinguish critical theory from philosophical hermeneutics: 'It is not only the neurotic patient who, in defence of his neurosis, suffers from systematically distorted communication. Indeed every social consciousness that finds itself in agreement with the ruling social system, thereby supporting its coercive character, also suffers fundamentally from such systematically distorted communication. This is the presupposition, itself never discussed, of Habermas' argumentation.' Gadamer, *Philosophical Hermeneutics*, p. 279.

[44] Gadamer, *Truth and Method*, p. xxxviii.

Or, in another vein, he states '[I] am concerned with the fact that the displacement of human reality never goes so far that no forms of solidarity exist any longer. Plato saw this very well: there is no city so corrupted that it does not realize something of the true city . . .'[45] The *Stimmung* of philosophical hermeneutics, therefore, is one of 'good will' and openness towards the possibilities of the other, be it a text, an individual, the past or a culture. In this way it balances critical theory and poststructuralism by presenting an account of understanding that emphasises the *possibilities* for the exchange of meaning and mutual comprehension between different agents. The pursuit of a conception of universal community which does justice to difference requires both these moments. It requires both the awareness of discontinuity and misunderstanding *and* the possibility of continuity and understanding. Indeed, it is the interaction between these two moments which makes for productive conversation and the possibility of learning.

Conversation and dialogue revisited

Having outlined the philosophical hermeneutic contribution to the project of community in international relations, and having reflected on how critical theory, poststructuralism and philosophical hermeneutics all serve to provide mutually illuminating perspectives on the possibilities for understanding and conversation, the task now is to revisit the model of conversation itself and to attempt to spell out the conclusions that can be drawn from the above discussions.

The first task is to identify some of the shared goals, themes and aspirations common to the literature surveyed above.[46] The discussion of the mutually illuminating dimension of critical theory, poststructuralism and philosophical hermeneutics outlined here leads to the conclusion that they should not be understood as necessarily conflicting approaches.

The following discussion briefly outlines the manner in which these approaches converge on some common ground in relation to the issues of conversation and community. In this, it depicts the manner in which they can be understood as attempts to explore a similar problematic: how to approach the tension between community and difference?, or

---

[45] Gadamer, 'A letter from Hans-Georg Gadamer', p. 269.
[46] The areas of common concern identified here by no means constitute an exhaustive list. They are merely what appear to me to be the most relevant in terms of the investigation being undertaken here.

alternatively, how is it possible to achieve justice through recognition in a world of differently constituted agents?

As a corollary to a commitment to communication, there is a general consensus that good dialogue is not compatible with the maintenance of hard and fast boundaries between individuals, communities, states or cultures. While pragmatic considerations may arise which justify the construction of boundaries in certain circumstances, boundaries should not, in principle, prevent dialogue and discourse. There is also a clear sense in which the principle of communication works actively to subvert such boundaries and the exclusionary and unequal relationships they maintain. Unlike theories of justice or community which justify themselves according to pre-existing shared values, physical proximity, bloodlines, history or family, the emphasis on dialogue and discursive construction of community is inherently more universalistic, and inclusive, because it seeks justification in a universal capacity or potential.

The questioning of boundaries in philosophical hermeneutics, poststructuralism and critical theory is also consistent with the common hermeneutic starting point. A hermeneutic emphasis on meaning amounts to recognition of the social construction of reality or, in Linklaters terms, the recognition that social forms are not dictated by nature, but are, rather, the effect and consequence of human volition. This recognition allows for a critical and questioning attitude to the boundaries which divide the species. This concern with critical appraisal can be witnessed in the account of autonomy in critical theory, the idea of deconstruction and disturbance in poststructuralism, or the idea of the critical appropriation of the historical horizon of tradition, in philosophical hermeneutics. In this way, a commitment to a dialogic community that seeks justice to difference necessarily involves a critical disposition towards the boundaries of moral community.

The questioning of boundaries, and emphasis on critique, lead directly to another common theme: reason. By their own accounts, critical theory, poststructuralism and philosophical hermeneutics all are concerned to rescue reason from the idea and practice of *techne* (technical instrumental rationality). There is a significant sense in which they share a preoccupation with the conditions under which non-instrumental reasoning can occur, and with expanding the realms in which reason and critique, however defined, can operate. However, the common engagement in the critique of technical and instrumental rationality does not preclude the development of a variety of conceptions of reason, and its relationship to agency. In all three meditations on communication, justice, agency and practice are determined by the possibility of reason, and the definition of reasoning agents. The development of forms of community in which reason, and, therefore, freedom, can be exercised and flourish, underlies the critical dimension of these approaches, and supports their critiques of the inscription of absolute and sovereign boundaries. Where they differ, from the strictly universalist form provided by Habermas, to the fluid interpretations and practices in poststructuralist writings, is in their understandings of what reason actually amounts to, how it is defined, what it can achieve and how it is practised. In particular, it is the relationship between reason, agency and praxis that helps make for the key distinctions between philosophical hermeneutics, critical theory and poststructuralism.

Thus, it can be suggested that critical theory, philosophical hermeneutics and poststructuralism all share a desire to increase or expand the realms in which conversation can take place and 'reason' be exercised, but differ in their understanding of the meaning and purpose of dialogue.

Beyond this common ground the most significant area of agreement that emerges is the confirmation of the centrality of discourse and conversation in realising a relationship of justice based on recognition. Critical theory, philosophical hermeneutics and poststructuralism all concur that recognition through dialogue, in which the other is seen to be equal and yet different, is an essential component of doing justice to difference. In conversation, the other is allowed to express and articulate their individuality and particularity. It can be suggested that this apparent consensus stems from the shared interpretive or hermeneutic orientation of critical theory, philosophical hermeneutics and poststructuralism, and the recognition of the centrality of language this entails. This amounts to an acceptance that human lives are constructed in terms of meaning in important ways. Stemming from this acceptance, justice is achieved by the recognition of the particularities of individual or collective meanings. Conversation, therefore, becomes the obvious place in which recognition is achieved or aspired to. While different perspectives make different contributions to the understanding of the meaning of dialogue, and emphasise different aspects of communication, they nonetheless concur that communication, rather than coexistence or assimilation, is central to any concept of a just community.

Linklater, for instance, has identified a recognition of good dialogue in the work of Lyotard, and especially in his Amnesty International

Lectures in 1993. There, Lyotard emphasised that 'all human beings have an equal right to take part in dialogue and to "establish their community by contract" using "reason and debate" '.[47]

Likewise, a commitment to open dialogue and to certain rules of engagement in conversation, can be seen in Derrida's writings. In particular, in the afterword to *Limited Inc.*, which is subtitled 'Towards an Ethic of Discussion', Derrida suggests how discussion can or should be conducted. This piece aims 'to serve as an invitation to others, in the course of a discussion that is both open and yet to come'.[48] Indeed the value of an open dialogue informs much of Derrida's work, and helps us understand the aim of deconstructive readings, which is the identification and recognition of the role of violence in communication and discussion. The recognition of violence, he argues, will not necessarily remove it entirely, but may nonetheless serve to make for a less violent discussion. The afterword draws attention to that aspect of his work which is directed towards identifying the violence in academic discourse:

> [T]he violence political or otherwise at work in academic discussion or in intellectual discussions generally, must be acknowledged. In saying this I am not advocating that such violence be unleashed or simply accepted. I am above all asking that we try to recognise and analyze it as best we can in its various forms: . . . And if as I believe violence remains in fact (almost) ineradicable, its analysis and the most refined ingenious account of its conditions will be the least violent gestures, perhaps even nonviolent, and in any case, those which contribute most to transforming the legal ethical–political rules: in the university and outside the university.[49]

In this way, there is evidence to suggest that Derrida also appeals to the Socratic ideal of a nonviolent discussion, in which all participants aspire to speak and to be heard without violence. His focus is on the violences which accompany any mode of expression. This aim appears to be compatible with the goal of envisioning a form of inclusive conversation that allows all to speak and be heard free from violence. Therefore, there is in Derrida's work a commitment to an idea of communication as freedom and justice to difference, through openness in dialogue, even if at the same time he problematises the rules of any particular dialogue. In this way Derrida asks: what does it mean to speak freely and what obstacles are put in the way of free thought and discussion?

---

[47] Lyotard quoted in Linklater, *The Transformation of Political Community*, p. 98.
[48] Derrida, *Limited Inc.* p. 111.   [49] *Ibid.*, p. 112.

Further support for an ethics of good dialogue can also be found in some comments made by Foucault. When asked why he doesn't engage in polemics, he answered that polemics essentially deny the equality of those to whom they are addressed, and the goal of mutual truth seeking. He states that a conversation is preferable over polemic because

> In the serious play of questions and answers, in the work of reciprocal elucidation, the rights of each person are in some sense immanent in the discussion . . . The person asking the questions is merely exercising the right that has been given him: to remain unconvinced, to perceive a contradiction, to require more information, to emphasise different postulates, to point out faulty reasoning etc. As for the person answering the questions, he too exercises a right . . . by the logic of his own discourse he is tied to what he has said earlier, and by the acceptance of dialogue he is tied to the questioning of the other . . . The polemicist, on the other hand, proceeds encased in privileges that he possesses in advance and will never agree to question . . . the person he confronts is not a partner in the search for the truth, but an adversary, an enemy who is wrong, who is harmful and whose very existence constitutes a threat. For him then, the game does not consist of recognising this person as a subject having the right to speak, but of abolishing him, as interlocutor from any possible dialogue; and his final objective will be, not to come as close as possible to a difficult truth, but to bring about the triumph of the just cause he has been manifestly upholding from the beginning.[50]

In referring to the rights of speakers and the confrontation with truth, Foucault reflects an understanding of conversation as a mutual process of truth seeking, in which self and other are accorded equal rights. Therefore, while this statement cannot necessarily be said to prove that Foucault endorses the idea of universal communication community, it nonetheless resonates with the words of both Gadamer and Habermas.

The understanding of dialogue as a means of achieving recognition and equality between participants can be said to be common to a number of approaches concerned with achieving justice to difference. This common understanding of dialogue argues that in dialogue all participants must be free to speak and to be heard; no position can be excluded or judged prior to its articulation in conversation. By participating in discourse in this way agents are recognised and their equality and difference simultaneously confirmed. A sense that no agent should be excluded, that arguments cannot be judged prior to the articulation

---

[50] M. Foucault, 'Polemic, Politics and Knowledge', in P. Rabinow, *The Foucault Reader* (London: Penguin, 1984), pp. 381–2.

and that understanding involves being open to the possibility that one might learn from the other, that they may have a truth to communicate in regard to a common matter of discussion, are all components of a model of dialogue which seems to have broad support from a variety of perspectives, including those which are critical of the philosophical hermeneutic project. In this way, the criticisms of philosophical hermeneutics discussed here do not necessarily amount to an opposition to the possibility of developing a thin dialogical cosmopolitanism based on its model.

Conclusion

The recreation of the Aristotelian *polis* on the global scale is a common aim of philosophical hermeneutics and critical theory. Habermas and Gadamer share an understanding that the chief virtue of the Greek *polis* was the aspiration to develop a realm in which discussion, persuasion and argument could occur free from the threat of violence. However, proceeding from this general recognition, larger differences emerge regarding what counts as good discussion and what the discussion should be oriented towards. Habermas, we have seen, has sought to redefine the meaning of good conversation in terms of a universal communication community, in which discussion relates only to principles of obligation. Although the meaning of justice was debated in the Athenian *polis* and problematised by its philosophers, the deontological account given by Habermas would be largely alien to them. In contrast, the account of conversation oriented towards understanding and associated norms of practical reason provided by Gadamer would, on first glance, appear to be more familiar to its ancient Greek predecessors. To this extent, philosophical hermeneutics suggests a form of neo-Aristotelianism. However, the form of this return to Aristotle provided by Gadamer, is not one which refutes the goal of a universal communication community. On the contrary, philosophical hermeneutics is explicitly universal in scope and ambition. Philosophical hermeneutics, Gadamer argues, seeks to create a universal realm in which practical reasoning or *phronesis* can work again. The virtues of the Aristotelian *polis*, and the virtue of practical reasoning, he argues, are the most appropriate for the challenges facing the culturally and normatively fractured international realm. Philosophical hermeneutics, Gadamer suggests, is essential to the expansion of human solidarity and the expansion of 'we' feeling. In this way, philosophical hermeneutics shares a concern with the expansion of human community and the creation of universal communication community with critical theory, while emphasising different aspects of conversation and communication.

The overall argument thus far can now be summed up as follows. For philosophical hermeneutics, the *telos* of conversation is understanding oriented towards agreement, understood as solidarity. Understanding, conceived this way, requires a conversation in which differently situated participants engage in a process of question and answer in relation to a subject matter of conversation. The participants in conversation, in order to achieve recognition must be open to the possibility of learning, and recognising the possibility of truth in what the other participants have to say. Conversation oriented towards understanding, in the Gadamerian sense, is not necessarily agonal or argumentative. Instead, in dialogue participants attempt to come to share an understanding in relation to a subject matter of conversation, and they do so by trying to strengthen each other's argument. Through this openness to the potential truth communicated by the other, a form of equality is achieved without assimilation. From a philosophical hermeneutic perspective, this is possible because of the situatedness of all linguistically constituted subjects within traditions or horizons of meaning. The act of conversation also brings about the basis of shared language, or horizon of meaning, as participants come to reach an understanding on the subject matter. The understanding achieved does not necessarily involve the development of substantive agreement, but may involve merely the coming to inhabit a similar frame of reference, or coming better to understand the differences between the respective horizons. However, no matter what the 'outcome' in this sense, the deeper outcome is the enabling and experience of solidarity between the discursive partners as they struggle to achieve understanding. In the conversation oriented towards understanding, in this sense, no topics of conversation can be ruled out *a priori*. Achieving an understanding of another's horizon requires being open to the entire particularity of what it is the other has to say. In Benhabib's terms, it requires an openness toward both the 'generalised' and the 'concrete' dimensions of otherness. In this sense, the philosophical hermeneutic model of conversation precedes the model of conversation outlined by discourse ethics, which presupposes and requires a degree of human solidarity, which its procedures cannot supply. As Habermas himself notes

> [J]ustice conceived deontologically requires solidarity as its reverse side . . . Justice concerns the equal freedoms of unique and self

determining individuals, while solidarity concerns the welfare of consociates who are intimately linked in an intersubjectively shared form of life – and thus also to the maintenance of the integrity of this form of life itself. Moral norms cannot protect one without the other; they cannot protect the equal rights and freedoms of the individuals without protecting the welfare of one's fellow man and of the community to which the individuals belong.[51]

The hermeneutic conversation is oriented towards the creation of shared meanings where possible, of a sense of human solidarity, in the absence of, and in anticipation of, more substantial agreement. The form of conversation necessary for such solidarity building must of necessity be thinner than the strictly deontological conversation outlined by Habermas. The philosophical hermeneutic *telos* of understanding is better suited to building solidarity, because it provides a broader definition of conversation. The goal of communication is understanding; that is, the coming to share aspects of a world-view. Of course, understanding may not lead to agreement regarding concrete detail or belief, but in the act of trying to understand or engage with the other in conversation oriented towards understanding, a different, thinner, shared understanding is delivered nonetheless. Through engaging in the goal of understanding a common language or horizon is made possible. While this common horizon cannot be guaranteed nor assured of permanence, it nonetheless creates the possibility of further agreement or consensus and solidarity.

The expansion of human solidarity is the necessary prerequisite for the flourishing of practical reasoning understood as *phronesis*. That a community in which practical reasoning of this type, involving the mediation between universal and particular, reflection on questions of justice and the good life, and the cultivation of a sense of human finitude and openness towards others, can flourish provides the basis for a more adequate relationship between identity and equality amongst diverse human beings. Practical reasoning, as understood by Gadamer, is the orientation towards political practice and community that is consistent with the philosophical hermeneutic description of human being in the world. The philosophical hermeneutic description of human 'being in the world' is one which emphasises the finitude and plurality of human experience, while simultaneously recognising unity of the quality

---

[51] J. Habermas, 'Justice and Solidarity' in M. Kelly (ed.), *Hermeneutics and Critical Theory in Ethics and Politics* (Cambridge: MIT Press, 1990), pp. 32–52, p. 47.

and capacity of linguisticality. In other words, the practice of *phronesis* in the Aristotelian *polis*, as understood by Gadamer, is consistent with linguisticality, which is both bridge and barrier to understanding.

The participants of conversation aspiring to universal inclusiveness must always be mindful and attentive to those of their practices, values and procedures which are exclusive or potentially exclusive. They must also be mindful of the attempts to 'close down' and end conversation and practices of practical reasoning. The thin cosmopolitan conversation concerned with achieving justice to difference must constantly be concerned with increasing the inclusiveness of the conversation through being forever open to new arguments, new modes of argument and alternative truths, but must also include moments of suspicion towards the agreements reached. The recognition of human finitude, which is central to both philosophical hermeneutics and poststructuralism, should be cultivated and used to remind the participants of the limits of their own understandings and of the possibility of new interpretations emerging.

Despite the concerns associated with the Kantian paradigm, and the paradox of limitation and legislation associated with it, the model of conversation and political community developed by philosophical hermeneutics is one that is consistent with and which seeks to expand the realm of human freedom. The exercise of practical reasoning in the 'thin' universal *polis* requires and embodies the ability of reasonable agents to engage in free discussion. Conversation in which justice to difference is achieved strives to embody the goals of equality and freedom, without this involving the ascription of substantive identity between agents. The philosophical hermeneutic model of conversation and its development into a thin model of cosmopolitan community, therefore, can be seen to aspire to keep the promise of both the Athenian *polis* and the European enlightenment by seeking to create a realm in which freedom reigns. The next question is, how to realise and translate this understanding of good dialogue into international relations? This question forms the starting point of the next chapter.

6 Towards a thin cosmopolitanism

> Communities are to be distinguished, not by their falsity/genuineness, but by the style in which they are imagined.[1]

This enquiry began with the words of Paul Ricouer, who suggested that a genuine conversation between the cultures of the world, which was not an act of violence or assimilation, has yet to take place. This book has taken the development of a model of such a conversation as its motivating goal. It has argued that if such a 'genuine' conversation of cultures and civilisations is to occur, then Gadamer's account of philosophical hermeneutics provides an appropriate model of how it might proceed. Having outlined the meaning of philosophical hermeneutics and its contribution to our understanding of communication, the task of this chapter is to chart the implications of the preceding argument for the nature of political community and ethical action in international relations.

This chapter begins, in a preliminary fashion, to outline a more complete account of the philosophical hermeneutic contribution to the cosmopolitan project. The principal insight to draw from this discussion is that the essential task of a thin cosmopolitanism is to enable a genuine conversation between different cultures and civilisations. Cosmopolitanism, then, is reconstituted, or re-imagined, as a vehicle for intercultural conversation. This chapter also argues that the philosophical hermeneutic account leaves open the possibility that thicker cosmopolitan communities may develop.

The chapter is divided into two sections. The first offers some general reflections and provides a broad brushstroke sketch of what the

[1] B. Anderson, *Imagined Communities: Reflections on the Origins and Spread of Nationalism*, 2nd edn (London: Verso, 1991), p. 6.

thin dialogic cosmopolitanism might look like, and how it might be related to contemporary trends and, in particular, to the apparent moves towards a more solidarist interpretation of international society. The second section of the chapter explores in more detail how the approach developed in this book might contribute to thinking about human rights. A thin cosmopolitanism informed by philosophical hermeneutics suggests understanding the issue of human rights as both a political and philosophical issue. It also suggests that conversation and dialogue have an important place in any resolution of both these aspects.

The chapter concludes with the suggestion that communicative ethics do not exhaust the scope for thinking about justice and ethics in IR, but rather, provide a starting point for the development of more concrete practices of ethical engagement.

Opening and enhancing communication

The model of conversation informed by philosophical hermeneutics and outlined in the preceding chapters is directed towards the development of 'thin' understanding of cosmopolitan community, which nonetheless aspires to something like the recreation of the Aristotelian *polis* on the global scale. Dialogical communication was understood as both a means and an end in the achievement of this form of community. In particular, conversation was understood as enabling a more just relation between self and other, and helping to create the conditions necessary for ongoing relationships of equality, by contributing to the building of solidarity between differently situated agents. Several questions arise at this juncture. The first is: how to achieve such a thin cosmopolitanism and the expansion of the realm of human solidarity, or in other words, how to achieve and encourage communication between differently situated agents? The second question is: in addition to embodying communicative relations, what then would such a thin cosmopolitanism entail, that is, what might such a thin cosmopolitan community actually look like?

The most important answer to these questions, given the primacy of communication as both means and ends, is to search to find the means for opening and institutionalising channels of communication between differently situated agents. The goal of justice to difference supports the erosion, transgression or transcendence of boundaries which prevent communication between differently situated people (and peoples). This requires reflection on how cultural and sociological aspects prevent 'the other' from being seen as equal and capable of communication. Such a task requires, at the very least, an analysis which seeks to understand how communication becomes closed, and how difference comes to be understood as inferiority or threat. It also requires an effort to remove the obstacles to communication which are institutionalised in political practices, such as state sovereignty. The difficulty associated with both of these tasks should not be underestimated.

It was argued in the previous chapter that critical theory and post-structuralist approaches were particularly adept at drawing attention to, and analysing, the ways in which communication between different agents can be blocked. Crucial to these analyses is the identification of the way in which difference is cast as inferiority or incommensurability, and the way in which such perceptions function to close down the avenues for communication. A recent example of how such identification works to prevent communication has been supplied by David Campbell's analysis of the 'deconstruction' of Yugoslavia.[2] The wars in the former Yugoslavia are perhaps paramount cases of the breakdown of communicative relations. The 'deconstruction' of Yugoslavia, in Campbell's appropriate term, is testimony to the triumph of non-communicative relations based on the perception of 'the other' as different and inferior. In the case of situations such as this, genuine dialogue indeed has a hard task. However, it is precisely in such situations that justice, understood as communication, is most desperately required, and every effort should be made to create the conditions whereby communication is possible. Central to this task is reflection on how the difference between self and other came to be seen as morally important. This task requires reflection on the communicative dimensions of prior understandings of self and other. The breakdown of the former Yugoslavia was facilitated by both the triumph of non-communicative relations within and between its members, but also, in inadequate communication between the former Yugoslavia and the 'outside' world.

Campbell's reading emphasises the degree to which handicapped communications between policy makers and analysts outside the former Yugoslavia and the communities within the former Yugoslavia, Bosnia in particular, in turn handicapped the perception of how to engage with the conflict by those same people. Campbell's analysis can be read to suggest that these actors, rather like Las Casas, saw what they expected to see. In his account, the preconceptions, prejudices and blindness of these 'outside' actors' perceptions of what Yugoslavia consisted of, who the warring parties were, and why they were fighting,

---

[2] D. Campbell, *National Deconstruction* (University of Minnesota Press, 1998).

overdetermined their responses. Dominant perceptions of the war in the former Yugoslavia, and Bosnia in particular, were that it consisted of a realm of 'ancient hatreds' which had been simmering away, or had lain dormant, and which now were re-awoken and prodded into life. It suggests a perception of Bosnians, Croats, Serbs, and other inhabitants of the region as possessing a chronic, almost natural, inability to communicate as equals. This understanding tended to characterise the people of the Balkans as 'backward' or rooted in ancient tribalism, This in turn suggested a characterisation of them as different and inferior. Most importantly, Campbell emphasises, these preconceptions reflected a failure of communication, in the sense that they were both the result of an incomplete familiarisation with the circumstances, and acted to prevent further familiarisation.

These preconceptions indicate the extent to which understanding of the situation in the former Yugoslavia was inhibited by a lack of genuine communication. This lack of communication in turn handicapped responses and maintained a situation in which division rather than understanding and communication were fostered. The solution achieved at Dayton, many have suggested, entrenched the ethnic divisions between the parties and rewarded the separatists rather than sought to overcome them.[3] The implication here is that the sponsors of the Dayton accords were informed by their understanding of the situation as irredeemable, and the protagonists as incapable of arriving at less divisive arrangements. Put simply, if one understands the wars to have been caused by 'ancient ethnic hatreds' which are unresolvable, then the best solution is partition between these communities. In other words, understanding how to increase communicative relations requires reflection to extend to the solutions envisioned for such crises. It requires that such thinking is extended, not merely to the participants 'inside the conflict' – that is the warring parties – but also to those 'outside' it. A more informed understanding of the situation in the former Yugoslavia, one informed by reflection on the adequacy of perceptions of self and other in this conflict, may have led to a better solution, or even an entirely different scenario. Thus, pursuing the goals of a thin cosmopolitanism requires opening the channels of communication, which in turn requires reflection on perceptions of self and other, and enquiry into the dialogical basis of those perceptions and whether they reflect genuine or unjustifiable (non-dialogical) prejudices. The telos of understanding reminds

[3] J. M. O. Sharp, 'Dayton Report Card', *International Security*, 22. 3 (1997/8).

us not to close the door to communication too early, and the task of practical reasoning directs us towards inquiring into the conditions in which actions and beliefs enable or disable communicative responses.

Such reflections form only part, and a preliminary part, of the meaning of communication between equals in a thin cosmopolitan community. The goal of inclusion also requires reflection on how the political/institutional channels of communication between differently situated actors can be opened and explored. The first thing to note about such a task is that opening the channels of communication between individuals and political communities requires that the divisions and differences between them are not seen as absolute. It requires pursuing the argument that communal and individual rights to autonomy and independence need to be negotiated, and must take into account the effects of these claims on those excluded from them. It means understanding claims to independence and autonomy as intersubjective claims between equals, and not unilateral and non-negotiable ones carried out in isolation. It means understanding claims to sovereignty as non-absolute and contingent. A commitment to creating a communicative community requires understanding the boundaries between communities as negotiable and flexible. It requires a willingness to question arrangements which exclude outsiders from dialogue or which unjustifiably restrict communication. In this sense, this 'thin' cosmopolitanism is, therefore, subversive of the sovereign state's exclusive claim to communicative legitimacy. At the same time, however, it is not necessarily subversive of the maintenance of a relatively bounded community. Instead, what makes this 'thin' community cosmopolitan is the refusal to identify the state as the only representative voice, or form, of bounded community. Such a principle constitutes a cosmopolitan community in only the thinnest possible sense.

A thin cosmopolitanism is, therefore, consistent with the creation of multiple channels of communication between its members. It is consistent with the creation of 'global civil society' and the supplementing of interstate discourse with intersocietal discourse as the medium for intercommunal communication. In turn, this requires reflection on the communicative dimension of policy-making in international institutions, non-governmental organisations (NGOs), and states. It requires the incorporation of dialogical relations into all such bodies, ensuring that policies, practices and procedures are oriented towards achieving maximum communicative input from all affected by their actions. It requires that international institutions and NGOs reflect on the relations between themselves and those whose interests they advocate, and those who are excluded from their self-definition. An example, though perhaps a difficult one, is in the area of emergency relief and humanitarian aid. In such situations a communicative relationship suggests that it is vital for aid agencies and other institutions to communicate with those whom they wish to provide relief and aid to. This, in turn, requires that the beneficiaries of aid be seen not merely or only as victims in need of rescue, but as dialogical equals who have a say in the arrangements which govern the distribution of aid and humanitarian relief. It is especially vital that the loss of agency, which is arguably experienced by refugees and the victims of natural disasters, not be replicated or compounded by the very agencies seeking to remedy the situation.[4]

Beyond international society

Beyond the reform of such practices to include communicative dimensions, the opening of channels of communication consistent with a thin cosmopolitanism has significant implications for the current institutions whereby order is maintained. If the current form of universal community can be understood as being restricted to international society of states, as suggested by Mervyn Frost and Chris Brown, then a commitment to building solidarity and opening the channels of communication necessarily requires both building upon and superseding the achievements of international society. In the *Transformation of Political Community* Andrew Linklater pointed to Richard Rorty's argument that thinking about matters of universal moral community must begin, not from the defence of the 'epistemological foundations' in a transcendental subject, but from 'where we are'.[5] Rorty argues that western liberals must acknowledge the historicity of their own beliefs in universality and not assume universal grounds for them. Rorty's emphasis on starting from where we are now suggests a compatibility with Gadamer's insight that understanding takes place only within a pre-given, if problematic, tradition. In the context of international relations and the re-thinking of political community, a recognition of 'where we are now' involves a recognition of the roles played by international society and its most important institutions, both now and in the past. In other words, whether or not there are epistemological or transcendental foundations

---

[4] See the comments in J. Edkins, 'Sovereign Power, Zones of Indistinction, and the Camp', *Alternatives*, 25. 1, Jan–Mar. (2000), 3–25.

[5] See A. Linklater, *The Transformation of Political Community: Ethical Foundations of the Post-Westphalian Era* (Cambridge: Polity Press, 1997), p. 77.

for human community is, to a certain extent, beside the point. Recognising where we are now involves recognising that the institutions of international order have in the past, and will in the future, play a role in maintaining and expanding the human conversation. Therefore, any attempt to engage in the transformation of human community, so that it might approximate a thin cosmopolitanism, can start from the current situation which involves the existence of an international society of which states are the primary members. If the development of international society suggests a process of cultural interaction, allowing the development of minimal, universal principles, then it is possible to conceive that a 'thin' cosmopolitanism may develop out of that process. Such a transformation, however, requires moving beyond international society as it is currently conceived.

In order to understand this progression an examination of the historical contexts of inter-cultural communication and an understanding of the current international order is required. Samuel Huntington has argued that the possibilities of inter-cultural conversation are virtually non-existent.[6] Instead, in the future, different cultures and civilisations will (almost inevitably) continue to clash and engage in violent and unequal relations. For Huntington, the near total incommensurability of the major civilisational groupings guarantees a future of conflict and a withdrawal from understanding. This incommensurability stems, he argues, from the fact that these clashes will be between different identities. In the future, conflicts will no longer be over what a person believes, but over who they *are*. In the dimension of identity, according to Huntington, there is no room for negotiation or accommodation.

Despite Huntington's assertions, there exists enough evidence to suggest that culturally different societies have, over the course of history, been able to come to agree on certain principles and engage in a practice of mutual coexistence, if not always of understanding. According to Bull, Wight, Watson and others, different civilisations and societies have been able, through the institutions of international society and over time, to come to share certain understandings and norms and even identities.[7] For writers, such as the early Bull, these norms have principally been restricted to the norms of sovereignty and non-intervention

---

[6] S. P. Huntington, 'The Clash of Civilizations?' *Foreign Affairs*, Summer (1993), 22–49.
[7] See especially H. Bull and A. Watson (eds.), *The Expansion of International Society* (Oxford University Press, 1983), also M. Wight (G. Wight, and B. Porter, eds.), *International Theory: The Three Traditions* (Leicester University Press, 1991); M. Wight, *Systems of States* (Leicester University Press, 1977).

and, on occasion, extended further to include the rules for both *Jus in bello* and *Jus ad bellum*. Some, such as Mervyn Frost, as seen in chapter 2, have argued that the norms of international society now exceed those minimal goals of mere coexistence and incorporate thicker values such as the recognition of universal human rights. Bull's comments on the need for international society to be more inclusive of the 'third world's' demands are often cited in this regard.[8]

This suggests that international society can be understood as an arena in which states have not only negotiated their interests but also one in which different societies, cultures and civilisations are able to engage with each other in relative equality. Bull and Watson's investigation into the expansion of international society demonstrates this point. The establishment of international principles of order has involved a process of inter-civilisational learning and dialogue, though not necessarily a conversation between equals. It is certainly true that the norms and principles of international society have been and continue to reflect the norms and values of the most powerful societies, and it is true that the norms of international society were spread through the use of force and unequal conversations. However, it is also true that appeal to international society has also been a means by which some communities have in turn attempted resistance to assimilation, and have attempted to articulate their resistance to the dominance of the most powerful.[9] In articulating their claims in this way, these communities are acknowledging the necessity and desirability of maintaining channels of communication. Furthermore, as Bull's comments on the 'revolt against western dominance' suggest, international society has in recent decades come to be seen as a forum in which those subject to western dominance now pursue their equality. Thus, while acknowledging the deeply assimilatory history of this encounter, it is nonetheless possible to conceive of the institutions of international society as having served the purpose of maintaining international political order while allowing a greater intercivilisational conversation of humankind to emerge.

Furthermore, to proceed from 'where we are' requires an acknowledgement of the existing tension between pluralist and solidarist forms of international society. Starting from 'where we are' means starting from an international society in which pluralist and solidarist tendencies

---

[8] See H. Bull, *Justice in International Relations* (The Hagey Lectures), (University of Waterloo, 1983) and H. Bull, 'The Third World and International Society', *Yearbook of World Affairs* (1979), 15–31.
[9] Again see Bull's discussion of 'The Revolt Against Western Dominance' in Bull, *ibid.*

exist, and in which non-state actors claim an important role, and struggle to be recognised.

A pluralist interpretation of international society emphasises its role in providing order between disparate political communities who lack consensus amongst them, regarding substantive conceptions of the good life and morality. This is the 'egg-box' conception of international society discussed in chapter 1. However, in the period since the end of the Cold War, international society has arguably moved in what Bull labelled a solidarist, or interventionist, direction.[10] Specifically, the international order in the 1990s has been characterised by a number of circumstances which have challenged international society to develop and uphold some minimal standards for state behaviour which go beyond merely the mutual recognition of sovereignty, and which require its members to act together to enforce these standards. Such a move goes beyond the pluralist principles of coexistence. To move in a solidarist direction necessarily involves a shift away from the foundational principle of sovereignty. This is so because the central feature of solidarism is a commitment to the principle of consensus rather than consent. The principle of consensus means that international society can act against recalcitrant or criminal states when there is an 'overwhelming majority, a convergence of international opinion'.[11] The shift to a consensus interpretation of international law has an impact upon the norms of international society because it suggests that something like 'the will of the international community' can, under certain circumstances, override the sovereignty of states. This is a demotion of sovereignty from its status as a 'primary goal' to a somewhat secondary one.

The move to a more solidarist international society suggests the need to develop new means for assuring the legitimacy of international law and of international society in general, through the establishment of a genuine international consensus on the values underlying solidarism. If the shift to a solidarist international society replaces a consent-based international law with a consensus based one, then that consensus must be

[10] See H. Bull 'The Grotian Conception of International Society', in H. Butterfield and M. Wight (eds.) *Diplomatic Investigations* (London: Allen and Unwin, 1966) and also Bull, *Anarchical Society;* also N. Wheeler and T. Dunne, 'Hedley Bull's Pluralism of the Intellect and Solidarism of the Will', *International Affairs,* 72 (1996), 1–17.

[11] Richard Falk quoted in Bull, *The Anarchical Society,* p. 148. This is opposed to the principle of consent in which international law is upheld only by states willing to do so, i.e. international law requires the consent of those affected by it. For a discussion of the norm of consent see Christian Reus-Smit, 'The Constitutional Structure of International Society and the Nature of Fundamental Institutions', *International Organisation,* 51. 4, Autumn (1997).

assured and genuine. In the context of Bull's and others' long-standing reservations about such projects, the normative and practical questions revolve around the task of pursuing and achieving consensus on international norms of behaviour.

From a cosmopolitan position, it stands to reason that, if the principles and practices of international society are moving in a more interventionist and solidarist direction, involving a shift beyond principles of mere coexistence, then forms of legitimation are required which rest on the consent of citizens as well as states. For international society to take a solidarist turn and its members to act on the basis of consensus, then the legitimacy of this consensus must be assured. Therefore the replacement of state consent by a principle of consensus requires in turn the extension of consent, that is that laws should be made by those subject to them, to the citizens of states. If the institutions of international governance and the practices of international society are to be truly global in their scope, then they are in need of universal, cosmopolitan, forms of legitimation.

Such forms of legitimation must necessarily be inclusive of a wide variety of cultural differences. The model of conversation deployed above provides one principle with which to engage in thinking about these questions. The model of conversation oriented towards understanding and recreation of the Aristotelian *polis*, and embodying the logic of practical reasoning, is one means of thinking about how to legitimate solidarist practices of international society.

The shift from pluralist to solidarist international society suggests the possibility that more solidaristic and communicative arrangements may be aspired to, and may develop out of the current order. However, for a thin cosmopolitanism to be developed out of international society, it must move beyond both pluralist and solidarist forms of international society. Furthermore, a moral community in which justice to difference is pursued requires the transformation of international society into a thin cosmopolitanism. International society as it currently stands remains state-centric. Even the incorporation of thicker principles such as human rights into the realm of agreement does not undermine the fact that it is states who are the members of international society. For international society to become more just, it needs to become more cosmopolitan and move beyond the principle of state-centrism. While the presence of international society provides evidence of the possibility of developing transcultural normative discourses and principles, 'international society' itself must be transcended if the goal of justice to difference is to be pursued further.

As such, new agreements recognising these dimensions are required. However, doing so requires that international society envisage the difficult task of moving beyond the question of sovereignty; or, alternatively, redefining it so as to be more inclusive and less restrictive. Thus, a concern with justice to difference requires acknowledging the gains of international society, while at the same time transcending its limitations and transforming it into a 'thin' cosmopolitanism, in order to achieve a more equal conversation between different cultures.

A variegated cosmopolitanism

The previous discussion has outlined some of the implications of a commitment to inclusion, through dialogue, to current understandings of international society and international institutions. This section turns to a discussion of the broad features of a thin cosmopolitanism informed by philosophical hermeneutics and constituted by the goal of dialogical inclusion. In other words, this section addresses the question 'what might such a thin cosmopolitanism look like?'

The first and most important answer to this question is that the primary characteristic of such a thin cosmopolitanism is that it does not prescribe the 'thick' moral content of the community prior to dialogue between those concerned. Instead, it allows that content to be filled in by the participants themselves. It is in this manner that the cosmopolitanism community is 'thin', because it does not prescribe the thick norms associated with other forms of cosmopolitanism, such as the model advanced by Beitz and discussed in chapter 1. In this way the thin cosmopolitan informed by philosophical hermeneutics shares a similar goal to that outlined by Linklater. A thin cosmopolitanism is a form of dialogical universal moral community where the moral content and norms which govern the relations between its members are the product of discursive engagement between the members themselves, and are not delivered by philosophic fiat or acts of 'monological reasoning'.[12] Likewise, such a realm is one in which norms are not simply imposed by the strongest over the weakest, and do not necessarily reflect the thick norms of any

---

[12] Such justification extends to a substantive morality of communication itself. The goal of universal community in which justice to difference is achieved through dialogue is itself a 'thick' goal. It represents an interpretation of the values arising from within European/Christian traditions of thought and seeks to extrapolate those values to the world. The claim that is being made here is that the formulation offered here is substantively 'thinner' than some other interpretations. As has been suggested in the introduction and again in chapter 4 it is impossible to formulate a conception of community that is without substance (i.e. in some degree thick) at all.

particular moral horizon, tradition or political power. With these insights in mind it is possible to reflect further on the forms which a thin cosmopolitanism may take.

The global moral community envisioned here and consistent with these principles is compatible with the idea that, rather than one cosmopolitan community, it might be possible to develop a variety of cosmopolitanisms. A thin cosmopolitanism involves, not necessarily a single conversation, generating a single universally thick or thin community, but the possibility of many conversations developing forms of community in which some parts are more 'cosmopolitan' and others less so. Rather than one cosmopolitan community, it might be possible to develop a variety of 'cosmopolitanisms', characterised in different ways in different times and places.

The traditional account of cosmopolitan community suggests that it is a reproduction of the supposedly unitary domestic community at the global level. However, the emphasis on a community constituted by understanding and solidarity between radically different agents, means that it is openness to conversational engagement, rather than the production of specific arrangements, which announces the presence of a cosmopolitan ethos. Therefore, a commitment to conversation, informed by practical reasoning, does not require that every social arrangement in every community be submitted to impartial universal approval, and does not produce a single 'community'. What it does suggest, instead, is that a commitment to universal community and to recognition of difference in conversation might result in a cosmopolitanism characterised in different ways in different times and places.

The thin cosmopolitanism envisioned here is thin in the same sense intended by Linklater, because it is consistent with a variety of different forms of association. According to Linklater, there is no reason for thinking that discourse between differently situated agents will necessarily bring about a uniform cosmopolitan community, in the thick or solidarist sense.[13] There are reasons for believing, on the contrary, that certain parts of the system would, under conditions of a free and open dialogue, resist this movement and agree to disagree, limiting the obligations each demands of the other. Linklater argues that international society, for example, may develop along either pluralist and solidarist routes, indicating the manner in which different parts of the international system may develop according to different

---

[13] See Linklater, *The Transformation of Political Community.*

logics, while nonetheless, remaining consistent with the principles of open and universal discourse.[14] Such a conception would require a conversation that is sufficiently flexible and open, while at the same time acknowledging the pragmatic and practical limits of such conversation in any given situation. The advantage of the account of conversation and praxis informed by philosophical hermeneutics is that it is flexible enough to allow this, because it does not legislate the dimensions of the cosmopolitan community that it aspires to.

Such a model suggests that, while some parts of the globe may be willing and able to engage in something resembling either Beitz's liberal cosmopolitanism or Linklater's Post-Westphalian community, others may choose to restrict interaction to a mode of coexistence which does not move beyond, say, the rules of coexistence currently operative in international society as articulated by Brown. Thus, some communities may discover or achieve a higher, or 'thicker', level of solidarity than others. It may be possible that some societies may identify areas of common agreement that extend to principles of citizenship, including a high degree of specificity of rights and responsibilities. On the other hand, some communities may not be able or wish to develop such arrangements, and may agree to restrict the level of transnational agreement to principles of orderly interaction. The important point here, is that a principle of discursive inclusion does not legislate the outcome of conversation itself, nor the procedures in which agreement can be pursued. What constitutes these different arrangements as cosmopolitan, is that they should result from, and be consistent with, a commitment to open communication between members of human society as a whole.

An approach taking into account the variety of engagements between different societies, cultures and groups, must, if it is to remain committed to doing justice to difference, also be sensitive to, and aware of the degree to which these bodies themselves are not cohesive, and contain disputes between their members. A principle of communication, therefore, does not restrict conversation to the acknowledged representatives of a given community, but must be inclusive of the wide range of voices *within* any group. This conversation is attentive to the voice of different groups and cultures, while aspiring to universal inclusion, and is, therefore, consistent with a variety of 'cosmopolitanisms'.

---

[14] See A. Linklater, 'Citizenship and Sovereignty in the Post-Westphalian State', *European Journal of International Relations*, 2. 1, March (1996) 77–103 and Linklater, *The Transformation of Political Community*.

This formulation of community is suited to a world of radical difference because it settles for *neither* coexistence *nor* assimilation and, instead, investigates the possibilities of a communicative cosmopolitanism. Such a thin, variegated, cosmopolitanism is more attuned to the realities of the present world order because, while this order is dominated by states and societies engaged in modernisation and partaking in the capitalist world economy, it also contains interactions between cultures and groups that are not commensurate with states, or whose engagement with modernity might be more limited. The contemporary world can be understood as involving interactions between varieties of levels, and types of social organisations and individuals requiring different conversations. Some societies, cultures, religious or ethnic groups are universalistic in aspiration, while others are perhaps content to remain parochial; some wish to resist the worst aspects of modernisation, while holding onto and using some of its advantages, in order to secure their own survival.[15]

In such a context, it is necessary to be attentive to the different types of relations which may exist between the different aspects of this world society. The relations between societies which are dominated by what we might call universalising cultures are likely to be different, in some ways more confrontational and in others less, than relations between universalising cultures and parochial or particularistic ones. For example, the type of conversation and community that may come about in relations between west-European societies is likely to be different from that which may come about in relations between west-European societies, dominated by the universalism of Christianity and the enlightenment and societies dominated by Islamic teachings and practices. Likewise, conversations between Islamic societies and indigenous peoples are likely to produce different results again. This being the case, then, a thin cosmopolitanism aims to be inclusive of the full variety of societies, cultures and different normative universes and flexible enough to recognise that different societies have different agendas and are likely to have different concerns in relation to each other. The point of this argument is that any account of a universal ethical life which aspires to do justice to

---

[15] An example of this might be the use of modern media and political institutions by certain indigenous groups, such as the Yanomani of the Amazon and the Penan of Borneo, to articulate their claims to a wider universal audience. These claims are largely claims to a form of self-determination in relation to a dominant state, but also include a claim to resist the intrusion of certain aspects of modernity into their relatively bounded societies. In this way, these people both exploit and resist 'modernity'.

difference should take into account the possibilities for different types of relations between communities, states, societies and the universal community. Where thicker universalism is aspired to, the hermeneutic account would require it to be the product of 'genuine' conversation. What this would mean is that, rather than the expression of any particular culture, any thicker universal agreements must be just that, the result of inclusive conversation. Such agreements may be a fusion of a number of positions, or the creation of something new that is not unique to any culture. It may even be possible that one culture or society has been able to persuade the others of the universal merit of a given norm, for example freedom from torture, or even the concept of human rights. What is certain is that the participants in the conversation must be open to the possibilities for learning from others, and any substantive agreement should reflect that learning. The argument of this book has been that the model for such a conversation is provided by philosophical hermeneutics.

By way of further comparison, this thin cosmopolitanism can be differentiated from the account of cosmopolitan conversation provided by Charles Taylor. In 'The Politics of Recognition'[16] Taylor argued that the fusion of horizons resulting from a conversation between different cultures will not only aid mutual understanding but also create the categories whereby we can judge their relative contributions and worth. Taylor argues that, in order to ensure equal recognition, the 'starting hypothesis with which we ought to approach the study of any other culture [should be that] all human cultures that have animated whole societies over some considerable stretch of time have something important to say to all human beings'.[17] While Taylor's formulation captures much of the essence of the argument for recognition, and draws upon philosophical hermeneutics, there is nonetheless something troubling in his hypothesis that suggests a type of conversation different from that consistent with the thin cosmopolitan conversation being described here.

The goal of discovering the contribution of different cultures would seem to be another variation on the idea that there is something to be learnt from them in understanding. The problem is that, for Taylor, not only should we start with a presumption of worth, but the purpose of conversation is to endeavour to assess that worth. The purpose of understanding, therefore, is not merely coming to an understanding, but an assessment and judgement, in terms of an unspecified *contribution* to

---

[16] C. Taylor, 'The Politics of Recognition', in C. Taylor and A. Gutman, *Multiculturalism: Examining the Politics of Recognition* (Princeton University Press, 1994).
[17] *Ibid.*, p. 66.

a universal humanity. Taylor's account, therefore, seems to share with Kantian accounts, discussed in chapter 2, a rejection of the possibility that local truths may remain just that, local, and have no obvious universal applicability, truth or contribution. The unspoken presupposition that guides conversation is that cultures only have worth in so far as they are able to contribute to humanity as whole. In Taylor's account then, recognition is conditional rather than assumed.

This criticism is not meant to suggest that judgement and understanding are incompatible, and that participants in conversation should refrain from moral judgements of the practices or beliefs of others. Understanding does not require the abandonment of identity or of one's own beliefs or standards of judgement – these are always a condition of engagement. Conversation, however, allows different agents to come to understand the reasoning behind practices and beliefs, and then to make an informed judgement. Furthermore, conversation permits the development of a shared language of moral discourse in which judgements may be conducted. It is understanding which constitutes the moment of recognition as equality, not judgement. However, on the other hand to withhold from judgement, as in a practice of coexistence, involves a lesser form of equality, and so cannot be dispensed with altogether. The history of inter-cultural contacts, especially in the last four hundred years, has been dominated by too-hasty judgements and a lack of genuine dialogue between cultures. Given this history, and in the absence of any thick cosmopolitanism, a conversation which ignored the task of understanding would have significant limitations.

The thin cosmopolitanism being described here does not rule out the search for transcultural validity of moral claims or the possibility that different horizons have contributions to make to a global community. However, it does emphasise that the primary task of conversation is the building of solidarity through understanding, and this is not necessarily consistent with a conversation the aim of which is to rank different cultures according to their overall contribution to humanity, or in terms of their place in any 'great chain of being'. The goal of seeking to do justice to difference encourages the attempt to resist the language of hierarchy, while not surrendering the capacity to make reasoned judgements.

Human rights and dialogue

The reflections above have served to help clarify where a commitment to communicative inclusion based on philosophical hermeneutics might take the international order, and inform thinking about certain types of actions and institutions. This section offers an exploration of how a commitment to communicative inclusion might contribute to thinking about questions of human rights.

If there is one issue in international relations today which most directly speaks to the concerns of a thin cosmopolitanism it is the idea of universal human rights. The pursuit of universal human rights and their institutionalisation as an international norm since the end of the Second World War are of central importance to the goal of creating a thin cosmopolitan community for several reasons. First, it is the clearest expression of a moral universalism which goes beyond the morality of states, evident in the international realm today. As such, the incorporation of human rights into the norms of international society is, whether states perceive it this way or not, a commitment, however thin, to the idea of universal community of humankind. The commitment to human rights suggests that states, as well as individuals, have obligations and duties to humankind that are superior to the obligations they have to maintain order, or that individuals have to their states. Second, the norms of universal human rights, in a sense, underpin most other normative developments in international society, including the shift from a pluralist to a solidarist understanding. Third, human rights are also a key focus for debates regarding the rights to cultural difference and diversity. Just what human rights are, where they have their grounding and how they can be defended as universal, are central philosophical questions which have arisen alongside, and as part of, the usual political objections to universal moral projects. In this way, they can be seen as a paradigm case for how a communicative approach can inform moral debates in international relations. Finally, any conception of thin cosmopolitanism must be informed by some sense of universal human right to participate in dialogue. However, such a commitment must be accompanied by a recognition that it must itself be defended argumentatively and established discursively. The discussion below offers an attempt to think through how to proceed in this vein.

In a recent contribution the moral philosopher Bikhu Parekh has proposed an important and viable approach for thinking about human rights in international politics, which is largely consistent with the approach to community outlined in this book.[18] Parekh's argument begins

---

[18] B. Parekh, 'Non-ethnocentric Universalism' in T. Dunne and N. Wheeler, *Human Rights in Global Politics* (Cambridge: Cambridge University Press, 1999).

by examining the epistemological questions which are often seen as providing the grounding for human rights. The question which has dogged most discussion of human rights has been 'Are human rights universal?' This question is a version of another more important question, which is: 'What grounds can we provide for convincing others of the *a priori* universality of human rights?' Parekh's approach is based on the argument that epistemological questions do not actually constitute the core issue. He argues that the challenge facing those wishing to advocate universal human rights is not one of epistemology but persuasion. Parekh's approach is in keeping with a dialogical cosmopolitanism: 'If universal values are to enjoy widespread support and democratic validation and be free of ethnocentric biases, they should arise out of an open and uncoerced cross-cultural dialogue.'[19] He argues for a recognition that the attempt to use epistemological arguments in order to justify universal human rights has not been fully convincing, either within the west or outside it. As a result, arguments based on such foundations are no longer fully available to those who wish to pursue universal human rights. All attempts to ground or provide secure foundations for universal human rights, such as natural law arguments, have suffered similar fates, in remaining unconvincing to many. These insights sit well with post-war developments in the philosophy of the human sciences. The interpretive turn as argued in chapter 2 has emphasised the extent and manner in which human life, including its moral values, is socially constituted.

Parekh's argument suggests that, in keeping with this development, projects such as the defence of universal human rights should be seen as having their origins not outside the realm of human intersubjectivity, derived from some sort of transcendental insight, or existing in some sense outside of human values, that is, residing innately in human beings or natural law. In contrast, the values of universal human rights should be understood as part of the social constitution of reality. However, unfortunately for many, this recognition has, as with the communitarians, been seen to lead away from the defence of moral universalism in the form of human rights, rather than towards it. The communitarian approach can, with some qualification, be identified with this line of thinking. Communitarians, it was argued in chapter 1, hold that, because values are socially constructed then different societies construct them differently. This is then followed by a series of riders such as, that

---

[19] Parekh, 'Non-ethnocentric Universalism', p. 139.

these traditions are incommensurable, that different traditions have no ability to judge other cosmologies and their practices, and that furthermore, they have no right to do so. Therefore, in the communitarian philosophy the prospects and perhaps even the desirability of universal human rights are thin.[20]

However, the argument of this work has been that the recognition of the social construction of human rights, or the rootedness of human rights as a discourse, does not necessarily lead to a strictly relativist conclusion. On the contrary, it is the social and intersubjective, and ultimately linguistic basis of human rights, as discourse as well as practice, that provide the best hope for actually achieving universal recognition of human rights. If we understand social reality to be socially constituted then we can understand human rights like other values to be, as Parekh points out, the product of reasoning and agreement. Values, he argues 'are a matter of collective decision, and like any other decision it is based on reasons'.[21]

Therefore, instead of asking the question, 'are human rights universal?', and looking for an epistemological answer, the moral, as well as the political, questions that arise from a recognition of intersubjectivity should instead be posed thus: 'How can we achieve universal human rights?', or, 'How can we come to achieve understanding on human rights?', or as Onora O'Neill might put it, 'What type of universal human rights community can we construct?' In other words, agreement on universality can be achieved only through dialogue. The task is to build a dialogue on human rights and in that dialogue to ask what human rights are and which human rights are universal? At the same time, a universal dialogue which seeks to pursue understanding on the meaning of human rights serves to entrench the human rights of participation in conversation.

The challenge of communitarianism and the charge of incommensurability have been met by the attempt to think through the meaning of dialogue in a world of radical difference, or what Nick Rengger has called radical value incommensurability.[22] However, the model of dialogue is really only the starting place. There are at least three ways

[20] See for instance the discussion in C. Brown, 'Cultural Diversity and International Political Theory: From the Requirement to "Mutual Respect"', *Review of International Studies*, 26 (2000), 199–13.
[21] Parekh, 'Non-ethnocentric Universalism', p. 140.
[22] N. J. Rengger, 'Incommensurability, International Theory and the Fragmentation of Western Political Culture', in J. Gibbins, *Contemporary Political Culture* (London: Sage, 1988), pp. 237–50.

of understanding the way in which a dialogue on human rights might proceed. The first might be that it is a conversation in which the purpose is to persuade 'others' that 'our' conception of human rights is correct. Another is to understand the conversation as a search for transcultural validity of universal human rights; in other words, it may be possible to find or recognise common elements shared by different cultures. Such a conversation is engaged in discovering which pre-existing values can be found to be consistent with the conventional understanding of human rights. A further response is also possible, and this is the one most consistent with the model of conversation developed here and supported by Parekh's argument. This conversation proceeds from an assumption that shared commitments to and definitions of universal human rights are a matter to be constructed; that through dialogue a universal human rights consensus may be achieved. This model emphasises that dialogue may bring about a consensus on issues of human rights which may or may not stem from pre-existing cultural values and beliefs. This conversation is a search for transcultural validity, but understood as a transcultural validity that, in Rorty's words, should be 'shaped rather than found'. Such a conception does not rule out the possibility that pre-existing transculturally common norms may be found, but it does not direct the conversation exclusively in that direction.

This model of conversation understands universal human rights not as a truth which 'we' possess and must convince others of, but rather as a common subject of conversation, in the manner of '*die Sache*' in Gadamer's model. In this sense, the meaning of universal human rights is a subject placed before the participants in conversation and forms the focus of that discussion. Each participant possesses their own understanding of the meaning of this subject, and the conversation is oriented towards achieving further understanding. If we understand the conversation surrounding human rights as concerned exclusively with getting 'them' to agree with 'us' then it cannot be understood as a dialogue between equals. However, if we understand human rights as an issue or subject about which all are concerned, stemming, for example, from reflection upon what it means to be human and what constitutes proper treatment for those considered human, then a dialogue between equals becomes possible.[23]

---

[23] In their comments on Parekh's argument Dunne and Wheeler suggest that it suffers from a prior assumption of that which it seeks to achieve, i.e. a universal sense of the

Such a model of conversation proceeds from the assumption that the meaning of universal human rights is to be negotiated and that human rights may come to have different connotations in different times and places. What it might mean to uphold human rights, and indeed what human rights are, cannot always be understood in the abstract and in advance. What is meant here is that the answers to the question 'are human rights universal' can only be decided upon in conversation, and in the context of application of particular definitions in particular times and places.[24]

Such a dialogue provides no guarantees. Dialogic engagement and understanding may occur without producing any substantive consensus or shared values which the parties can agree upon. Alternatively, there may be limits to the degree of consensus achieved. Agreement upon universal human rights may only go so far or may not cover, for instance, the range of human rights covered by existing UN resolutions or organisations like Amnesty International. For example, amputation may not be seen as violation of human rights in some states ruled by Islamic Law, nor the use of the death penalty in the United States. Finally, such a conversation is not necessarily inconsistent with a search for, or advocacy of, particular accounts of human rights. The model of conversation drawn upon here in which all partake as equals, does not involve the complete surrender of one's own position nor necessarily prevent one from seeking to have one's own interpretation of human rights (and of which human rights are the most important) secure recognition or become adopted by others. It only requires that the 'other' may have something different to say and that one be open to the possibility of learning. In this way the conversation on universal human rights seeks to avoid becoming a repeat of the requirement (see Introduction) in which the meaning of human rights, or human dignity, is assumed and imposed rather than discursively proposed.

human. But this point runs the risk of absurdity if taken too far. In order to have a dialogue about human rights two things are necessary. The first is that there is something called the human to which these rights refer. What the definition of the human is may differ across cultures and individuals but the concept at least must be present and there must be some minimal recognition of the subject matter as having something in common for all. This is the opening of Socratic dialogue.

[24] In such a conversation a number of further questions arises. Instead of asking are human rights universal in the abstract, we can ask two further questions: can universal agreement on human rights be achieved and which human rights might be capable of such a consensus? Thus for instance there may be universal agreement that human rights are universal in the sense that everyone deserves the right to life but there may not be universal agreement on the proposition that everyone deserves free universal health care.

In all of these cases assessment of what may be achieved in dialogue can be made only after, or as, it takes place and not before. The upshot of this argument is that the task of pursuing universal human rights cannot proceed without a basis in dialogue, the question 'can we achieve universal human rights?' cannot be answered until dialogue has taken place.

Beyond reflection on the manner in which dialogue might proceed and how the issue of universal human rights should be understood philosophically, is the issue of how to think about human rights politically. Human rights is of course a deeply political issue, and a response to the above reflections might be that 'that's all very well but people are suffering now and human rights need to be defended and upheld now, we can't wait for a conversation to take place'. Another response might be to ask 'Who should partake in this conversation? Should it be a conversation between states when it is states who are mostly to blame for human rights violations?' The first reply to these questions is that any political practice oriented towards defending human rights will be more successful when supported both by sound philosophical starting points, defences and arguments, and by a shared understanding of what human rights consist of and how they should be defended. Without such defences, and it is suggested here these defences can be derived from a conversation, the programme for universal human rights becomes, indeed, just another version of the 'requirement'.

A second response is that from a thin cosmopolitan perspective there are no reasons for restricting the conversation to states alone. Indeed, as it is states who are the most likely perpetrators of human rights violations, there is every reason to be concerned with the voices of the victims. Booth is correct in reminding us that it is the victims of human rights abuses that we should listen to, rather than just the perpetrators of them.[25]

Furthermore, given that the world is now a world of states, we should not be surprised that it is states, or those who aspire to run them, who are resistant to universal human rights claims. Human rights, as universal doctrine, have their origins not only in the western philosophical tradition but also as a product of a political struggle for recognition and freedom over and against the state. It is, for the same reason, that they may and do appeal to many in the non-west, and why the voices of individuals should be listened to. This, in turn, supports Parekh's

---

[25] K. Booth, 'Three Tyrannies', in Dunne and Wheeler, *Human Rights in Global Politics*.

argument that we need to move beyond the epistemological defence of human rights, and opens up other means by which human rights might be made more persuasive. If the political and social circumstances in which human rights thinking evolved in the west are remembered, and cited as arguments in favour of them, then they are more likely to appeal to others who find themselves in similar situations, that is those resisting the encroachments of states and other agencies which seek to deny freedom to those who oppose them, or hold different conceptions of how to conduct themselves or their place in society. Thus, ironically, it might also be that it is the universality of the state form which provides the best ground for the universality of human rights. If human rights grew out of a resistance to the state, then those who are best served by human rights will be those who are suffering under them.

Finally to return to the question, 'what happens to the task of universal human rights, and more importantly, to the victims of human rights violations, in the meantime, that is, as conversation takes place?' Is it possible and justifiable to act against abusers in the absence of such a consensus? The political problems associated with human rights return us to Rorty's observation that we must begin from where we are. Where we are is a heterogenous international society with an incipient global civil society and not a pre-existing thin cosmopolitan community. How, then, to proceed from where we are? The first thing to acknowledge is that a conversation concerning human rights has been and is taking place. While this conversation is largely dictated by political agendas and processes, because it is carried out by means of the vehicle of international society and the institutions of the UN, it has produced both a series of documents and resolutions to which states can now be held accountable and a wider conversation between non-state actors, NGOs, religious organisations and others. This wider conversation might be less motivated by political jockeying and more by a search for genuine understanding. Such processes and agreements provide the starting point for action on human rights while the larger conversation continues. Finally, there is nothing in the philosophical hermeneutic model of thin cosmopolitanism which prevents concerned agents acting or seeking to condemn the actions of states or other bodies which do not respect universal human rights, where those actions stem from the pleas or requests of the victims of human rights. There is, on the contrary, every reason why their voices should be heard and acted upon.

These thoughts have been offered in the manner of preliminary reflections on how philosophical hermeneutics might inform thinking about the issue of universal human rights. They are not proposed as the definitive or even the right approach to addressing these issues. Instead, they should be understood as an attempt at a thinking through of possible implications. The philosophical hermeneutic model of conversation and the thin cosmopolitan ethics informed by it do not necessarily have the solution to all problems associated with human rights and moral universalism. However they do provide a means which is consistent with the aspirations, central to the project of achieving human rights, of universalism and the recognition of difference.

Conclusion

> Justice is like the pre-original, anarchic relation to the other, and akin
> to the undecidable. It represents the domain of the impossible and the
> unrepresentable that lies outside and beyond the limit of the possible
> and the representable.[1]

This investigation began by suggesting that the goal of reconciling community with the recognition of difference represented an impossible
task. The argument that followed was premised on the assumption
that the goal of achieving justice to difference in a universal community should be pursued nonetheless. This book has presented an account of a thin cosmopolitanism which endeavours to accommodate
the widest possible variety of cultures and cosmologies. It has argued
that philosophical hermeneutics in dialogue with liberalism, communitarianism, critical theory and poststructuralism can help to provide
such an account. While aspiring to a thin community in which difference is engaged with equally the model of conversation itself embodies
a substantive moral position which is not neutral, in the liberal sense of
impartiality.

Philosophical hermeneutics informs a particular variant of a communicative approach to addressing moral issues and conceiving of community. It is informed by an argument that communication provides a superior form of relationship to the alternatives of annihilation, assimilation
and coexistence. However, the argument has not rested here. The claim
made for philosophical hermeneutics in this book is that communication requires a rehabilitation of the concept of truth. It has been argued
that the achievement of dialogical equality between self and other rests

---

[1] D. Campbell, 'The Deterritorialisation of Responsibility: Levinas, Derrida, and Ethics
After the End of Philosophy', *Alternatives*, 19 (1994), 455–84, p. 472.

on the possibility of encountering or experiencing truth. A claim to have achieved understanding involves coming to experience a new, or different, truth. The moment of equality in conversation occurs at the point in which a participant acknowledges not only the limits of their own knowledge, but also the possibility that the other participant(s) may be able to bring to light new ways of seeing or understanding, which are of equal or greater validity. This encounter permits the other to be seen as both different and equal. The concept of truth is pivotal to this relationship of equality. Without it the relationship of understanding risks becoming one in which the knowledge of the other is objectified and employed for one's own ends. Alternatively, without the openness to truth there is a risk that both self and other's positions can be dismissed as mere opinion or prejudice. Truth plays the role of allowing one's own knowledge, and that of the other, to have some purchase or claim to be worth listening to.

Making a claim for the centrality of truth is not a fashionable pursuit in contemporary social and political theory. Often, and for good reason, truth is associated with unsustainable claims to have revealed, or to be able to reveal, some foundational knowledge or position with which to exclude others. The advantage of philosophical hermeneutics is that it provides a non-foundational account of truth which is deployed in order to include other positions. For philosophical hermeneutics, it is the possibility of truth, which allows the recognition of one's own finitude, which is the essential precondition for openness to the other. Furthermore, without this ingredient there is little or nothing to provide motivation for engaging with others, or to move beyond the practices of assimilation or coexistence. A commitment to the possibility of truth also provides the guidance and criteria, and something of a standard, as to how engagement and communication can be undertaken.

The rehabilitation of truth is also what distinguishes philosophical hermeneutics from other 'post positivist' or interpretivist positions, and which provides its unique contribution. It has been emphasised that no single account is, in itself, sufficient to the task of pursuing the possibility of justice. The pursuit of justice requires a mutually illuminating dialogue between a variety of perspectives. However, it has been the argument of this book that philosophical hermeneutics provides a particular, distinctive, contribution which, until now, has not been recognised. This contribution consists of the provision of a *via media*, a means for achieving a better reconciliation of universalism and particularism (or relativism), which seeks to incorporate the advantages, while rejecting the limitations, of each. Philosophical hermeneutics advances the prospect of a non-foundational universalism. To be more specific, it offers an alternative epistemology, ontology, and morality to the unproblematic universalism of liberal cosmopolitanism, to the slightly more problematised universalism of Frankfurt School critical theory, and to the perceived anti-universalism of poststructuralism/postmodernism. Philosophical hermeneutics incorporates the anti-foundational insights of poststructuralism while rejecting the relativist implications which follow. Likewise, it retains the universalism of liberal cosmopolitanism, while rejecting the foundationalism or quasi-foundationalism of liberal cosmopolitanism and critical theory. In this way philosophical hermeneutics celebrates the existence of differences, while providing hope that difference can be bridged and communication and agreement achieved. In so doing, it contributes to finding a way out of the interregnum, described by Ricoeur, 'in which we can no longer practice the dogmatism of a single truth and in which we are not yet capable of conquering the scepticism into which we have stepped'.[2]

The way out of this interregnum begins with a recognition that achieving communication means that we must start from 'where we are now'. An attitude towards communication informed by philosophical hermeneutics does not require the engineering of a new human being, nor an acceptance that human finitude rules out improvements in the human condition. Philosophical hermeneutics takes it that the capacity for cross-cultural understanding is real and accompanies the development of language itself. This means that movement towards a 'universal horizon' requires only the linguisticality of the human species. The capacity to reason and understand inhabit language itself, and are not the exclusive property of any particular sector of the human population. Language provides us with all the resources we need to understand each other, and to build commonality and solidarity. And at the same time, language, or languages, provide the obstacle(s) to, and limits upon, our ability to understand and communicate. Linguisticality points to the limits of human understanding of ourselves, others, and the world(s) which we inhabit and create. Philosophical hermeneutics brings this awareness to the forefront by reminding us of the capacity of language to act as both bridge and barrier. Furthermore, the insights of philosophical hermeneutics, as used here, suggest that, while there may well continue to be real and irresolvable political obstacles to the expansion

---

[2] P. Ricoeur, *History and Truth* (Evanston: Northwestern University Press, 1966), p. 283.

of human political community, at the 'philosophical' level there is little to prevent a universal moral conversation from taking place.

However, the claim has not been made that philosophical hermeneutics in particular, or a communicative approach, in general, either resolves all moral/ethical problems or exhausts the scope of ethical and moral activity in international relations. Certain situations do arise wherein communication has ceased or is not possible. Some of these situations nonetheless call for moral or ethical action. What has been argued here is that communication should, wherever possible, be aspired to and communicative approaches be incorporated into solutions to ethical/moral problems at all stages. While it is always possible, and indeed probable, that opportunities for communication will be excluded at an early stage where issues of 'national security', survival, or military intervention are required, there is a need to keep channels of communication open while recognising that sometimes moral/ethical demands might require a non-dialogical response.

In such cases, or cases where communication or dialogue are abused or used in order to gain strategic advantage, there is an obvious lack of good will between the partners. At least two responses are possible, both valid. The first is to recognise that communication between the major protagonists is not possible in a genuine sense, that is, that there is no goodwill between us and them. In such a situation it is possible that other actions, including coercive ones are required if justice is to be done. However, a commitment to a communicative ethic also requires that the results of such coercive or non-communicative actions be anticipated. In particular, it requires the much harder task of attempting to anticipate which actions will lead to a communicative closure and which will prevent such closure. In addition, none of this is to say that 'goodwill' should necessarily have been extended to all parties at all times.

A second response is to seek to find communicative responses, or modes of communicative engagement. This, in turn, requires seeking to achieve good will and to build the circumstances for solidarity. Creating the conditions of communication is especially difficult in the realm of international relations. Realists constantly remind us of the obstacles to successful communication engendered by a chronic systemic security dilemma. In places such as the former Yugoslavia these obstacles are heightened. However, rationalists have also emphasised the element of dialogue and intersubjective agreement between states, which reduce the tension associated with a security dilemma and lead to the creation of an international society of states. Likewise, the work of the constructivist approach has demonstrated the dialogical constitution of the components of the international system and the institutions of international order.

What these arguments suggest is that dialogue and communication cannot be put off until the security dilemma has been resolved, but rather that understanding based on communication (interpreted broadly) is crucial to ameliorating and, on occasions, escaping the security dilemma. Thus, what has not been offered in this book is an idealist recipe removed from international realities. On the contrary the argument is that the realities of international politics cry out for an enquiry into how communication can be furthered and solidarity built upon. In this sense, philosophical hermeneutics lives up to its aim to be a practical philosophy.

The argument presented in this book does not exhaust the possible applications of philosophical hermeneutics to international relations. Little has been said here about how Gadamer's thought might apply to the issues of methodology which arose in the so-called third debate. Needless to say, the insights contained in *Truth and Method* add another voice to the debate about the nature and possibilities for theorising and understanding international relations, which might serve to indicate possibilities and interpretations other than those provided by critical theory and poststructuralism. Amongst the possible contributions of philosophical hermeneutics to this debate is that it provides a means of reflecting and reinterpreting the concerns of the English school. It is possible to interpret the English school's concerns with history of the development of international society as the development of a tradition of thought oriented towards the possibilities for communication across cultural barriers.[3] Beyond that it might be possible to see the mode of theorising undertaken by authors such as Hedley Bull and R. J. Vincent as examples of a form of practical reasoning in the Aristotelian sense. Bull's reflections on justice serve as illustrations of a mode of thought which seeks to accommodate change within the context of a pre-existing tradition and to reflect on universal principles in the light of particular issues.

This interpretation of Bull's approach brings the attention back to the issue of *phronesis* and practical reasoning and the argument presented in this book. The development of thin cosmopolitanism informed by

---

[3] See R. Epp, 'The English School on the Frontiers of International Society: A Hermeneutic Reflection', *Review of International Studies*, 24, Dec. (1998), 47–53.

philosophical hermeneutics has raised the issue of the nature of practical reasoning or *phronesis* and suggested that this mode of reasoning presents a suitable model for thinking about how to approach moral and ethical issues in international relations. If this is the case, then further enquiry should explore this avenue. A crucial part of any investigation into these concerns would be an exploration of the relationship between neo-Aristotelianism and more emancipatory approaches. It is in the dialogue between these two and the negotiations of their tension that a productive future for moral/ethical thinking in international relations might lie.

This book has been dedicated to the task of conceiving a form of universal human community which can include, celebrate and facilitate conversation between all the cultures and individuals of the world. The fundamental premise on which it is based is that membership of a particular community does not have to exclude membership of a larger community. The capacity of human beings to engage in reasoned understanding of each other creates the basis for a cosmopolitan order and suggests that to be situated in a particular community does not have to make one the enemy of humankind.

Bibliography

Anderson, B. *Imagined Communities: Reflections on the Origins and Spread of Nationalism*, London: Verso, 1991 (2nd edn).

Apel, K. O. *Analytic Philosophy of Language and the Geisteswissenschaften*, Dordrecht: Reidel, 1967.

'The A Priori of Communication and the Foundation of the Humanities', *Man and World*, 5. 1 (1972), 3–37.

Ashley, R. K. 'Untying the Sovereign State: A Double Reading of *The Anarchy Problematique*', *Millennium*, 17. 2 (1988), 227–62.

'Political Realism and Human Interests', *International Studies Quarterly*, 25. 2 (1981), 204–36.

'Living on Border Lines: Man, Poststructuralism and War', in Der Derian J. and Shapiro. M. J. (eds.), *International/Intertextual Relations*, pp. 259–321.

Ashley, R. K. and Walker, R. B. J. 'Reading Dissidence / Writing the Discipline: Crisis and the Question of Sovereignty in International Studies', *International Studies Quarterly*, 34 (1990), 367–426.

Bauman, Z. *Hermeneutics and Social Science: Approaches to Understanding*, London: Hutchinson, 1978.

Postmodern Ethics, Oxford: Blackwell, 1993.

Beitz, C. R. 'Cosmopolitan Ideals and National Sentiment', *Journal of Philosophy*, 80 (1983), 591–600.

'Sovereignty and Morality in International Affairs', in Held, D. (ed.), *Political Theory Today*, 236–54.

'Democracy in Developing Societies', in Brown and Shue(eds.), *Boundaries*, pp. 178–205.

'Cosmopolitan Liberalism and the States System', in Brown, C. (ed.), *Political Restructuring in Europe*, pp. 123–36.

Political Theory and International Relations, Princeton University Press, 1979.

Benhabib, S. *Situating the Self*, Oxford: Blackwell, 1992.

(ed.), *Democracy and Difference: Contesting the Boundaries of the Political*, Princeton University Press, 1996.

Bibliography

Benhabib, S. and Dallmayr, F. *The Communicative Ethics Controversy*, Cambridge: MIT Press, 1990.

Bernstein, R. *The Restructuring of Social and Political Theory*, London: Methuen, 1976.

Beyond Objectivism and Relativism, Philadelphia: University of Pennsylvania Press, 1983.

The New Constellation, Oxford: Polity, 1991.

Blaney, D. and Inayatullah, N. 'Prelude to a Conversation of Cultures in International Society? Todorov and Nandy on the Possibility of Dialogue', *Alternatives*, 19 (1994), 23–51.

Bleicher, H. *Contemporary Hermeneutics: Figures and Themes*, London: Routledge and Kegan Paul, 1980.

Booth, K. and Smith, S. (eds.), *International Relations Theory Today*, Cambridge: Polity, 1995.

Brown, C. 'Turtles All The Way Down: Antifoundationalism, Critical Theory and International Relations', *Millennium*, 23. 2 (1994), 213–38.

International Relations Theory: New Normative Approaches, London: Harvester Wheatsheaf, 1992.

'Ethics of Coexistence: The International Theory of Terry Nardin', *Review of International Studies*, 14 (1988), 213–22.

'The Modern Requirement?: Reflections on Normative International Theory in a Post-Western World', *Millennium*, 17, 2 (1988), 339–48.

(ed.), *Political Restructuring in Europe: Ethical Perspectives*, London: Routledge, 1994.

'Cultural Diversity and International Political Theory: From the Requirement to "Mutual Respect"?, *Review of International Studies* (2000), 26, 199–213.

Brown, P. G. and Shue, H. *Boundaries: National Autonomy and its Limits*, New Jersey: Rowman and Littlefield, 1981.

Bull, H. *The Anarchical Society*, London: Macmillan, 1977.

'The Grotian Conception of International Society', in Butterfield, H. and Wight, M. (eds.), *Diplomatic Investigations*, London: Allen and Unwin, 1966.

Justice in International Relations (The Hagey Lectures), University of Waterloo, 1983.

'The Third World and International Society', *Yearbook of World Affairs* (1979), 15–31.

Bull, H. and Watson, A. (eds.) *The Expansion of International Society*, Oxford University Press, 1984.

Burchill, S. and Linklater, A. (with Richard Devetak, Matthew Paterson and Jacqui True), *Theories of International Relations*, London: Macmillan, 1996.

Campbell, D. 'The Politics of Radical Interdependence: A Rejoinder to Daniel Warner', *Millennium*, 25. 1 (1996), 129–41.

'Violent Performances: Identity, Sovereignty, Responsibility', in Lapid, Y. and Kratochwil, F. (eds.), *The Return of Culture and Identity*, pp. 163–80.

'The Deterritorialisation of Responsibility: Levinas, Derrida, and Ethics After the End of Philosophy', *Alternatives*, 19 (1994), 455–84.

National Deconstruction, University of Minnesota Press, 1998.

Politics Without Principle, Sovereignty, Ethics and the Narratives of the Gulf War, Boulder: Lynne Rienner, 1996.

Car, E. H. *The Twenty Years Crisis*, London: Macmillan, 1939.

Cochran, M. 'Cosmopolitanism and Communitarianism in a Post-Cold War World', in Macmillan J. and Linklater, A (eds.), *Boundaries in Question*, pp. 40–53.

'Postmodernism, Ethics and International Political Theory', *Review of International Studies*, 21 (1995), 237–50.

Normative Theory in International Relations, Cambridge: Cambridge University Press, 1999.

Connolly, W. 'Identity and Difference in Global Politics', in Der Derian J. and Shapiro, M. J. (eds.) *International/Intertextual Relations*, pp. 323–42.

Identity/Difference: Democratic Negotiations of Political Paradox, Cornell University Press, 1991.

The Ethos of Pluralization, University of Minnesota Press, 1995.

'Democracy and Territoriality', *Millennium*, 20. 3 (1991), 463–84.

Cox, R. W. 'Social Forces, States and World Orders: Beyond International Relations Theory', *Millennium*, 10. 2 (1981), 126–55.

Dallmayr, F. R. *Polis and Praxis: Exercises in Contemporary Political Theory*, Cambridge: MIT Press, 1984.

Beyond Orientalism: Essays on Cross Cultural Encounter, Albany: SUNY, 1996.

Margins of Political Discourse, Albany: SUNY, 1989.

Dallmayr, F. R. and McCarthy, T. *Understanding and Social Inquiry*, Notre Dame University Press, 1977.

Der Derian, J. and Shapiro, M. J. *International/Intertextual Relations: Postmodern Readings of World Politics*, Toronto: Lexington, 1989.

Derrida, J. *Limited Inc.*, Evanston: Northwestern University Press, 1988.

Margins of Philosophy (trans Alan Bass), Brighton: Harvester, 1982 (Paris 1972).

'Three Questions to Hans-Georg Gadamer', in Michelfelder, D. P. and Palmer, R. E. (eds.), *Dialogue and Deconstruction: The Gadamer–Derrida Encounter*.

Devetak, R. 'The Project of Modernity in International Relations Theory', *Millennium*, 24. 1 (1995).

'Critical Theory', and 'Postmodernism' in Burchill, S. and Linklater, A. *Theories of International Relations*.

Donelan, M. 'The Political Theorists and International Theory', in Donelan, M. (ed.), *The Reason of States*, London: Allen and Unwin, 1978.

Dreyfus, H. L. and Rabinow, P. *Michel Foucault: Beyond Stucturalism and Hermeneutics*, University of Chicago Press, 1982.

Dunne, T. and Wheeler, N. *Human Rights in Global Politics*, Cambridge: Cambridge University Press, 1999.

Edkins, J. 'Sovereign Power, Zones of Indistinction, and the Camp', *Alternatives*, 25, 1, Jan-Mar. (2000).

Bibliography

Epp, R. 'The English School on the Frontiers of International Society: A Hermeneutic Reflection', *Review of International Studies*, 24, Dec. (1998), 47–53.

Foucault, Michel. *Discipline and Punish: The Birth of the Prison*, London: Penguin, 1977.

'What is Enlightenment', in Rabinow, P. *The Foucault Reader*.

Frost, M. *Ethics in International Relations: A Constitutive Theory*, Cambridge: Cambridge University Press, 1996 (originally published as *Towards a Normative Theory of International Relations*, 1986).

Gadamer, H. G. 'The Problem of Historical Consciousness', in Rabinow, P. and Sullivan, W. M., *Interpretive Social Science, A Reader*.

'A Reply to My Critics', in Bleicher, H., *Contemporary Hermeneutics*.

'Interview: The 1920s, 1930s and the Present: National Socialism, German History and German Culture', pp. 135–53 and 'The Future of the European Humanities', pp. 193–208, 'The Diversity of Europe: Inheritance and Future', pp. 221–36, in Misgeld, D. and Nicholson, G., *Hans-Georg Gadamer on Education, Poetry and History*.

The Enigma of Health, Cambridge: Polity, 1996.

'Text and Interpretation', 'Reply to Jacques Derrida', 'Letter to Dallmayr', 'Destruktion and Deconstruction', 'Hermeneutics and Logocentrism', in Michelfelder, Diane P. and Palmer, R. E. (eds.), *Dialogue and Deconstruction: The Gadamer-Derrida Encounter*, pp. 21–51, 55–7, 93–101, 102–13, 114–28.

Philosophical Hermeneutics (trans D. E. Linge), Berkeley: University of California Press, 1977.

Reason in the Age of Science, Cambridge: MIT Press, 1981.

The Knowledge of the Good in Platonic–Aristotelian Philosophy, Yale University Press, 1986.

Truth and Method, 2nd edn (trans. Weinsheimer, J. and Marshall, D.), London: Sheed and Ward, 1989.

George, J. and Campbell, D. 'Patterns of Dissent and the Celebration of Difference: Critical Social Theory and International Relations', *International Studies Quarterly*, 34 (1990), 269–93.

Gibbons, M. (ed.), *Interpreting Politics*, New York University Press, 1987.

Habermas, J. *Moral Consciousness and Communicative Action*, Cambridge: Polity, 1990.

Justification and Application, Cambridge: Polity, 1993.

'A Review of Gadamer's Truth and Method' (trans. T. McCarthy and F. Dallmayr), in Wachterhauser, B. R. (ed.), *Hermeneutics*, pp. 243–76.

'The Hermeneutic Claim to Universality', in Gibbons, M. (ed.), *Interpreting Politics*, pp. 175–202.

Knowledge and Human Interests (trans. Jeremy Shapiro), London: Heinemann, 1972.

'The Unity of Reason in the Diversity of its Voices', in Schmidt, J. (ed.), *What is Enlightenment*, pp. 399–425.

'Justice and Solidarity', in Kelly, M. (ed.), *Hermeneutics*, pp. 32–52.

The Past as Future, Cambridge: Polity, 1994.

Hekman, S. J. *Hermeneutics and the Sociology of Knowledge*, Cambridge: Polity, 1986.

Held, D. (ed.), *Political Theory Today*, Stanford University Press, 1991.

Held, V. (ed.), *Justice and Care: Essential Readings in Feminist Ethics*, Boulder: WestView, 1995.

Hoffman, M. 'Critical Theory and the Interparadigm Debate', *Millennium*, 16. 2 (1987).

'States, Cosmopolitanism and Normative International Theory', *Paradigms*, 2. 1, 60–75.

Hoffman, M. and Rengger, N. J. R. (eds.), *Beyond the Inter-Paradigm Debate: Critical Theory and International Relations* (forthcoming).

Hoffmann, S. *Duties Beyond Borders*, Syracuse University Press, 1981.

Hollis, M. and Smith, S. *Explaining and Understanding International Relations*, Oxford: Clarendon Press, 1990.

Hoy, D. C. *The Critical Circle*, Berkeley: University of California Press, 1978.

(ed.), *Foucault: A Critical Reader*, Oxford: Blackwell, 1986.

Hoy, D. C. and McCarthy, T. *Critical Theory*, Oxford: Blackwell, 1994.

Huntington, S. P. 'The Clash of Civilizations?' *Foreign Affairs*, Summer (1993), 22–49.

Hutchings, K. *Kant, Critique and Politics*, London: Routledge, 1996.

'Feminism, Universalism and Ethics', in Jabri V. and O'Gorman, E. (eds.), *Women Culture*, pp. 23–40.

Jabri, V. and O'Gorman, E. (eds.) *Women, Culture and International Relations*, Boulder: Lyne Rienner, 1999.

Jahn, B. 'The Power of Culture in International Relations: The Spanish Conquest in the Americas and its Theoretical Repercussions.' Paper prepared for ISA Annual Conference, April (1996), San Diego, USA.

Kamuf, P. *A Derrida Reader: Between the Blinds*, New York: Columbia, 1991.

Kearney, R. (ed.), 'Dialogue with Jacques Derrida', in Kearney, R. *Dialogues with Contemporary Thinkers*, Manchester University Press, 1984.

Kelly, M. (ed.), *Hermeneutics and Critical Theory in Ethics and Politics*, Cambridge: MIT Press, 1990.

Keohane, R. O. (ed.), *Neorealism and its Critics*, New York: Columbia University Press, 1986.

Kögler, H. H. *The Power of Dialogue: Critical Hermeneutics after Gadamer and Foucault*, Cambridge, Mass.: MIT Press, 1996.

Lapid, Y. and Kratochwil, F. (eds.), *The Return of Culture and Identity in IR Theory*, London: Lynne Rienner, 1996.

Linklater, A. 'The Achievements of Critical Theory', in Smith, S. Booth, K. and Zalewski, M. (eds.), *International Theory*, pp. 279–98.

'The Question of the Next Stage in International Relations: a Critical Theoretical Point of View', *Millennium*, 21. 1 (1992), 77–98.

Beyond Realism and Marxism: Critical Theory and International Relations, London: Macmillan, 1990.

'Rationalisation Processes and International History', in Hoffman, M. and Rengger, N. J. R. (eds.), *Beyond the Inter-Paradigm Debate: Critical Theory and International Relations* (forthcoming).

'The Problem of Community in International Relations', *Alternatives*, 15 (1990), 135–53.

Men and Citizens in the Theory of International Relations, 2nd edn. London: Macmillan, 1990.

The Transformation of Political Community: Ethical Foundations of the Post-Westphalian Era, Cambridge: Polity Press, 1997.

'Citizenship and Sovereignty in the Post-Westphalian State', *European Journal of International Relations*, 2. 1 (1996), 77–103.

'Transforming Political Community: A Response to the Critics', *Review of International Studies* 25. 1 (January 1999), 165–75.

Lyotard, J. F. *The Postmodern Condition, A Report on Knowledge* (trans., Bennington, G. and Massumi B.), University of Minnesota Press, 1984.

Macintyre, A. *After Virtue*, University of Notre Dame Press, 1984 (2nd edn).

Macmillan, J. and Linklater, A. (eds.), *Boundaries in Question: New Directions in International Relations*, London: Pinter, 1995.

Madison, G. B. *The Hermeneutics of Post-Modernity: Figures and Themes*, Bloomington: Indiana University Press, 1988.

Mapel, D. R. 'The Contractarian Tradition in International Ethics', in Nardin, T. and Mapel, D. R. (eds.), *Traditions*, pp. 180–200.

McInlay, P. F. 'Community and/or Difference: Gadamer on Sensus Communis.' Paper presented at APSA Conference, New York, Hilton, 1–4 September 1994.

Michelfelder, D. P. and Palmer, R. E. (eds.), *Dialogue and Deconstruction: The Gadamer–Derrida Encounter*, Albany: SUNY, 1989.

Misgeld, D. 'Poetry, Dialogue and Negotiation: Liberal Culture and Conservative Politics in Hans-Georg Gadamer's Thought' in K. Wright (ed.), *Festivals of Interpretation*, pp. 136–60

Misgeld, D. and Nicholson, G. *Hans-Georg Gadamer on Education, Poetry and History*, Albany: SUNY, 1992.

Morgenthau, H. *Politics Among Nations: The Struggle for Power and Peace*, New York: Alfred A. Knopf, 1954.

Morrice, D. 'The Liberal–Communitarian Debate in Contemporary Political Philosophy and its Significance for International Relations', *Review of International Studies*, 26 (2000), 233–51.

Mueller-Vollmer, K. *The Hermeneutics Reader*, London: Basil Blackwell, 1985.

Mulhall, S. and Swift, A. *Liberals and Communitarians*, Oxford: Blackwell, 1992.

Nardin, T. *Law, Morality and the Relations of States*, Princeton University Press, 1983.

Nardin, T. and Mapel, D. R. *Traditions of International Ethics*, Cambridge: Cambridge University Press, 1992.

Neufeld, M. 'The Right and the Good in International Ethics'. Paper Presented for the ISA Annual Convention. San Diego, April. 1996.

'Interpretation and the "Science" of International Relations', *Review of International Studies*, 19 (1993), 39–61.

'Reflexivity and International Relations Theory', *Millennium*, 22. 1 (1993), 53–76.

The Restructuring of International Relations Theory, Cambridge: Cambridge University Press, 1994.

Oakeshott, M. *On Human Conduct*, Oxford University Press, 1975.

O'Neill, O. *Faces of Hunger*, London: Allen and Unwin, 1986.

'Ethical Reasoning and Ideological Pluralism', *Ethics*, 98, July (1988), 705–22.

'Justice and Boundaries', in Brown, C. (ed.), *Political Restructuring*, pp. 69–88.

'Justice, Gender and International Boundaries', *British Journal of Political Science*, 20 (1989), 439–59.

'Transnational Justice', in Held, D. (ed.), *Political Theory Today*, pp. 276–304.

Ormiston, G. L. and Schrift. A. D. (eds.), *The Hermeneutic Tradition: From Ast to Ricoeur*, SUNY, Albany, 1990.

Palmer, R. *Hermeneutics: Interpretation Theory in Schleiermacher, Dilthey, Heidegger and Gadamer*, Northwestern University Press, 1969.

Parekh, B. 'Non-ethnocentric Universalism', in Dunne, T. and Wheeler, N. (eds.), *Human Rights*, pp. 128–59.

Rabinow, P. *The Foucault Reader*, London: Penguin, 1984.

Rabinow, P. and Sullivan, W. M. *Interpretive Social Science, A Reader*, University of California Press, 1979.

Rawls, J. *A Theory of Justice*, Oxford University Press, 1972.

Political Liberalism, Columbia University Press, 1993.

Rengger, N. J. 'Going Critical: A Response to Hoffmann', *Millennium*, 17. 1 (1988), 81–9.

'Culture, Society and Order in World Politics', in Rengger N. J. and J. Bayliss (eds.), *Dilemmas*, pp. 85–106.

'Serpents and Doves in Classical International Theory', *Millennium*, 17. 2 (1988), 215–25.

'Incommensurability, International Theory and the Fragmentation of Western Political Culture', in Gibbins J., *Contemporary Political Culture*, London: Sage, 1988, pp. 237–50.

Rengger N. J. and J. Bayliss (eds.), *Dilemmas of World Politics*, Oxford University Press, 1992.

Reus-Smit C. 'The Constitutional Structure of International Society and the Nature of Fundamental Institutions', *International Organisation*, 51. 4 (Autumn 1997), 555–89.

Ricoeur, P. *Hermeneutics and the Human Sciences: Essays on Language, Action and Interpretation* (ed. Thompson, J. B.), Cambridge: Cambridge University Press, Editions de la Maison des sciences de l'homme, Paris, 1981.

History and Truth, Evanston: Northwestern University Press, 1966.

Risser, J. *Hermeneutics and the Voice of the Other*, Albany: SUNY, 1997.

Rosenblum, N. L. *Liberalism and the Moral Life*, Harvard University Press, 1989.

Schmidt, J. (ed.), *What is Enlightenment?: Eighteenth-Century Answers and Twentieth-Century Questions*, University of California Press, 1996.

Shapcott, R. 'Conversation and Coexistence, Gadamer and the Interpretation of International Society', *Millennium*, 23. 1 (1994), 57–83.

Sharp, Jane M. O. 'Dayton Report Card', *International Security*, 22. 3 (1997/8).

Shue, H. *Basic Rights*, Princeton University Press, 1980.

Shute, S. and Hurley, S. *On Human Rights: The Oxford Amnesty Lectures*, New York: Basic Books, 1993.

Sjolander, C. T. and Cox. W. S. (eds.), *Beyond Positivism: Critical Reflections on International Relations*, Boulder: Lynne Rienner, 1994.

Skinner, Q. (ed.), *The Return of Grand Theory in The Human Sciences*, Cambridge: Cambridge University Press, 1985.

Smith, S., Booth, K. and Zalewski, M. (eds.), *International Theory: Positivism and Beyond*, Cambridge: Cambridge University Press, 1996.

Such, P. 'Human Rights as Settled Norms: Meryn Frost and the Limits of Hegelian Human Rights Theory', *Review of International Studies*, 26 (2000), 215–31.

Sullivan, R. R. *Political Hermeneutics: The Early Thinking of Hans Georg Gadamer*, The Pennsylvania State University Press, 1989.

Taylor, C. 'Connolly, Foucault, and Truth', *Political Theory*, 13. 3 (1985), 377–85.

'Cross-Purposes: The Liberal–Communitarian Debate', in Rosenblum, N. L. (ed.), *Liberalism*, pp. 159–82.

'Foucault on Freedom and Truth', in Hoy D. C. (ed.), *Foucault*, pp. 152–83.

Philosophy and the Human Sciences: Philosophical Papers Volume Three, Cambridge: Cambridge University Press, 1985.

'Language and Human Nature' in Gibbons, M. (ed.), *Interpreting Politics*, pp. 101–32.

Taylor, C. and Gutman, A. *Multiculturalism: Examining the Politics of Recognition*, Princeton University Press, 1994.

Thompson, J. *Justice and World Order: a Philosophical Enquiry*, London: Routledge, 1992.

Thompson, J. B. *Critical Hermeneutics*, Cambridge: Cambridge University Press, 1981.

Todorov, T. *The Conquest of America*, New York: Harper, 1982.

Vincent, R. J. *Human Rights and International Relations*, Cambridge: Cambridge University Press.

Wachterhauser, B. R. *Hermeneutics and Modern Philosophy*, Albany: SUNY, 1986.

Walker, R. B. J. *Inside/Outside, International Relations as Political Theory*, Cambridge: Cambridge University Press, 1993.

One World, Many Worlds: Struggles for a Just World Peace, Boulder: Lynne Rienner, 1988.

Waltz, K. *Theory of International Politics*, Reading: Addison Wesley, 1979.

Walzer, M. *Spheres of Justice*, Oxford: Blackwell, 1983.
  Thick and Thin: Moral Argument at Home and Abroad, University of Notre Dame Press, 1994.
  'The Distribution of Membership' in Brown P G. and Shue, H. (eds.), Boundaries, pp. 24–40.
  On Toleration, Yale University Press, 1997.
Warnke, G. *Gadamer: Hermeneutics, Tradition and Reason*, Oxford: Polity, 1987.
  'Walzer, Rawls and Gadamer: Hermeneutics and Political Theory', in Wright, K. (ed.), *Festivals of Interpretation*, pp. 136–60.
Wheeler, N. and Dunne, T. 'Hedley Bull's Pluralism of the Intellect and Solidarism of the Will', *International Affairs*, 72 (1996), 1–17.
White, S. K. *Political Theory and Post-Modernism*, Cambridge: Cambridge University Press, 1991.
Wight, M., Wight, G. and Porter, B. (eds.), *International Theory: The Three Traditions*, Leicester University Press, 1991.
  'De Systematilus Civitatem', in *Systems of States*, Leicester University Press, 1977.
Wight, M. and Butterfield, H. (eds.), *Diplomatic Investigations*, London: Allen and Unwin, 1967.
Williams, B. *Ethics and the Limits of Philosophy*, London: Fontana, 1985.
Wright, K. (ed.), *Festivals of Interpretation: Essays on Hans-Georg Gadamer's Work*, Albany: SUNY, 1990.
Young, I. M. *Justice and the Politics of Difference*, Princeton University Press, 1990.

Index

abstraction, 40–1
agency, 27, 39, 40, 60, 61, 93, 104, 105, 110,
   121, 183, 202, 214
  communitarianism and, 42–3
  conceptions of, 40, 41
  cosmopolitan/communitarian divide
    and, 44
  discourse ethics and, 88–9, 116, 117,
    122, 126
  freedom and,
    ethics of, 100
    pursuit of, 120
  human, 34, 38, 69, 93, 119, 125
  Kantian approach to, 40–2
  philosophical hermeneutics and,
    161, 167
    relation to reason, 162, 166
  postconventional, 94, 122, 184
  poststructuralism and, 100
  reason and, 162
agreement, 170, 177, 189, 191,
   195, 196
  conversation and, 168, 173
  fusion of horizons and, 149
  philosophical hermeneutics and,
   168, 171–2
  understanding and, 25, 171
  universal, 173, 178
alterity, 15, 16
anarchy
  sovereignty and, 65, 66
annihilation, 15, 16, 17, 19, 22, 72, 139,
   197, 233
Aristotelian
  phronesis, 152, 154, 157, 176, 186
  polis, 82, 160, 204, 208, 210, 218
art
  importance of, 148–9

Ashley, Richard, 80, 93, 95, 99, 101, 102, 104
assimilation, 13, 15, 16, 18–19, 21, 34, 40,
   42, 61, 72, 77, 94, 96, 120, 126, 129,
   139, 174, 178, 199, 202, 206, 209, 216,
   222, 233, 234
  communication and, 50, 196
  identity and, 22
  impartiality and, 38
  veil of ignorance and, 39
autonomy, 120
  claims to, 213
  human, 124
  individual, 118

Being, 135, 136, 138
  hermeneutics of, 190
  truth of, 149
Being-in-the-world (*see Dasein*)
Beitz, Charles, 4, 5, 9, 27, 32, 34, 39, 42,
   89, 219
  cosmopolitan morality and, 36
  liberal cosmopolitanism and, 37, 161,
   221
Benhabib, Seyla, 88, 105, 106, 109–114,
   115, 128, 165, 167
  abstract other and, 69
  generalised and concrete other and,
   34–6, 42, 206
  universalism and, 108, 111, 116, 127
boundaries, 32, 34, 210
  communication and, 201
  communities and, 213
  dialogue and, 201
  moral, 26, 33
  philosophical hermeneutics and,
   201
  sovereign, 202
  sovereignty and, 65, 100

Index

validation
  of norms, 107–8
  of moral claims, 116
  of principles, 120
  purpose of, 107, 119
'veil of ignorance', 37, 88
  assimilation and, 39
  conversation and, 39–40
  other and, 39
violence, 203, 205, 209

Walz, Kenneth, 6, 80
Walzer, Michael, 9, 12, 27, 32, 34, 40,
  42–3, 46–7, 49, 60
wisdom, practical, _see_ phronesis

Young, Iris Marion, 10, 51, 107, 117
  generalized other and, 37–8
  impartiality and, 38
Yugoslavia
  deconstruction of, 211–12

CAMBRIDGE STUDIES IN INTERNATIONAL RELATIONS